TOTAL TRANSFORMATION
全 面 改 變

FROM HEALING THE BODY TO HEALING THE SOUL
從醫治身體到醫治靈魂

KENNETH KWONG CHEE SIU

WESTBOW
PRESS®
A DIVISION OF THOMAS NELSON
& ZONDERVAN

WestBow Press books may be ordered through booksellers or by contacting:

WestBow Press
A Division of Thomas Nelson & Zondervan
1663 Liberty Drive
Bloomington, IN 47403
www.westbowpress.com
1 (866) 928-1240

ISBN: 978-1-9736-2968-9 (sc)
ISBN: 978-1-9736-2969-6 (hc)
ISBN: 978-1-9736-2967-2 (e)

Library of Congress Control Number: 2018906388

Print information available on the last page.

WestBow Press rev. date: 7/5/2018

To
my children,
my grandchildren,
and
their children and grandchildren

Contents

PRELUDE

The word of the Lord came to me, saying,
"Before I formed you in the womb I knew you,
Before you were born I set you apart;
I appointed you as a prophet to the nations."

Jeremiah 1:5 NIV[1]

A prophet is a person called by God to serve as a conduit for the Word of God in two ways:

> First: as a *Foreteller* of God's *predictive prophecy*, and,
> Second: as a *Forthteller* of God's *prescriptive prophecy*.

> In turn, the prophet may serve as an intermediary between God's people and their God in two similar ways:
> First: to bring the *praises* of the people and offer them to God, and;
> Second: to bring the *prayers* of the people and offer them to God.

> *"[13] You shall be blameless before the LORD your God, [14] for these nations, which you are about to dispossess, listen to fortune-tellers and to diviners. But as for you, the LORD your God has not allowed you to do this.[15] [2f]"The LORD your God will raise up for you a prophet like me from among you, from your brothers—it is to him you shall*

---

[1]   *The NIV Study Bible*. Zondervan. Grand Rapids, MI USA. 1985.
[2] ʃJohn 1:21, 25, 45; Cited Acts 3:22; 7:37

listen— *16 just as you desired of the* Lord *your God at Horeb [3g]on the day of the assembly, when you said, [4h]'Let me not hear again the voice of the* Lord *my God or see this great fire any more, lest I die.' 17 And the* Lord *said to me, [5i]'They are right in what they have spoken. 18 [6f]I will raise up for them a prophet like you from among their brothers. [7j]And I will put my words in his mouth, and [8k]he shall speak to them all that I command him. 19 [9l]And whoever will [10m]not listen to my words that he shall speak in my name, I myself will require it of him. 20 [11n]But the prophet who presumes to speak a word in my name that I have not commanded him to speak, or[126] who speaks in the name of other gods, that same prophet shall die.' 21 And if you say in your heart, 'How may we know the word that the* Lord *has not spoken?'— 22 [13o]when a prophet speaks in the name of the* Lord, *if the word does not come to pass or come true, that is a word that the* Lord *has not spoken; [14n]the prophet has spoken it presumptuously. You need not be afraid of him."[15]*

The role of the prophet could readily be applied to those of the pastors of our day.

Similarly, we can see a physician joining the "Healing Arts"

---

3 [g]See ch. 9:10

4 [h]See Ex. 20:19

5 [i]ch. 5:28

6 [f][See ver. 15 above]

7 [j]Jer. 1:9; 5:14; [John 17:8]

8 [k][John 4:25; 8:28; 12:49, 50]

9 [l][Acts 3:23]

10 [m]Jer. 29:19; 35:13

11 [n]See ch. 13:5

12 [6]Or *and*

13 [o][ch. 13:1–3; Jer. 28:9]

14 [n][See ver. 20 above]

15 *The Holy Bible: English Standard Version.* (Wheaton: Standard Bible Society, 2001), Dt 18:13-22.

profession as one who is answering a "call" from God and this calling is as sacred as the "call" of a pastor. He or she is to learn, first and foremost, to "do no harm" because the salient fact is that human beings are created by the hand of God in the *imago Dei,* that they come to life through the in-breathing of God, and hence we firmly subscribe and resolutely believe in the "sanctity of life."

The following excerpt is a very appropriate reflection of what my life has been:

"If you found a cure for cancer,
Wouldn't it be inconceivable to hide it from the rest of mankind?
How much more inconceivable
To keep silent the cure from the eternal wages of sin?"

Dave Davidson

I have often tried to visualize what motivated my grandfather to migrate from Surabaya, Java, where he was born and grew up, to the little village of Song Tihn (Sangtian) 桑田 (Mulberry tree plantation) in Chiuh Yeuhng (Chaoyang) 潮陽 near Swatow, in Kwong Tung (Guangdong) 廣東 Province. I was even more intrigued when a distant relative told me that my grandfather was the "mayor" of Song Tihn before he retired to live in Swatow where he was finally buried. I don't have the answers to any of these questions and probably never will this side of eternity. And it is precisely for this reason that I want to write this book about my life so that my children and grandchildren will, at least, get a glimpse of what their father/grandfather was like and where he came from.

A Note Concerning the Use of Romanization in this Book

Throughout this book, I have endeavored to use the Yale system in the romanization of all proper names and nouns. On a number of occasions, when the name or noun has a familiar romanization commonly used in Hong Kong, I have included these in [] brackets. Finally, I complete the romanization by using the Pinyin Romanization in () brackets, for the equivalent word in Putonghua or Mandarin, e.g., my name is Siu Gwong Ji [Siu Kwong Chee] (Xiao Guangzhi) 蕭光祉. I assert that my manuscript contains an accurate English/Chinese translation (accurate in tone, meaning and content) of any and all Chinese text that is included in my manuscript.

Have you ever wondered how, where, when and why the word Mandarin came to be used to address a Chinese "court official" and, at the same time, also ended up being used to represent the spoken "official language" in China? I have a pet theory about it but I've not been able to corroborate it nor have I read anything written about the subject.

My theory is that when the first British traveler arrived in China, he inquired of his interpreter who the minister was and how he was to address the man. The interpreter said in reply, "Man, da ren." Da ren is the transliteration of the Chinese salutation for a minister, which is 大人.

I suppose, the Briton, therefore, coined the word Mandarin for a Chinese minister and also used it to represent the spoken language the minster spoke. Obviously, he noticed that the minister's spoken language was quite different from the vernacular among the common population. Anyway, this is just an aside, so take it for what it's worth.

ACKNOWLEDGEMENTS

I would like to thank my wife, Mary Elizabeth (Betty) for her love, care, support, and encouragement; for patiently putting up with me for over half a century; and for her encouragement in the completion of this book.

A very special and heartfelt thank you is offered here with my utmost and sincere gratitude to my cousin, Dr. Gloria M. Tang 蕭敏, Associate Professor Emeritus, University of British Columbia, British Columbia, Canada. She is the second child of my uncle Henry Hon Lit Siu, my father's youngest brother.

Gloria obtained her B.A. (hons) degree in English language and literature at the University of Hong Kong in 1960. She subsequently proceeded to attain a Master of Education degree in teaching and learning at HKU in 1981 and a Doctor of Education in second language acquisition at the University of British Columbia in Canada in 1989.

She held teaching positions in Hong Kong and Vancouver, culminating her career as Assistant Professor 1991-1996 and Associate Professor from 1996 until her retirement in 2006 at the University of British Columbia. During her professional career and her tenure as professor, she taught many classes and students on the art and science of teaching and writing, among other skills. She has published academic papers and authored four books.

You can imagine my pleasure and excitement when she agreed to write a Foreword for my book and also consented to edit it to make it more readable. As my "angelic" eight-year-old granddaughter Abigail would say, "I am really 'siked' (psyched) that you are willing to do it for me. Thanks."

Thanks are also due Kay Dinolfo, our oldest daughter, Dr. Stephen Siu, our son, and Captain Bruce Brosch, USN, our son-in-law, for their kindness and expertise with their editing and suggestions for this book to make it readable. If any part of the book is far from enjoyable, the fault lies completely with me.

Kenneth Kwong Chee Siu
September 7, 2008
My "Retreat" in Mountain View

FOREWORD

When Kenneth approached me to edit his book and write a Foreword, I was flattered. However, I declined the invitation, knowing full well I was neither adequate to take up the challenge nor worthy of such an important task. What do I know about healing? Be it body or soul! I have now accepted the invitation not because I feel I am any less inadequate or more worthy of the honor but because he impresses on me that he needs to meet a deadline and my service is urgently needed. So here I am struggling to make the Foreword worthy of the book and summoning all the keen sense of a teacher to detect typos and errors while being fascinated by the manuscript.

Total Transformation is an autobiography. It is about the life of the author, Doctor/Reverend Kenneth Siu, who he is, where he comes from and the people whose lives he has touched. Dave Davidson's quotable quote which Kenneth cited in his Prelude:

> If you found a cure for cancer,
> Wouldn't it be inconceivable to hide it from the rest of
> mankind?
> How much more inconceivable
> To keep silent the cure from the eternal wages of sin?

sums up Kenneth's mission in life – his compulsive commitment to heal and his obligation to communicate the cure he has found to all humankind.

Kenneth has always been looked upon as God's chosen by his family. As a young man, he was good-looking. He was in medical school at the then exclusive University of Hong Kong. With this background plus a rich sense of humour and an abundance of charm which he bestowed generously on all especially on those who were the right age and the right gender, he was considered one of the most eligible bachelors in Hong Kong by unmarried girls. He became a legend when he sailed to the United States of America to further his career and to better equip himself to serve the underprivileged. The legend of Kenneth continued when he married a lovely American woman, Betty. The marriage was not legendary but the fact that his parents learned about the marriage by mail in one of those romantic by-the-time-you-receive-this-I'll-have-wedded letters was. We, i.e., his cousins looked upon him as a Hollywood star! And on his triumphant return to Hong Kong bringing with him wife, a beautiful blonde as tall as he (she is now a beautiful 70+-year-old) and daughter (a more intelligent toddler I had yet to encounter), the whole Siu clan and the whole Choy clan (plus a couple non-Siu/non-Choy) stormed the greeting area at Kai Tak Airport to meet him and his young family.

He was a dedicated surgeon having achieved a bundle of higher degrees and qualifications and served in various positions in both Hong Kong and USA. He enjoyed an illustrious career until he retired in 1990. And the legend continued.

Again he became God's chosen, this time pursuing an education in theology. Having been healer of the body for close to 40 years, he thought he would become a healer of the soul. He earned a Master of Divinity and was offered a position as medical ministries administrator (a position which seemed to have been created exclusively for his benefit) in 1994. He later became pastor of Sha Lei Tau Baptist Church in Macau, a position he held until 2008 during which period he earned yet another degree, a Doctor of Ministry. He is at present Adjunct Faculty at Southwest Baptist University in Mountain View, Missouri waiting to take up an assignment as pastor in Sha Lei Tau Baptist Church, Macau in 2011 when he will again put to good use the bilingual and bi-literate skills (being preacher and interpreter simultaneously) which God has generously bestowed on him to serve Him.

He and his wife have raised five beautiful and successful children who (with their spouses) have given them ten grandchildren with two deceased. According to Kenneth, the purpose of writing this book is to allow his children and children's children a glimpse of his life. He has even included a full length translation of the genealogy of the Siu clan for those who may wish to trace their roots. Admirable! Furthermore, he has told his stories and the stories of his forebears against the backdrop of world history and Chinese history.

True to his philosophy that to bring up children to know God's existence is to travel that way himself, in *Total Transformation*, Kenneth testifies that he is always travelling in God's way. True to his role as intermediary between human and God, in *Total Transformation*, Kenneth justifies the way of God to his children, to his readers and to all humankind.

As you turn the pages, you'll meet Kenneth the father and grandfather, Kenneth the surgeon and, most of all, Kenneth the pastor. Follow where his stream of consciousness takes you. Laugh with him, be amused by his anecdotes, be touched by his testimony, and be inspired by his interpretation of the Word of God and...

Praise Him!

Gloria M. Tang
Vancouver, British Columbia
10-10-10

INTRODUCTION

Therefore, my brothers,
be all the more eager to make your calling and election sure.
For if you do these things,
you will never fall,
and you will receive a rich welcome
into the eternal kingdom
of our Lord and Savior Jesus Christ. [16]

所以弟兄們，
應當更加殷勤，
使你們所蒙的恩召
和揀選堅定不移。
你們若行這幾樣，
就永不失腳；
這樣，
必叫你們豐豐富富地
得以進入我們主─救主耶穌基督永遠的國。17

2 Peter 1:10-11

And do not think you can say to yourselves,
'We have Abraham as our father.'
I tell you that out of these stones
God can raise up children for Abraham.

---

[16] *The Holy Bible: New International Version*, electronic ed. (Grand Rapids: Zondervan, 1996, c1984), 2 Pe 1:10-11.

[17] *The Holy Bible. Chinese Union Version.*, Shangti Edition. (Hong Kong: Hong Kong Bible Society, 2005), 2 Pe 1:10-11.

The ax is already at the root of the trees
and every tree that does not produce good fruit
will be cut down and thrown into the fire

Mt 3:8-10. NIV[18]

---

[18] *The NIV Study Bible*. Zondervan. Grand Rapids, MI. U.S.A 1985.

GENEALOGIES IN ANCIENT ISRAEL

Genealogies feature prominently in both the early and later history of Israel. There are ten principal genealogical lists in Genesis alone. These records served to establish and protect identity in that they regulated a variety of social interactions, including marriage and land inheritance (Dt 25:5-20; Ezr 10:18-43). Thus, the registration of families who had returned from exile was a profound concern during the postexilic period (1Ch 1-9; Ezr 8:2-14; Ne 7:7-63). Genealogies were especially important in ancient Israel because the right to hold important offices was a hereditary privilege. The New Testament preserves two pertinent genealogical texts, both of which present the human ancestry of Jesus as the son of David (Mt 1:1-17; Lk 3:23-38).[19]

Lord, you have been our dwelling place
throughout all generations.
Before the mountains were born
or you brought forth the earth and the world,
from everlasting to everlasting you are God.

Ps 90:1-2 NIV[20]

---

[19] NIV Archaeological Study Bible, Zondervan, *Grand Rapids, Michigan, 49530, U.S.A.* 2005. 1559.
[20] *The NIV Study Bible*. Zondervan. Grand Rapids, MI. 1985.

CHINESE GENEALOGIES: JUKH POU (ZU PU)

What is Zu Pu? A comprehensive definition is found in an article by Kimberly Powell in *genealogy.About.com,* where she quoted the following article: *Jia Pu (Chinese Genealogical Record): An Introduction,* written by Danny Boey, *Chinese Roots.com.*[21]

"Zu Pu is a record of a clan's history and lineage. It documents the origins of the surname, the migration patterns of the clan, the family lineage, the ancestral biography, the story of the locality, etc...Jia Pu or Zu Pu has been found as early as the Shang Dynasty (1523-1028 B.C.).

A 'Jia Pu' usually begins with the primogenitor that first settled or moved to a place and started his family there...usually does not have prominent records of the women in the family...Recent works in the field have dispelled the myth that Chinese genealogical research is only a mere pastime hobby for the amateur genealogist."

> *Another generation grew up,*
> *who knew neither the LORD*
> *nor what He had done for Israel"*

Jdg. 2:10.

There is cause and effect in the spiritual as well as the physical universe. The cause of the failure of the next generation to know God was rooted in the incomplete obedience of its parents.[22]

You and I can't guarantee that our children will know the Lord or live for Him. But if we trust God enough to act on His Word, if we are

---

[21]   *http://genealogy.about.com/library/author/ucboey1a.html.*
[22]   Larry Richards, *The 365 Day Devotional Commentary,* Includes Index. (Wheaton, Ill.: Victor Books, 1990), 145.

obedient in our daily lives, our children will never be able to say of God, "I didn't know Him."

The reality of who God is, is displayed in the faith moms and dads put into practice, and in their obedience to His Word.

Personal Application

There's nothing more important we can do for our children than love, trust, and obey the Lord.

Quotable

"There is just one way to bring up a child in the way he should go and that is to travel that way yourself."—Abraham Lincoln

Seeing the Realities of a Transformed Life

Paul dwelt two whole years in his own rented house, and received all who came to him, preaching the kingdom of God and teaching the things which concern the Lord Jesus Christ with all confidence, no one forbidding him.

Acts 28:30–31

This verse shows that, while Paul was under house arrest "in his own rented house," he continued to minister. In spite of the circumstances, Paul continued to do what he had been called to do.

You may find yourself thinking, "I can't go and preach the gospel. I can't be an evangelist, or a Bible teacher. I'm stuck with my job." But it doesn't matter whether you're chained to a desk, an assembly line, a classroom, a car, or a sales position—they all provide opportunities for you to further the gospel. The less desirable your confinement, the greater the opportunity for a godly life to shine!

People often tell me how hard it is to witness where they work. My response is that it is generally harder to witness under ideal conditions than in a more difficult situation. That's because in difficult situations the reality of a transformed life is more apparent, and that can't help but be attractive to those who haven't experienced it.[23]

---

[23] John MacArthur, *Truth for Today: A Daily Touch of God's Grace* (Nashville, Tenn.: J. Countryman, 2001), 366.

I

蕭氏族譜
THE GENEALOGY OF THE SIU (XIAO) FAMILY

蕭   Siu   (Xiao)
1. Chinese family name.
2. Quiet, lonely, desolate.

氏   sih   (shi)
1. Family, clan.

族   juhk   (zu)
1. A tribe, a clan, a family.

譜   pou   (pu)
1. A register, a record.
2. Policies of a clan.
3. Family tree, lineage, genealogy.

Origin of Xiao*, Siu*, Siew*, Seow*, Hsiao*

According to the website *Yutopian.com* (*http://www.yutopian.com/names/16/16xiao30.html*), the surname Siu (Xiao) ranks as the 30th most common last name in China. The Xiaos are the descendents of the ancient king Ku Di (2,435-2,365 B.C.). The direct forefather of the Xiaos was Da Xin who suppressed the Nangong Zhangwan rebellion, during the Chun Qiu period. (Nangong Zhangwan was a prisoner of war who went on a killing spree in the palace, evicting the duke of Song and appointed a new duke). Because of this Da Xin was made the duke of Xiao, and was given the kingdom of Xiao (Xiao of Jiang Su).

Hometown: 50 miles east of Feng in Shandong Province山東省

II

序
PREFACE

It has commonly been said that a dependent branch would seek its root; and, when we see a river, we would want to trace its origin. This is because a root that is firm will always have luxuriant and vibrant branches; and a river that is deep will meander over a long distance. A study of legal texts and documents shows the surname Siu (Xiao) actually began after Sung Meih Ji (Song Weizi) 宋微子settled in Cheuih Jau [Hsuchow] (Xuzhou) 徐州 a city in Gong Sou [Kiangsu] (Jiangsu) 江蘇Province, in the old Siu (Xiao) 蕭 kingdom and took the name. Presently, Hsuchow (Xuzhou) 徐州is in Kiangsu (Jiangsu) 江蘇Province located south of the river.

The descendents of the Siu (Xiao) 蕭family settled in Siu (Xiao) County 蕭縣in Hsuchow (Xuzhou) 徐州in Kiangsu (Jiangsu) 江蘇, then branched out and settled in Kiangsi (Jiangxi) 江西 Province. The descendents in Kiangsi (Jiangxi) Province moved on to live in Jyu Gei Hohng (Zhuji Xiang) 珠璣巷 (Baroque Pearl Alley), in Ngauh Tihn Fong (Niutian Fang) 牛田坊 (Ox Field Subdivision) in Chi Hing Yuhn (Shixing Xian) 始興縣 (Happy Beginning County) in Naahm Huhng Fu (Nanxiong Fu) 南雄府 (Southern Hero Prefecture) on the Eastern side of Kwangtung (Guangdong) Province廣東省. Not long after that, because of the Concubine Sou (Su) Incident 蘇妃之變it was not possible to live there any longer.

Therefore, Sing Yuht Gung (Shengyue Gong) 聖悅公 went with Luhng Gahn Tin (Long Jintian) 龍近天, Loh Gwai (Luo Gui) 羅貴,

Mahk Sau (Mai Xiu) 麥秀 and the group, to avoid the catastrophe, escaped to Daaih Leuhng (Daliang) 大良 in Seuhn Dak (Shunde) 順德 in Canton (Guangzhou Prefecture) 廣州府. After a period when the situation had quieted down, he moved to a walled village in Si Daaih Tin (Sida Tian) 司大田in Mouh Dak Leih (Mude Li) 慕德里 (Admire Virtue Neighborhood) in Pun Yuh (Panyu) County番禺縣 to settle down.

Sing Yuht Gung (Shengyue Gong) 聖悅公 bore two sons. The older son was Syun Yee (Xuanyi) 宣儀 and the second son was Syun Muih (Xuanmei) 宣梅. The brothers went to settle in Sehk Taahm village (Shitan Xiang) 石潭鄉 (Rocky Pond Village) in Chung Fa County (Congfa Xian) 從化縣 (Follow Change County).

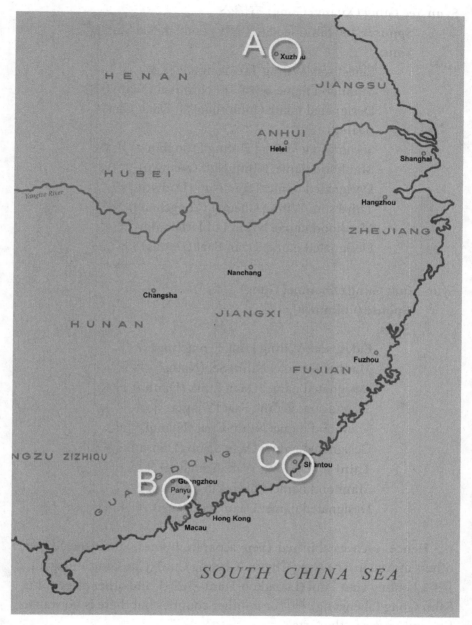

Figure 1. Migration map.
Our Primogenitor Sing Yuet Gung et al migrated from Hsuchow
(Xuzhou) (point A) to Seuhn Dak (Shunde) and Pun Yuh
(Panyu) (point B), then finally to Song Tihn (Sang Tian).

Syun Yee Gung (Xuanyi Gong) 宣儀公
> **Spouses**: Liu Sih (Liao Shi) 廖氏, Lou Sih (Lu Shi) 盧氏.
> **Sons:**
>> Eldest son: Wihng Tai (Yongtai) 永泰,
>> Manhood name Ji (Zi) 字: NihmYat (Nianyi) 念一,
>> Designated name Houh (hao)號: Daan Chat
>> (Danqi) 丹七.
>> Second son: Wihng Huhng (Yonghong) 永洪,
>> Manhood name: Nihm Ngh (Nianwu) 念五,
>> Designated name: Daan Ngh (Danwu) 丹五.
>> Third son: Wihng Cheung (Yongchang) 永昌,
>> Manhood name: Nihm Luhk (Nianliu) 念六,
>> Designated name: Daan Baat (Danba) 丹八.

Syun Muih Gung (Xuanmei Gong) 宣梅公
> **Spouse** (unknown)
> **Sons:**
>> Eldest son: Wihng Hing (Yongxing) 永興,
>> Manhood name: Nihm Sei (Niansi) 念四,
>> Designated name: Daan Luhk (Danliu) 丹六.
>> Second son: Wihng Faat (Yongfa) 永發,
>> Manhood name: Nihm Chat (Nianqi) 念七,
>> Designated name: Daan Saam (Dansan) 丹三.
>> Third son: Wihng Wah (Yonghua) 永華,
>> Manhood name: Nihm Yih (Nianer) 念二,
>> Designated name: Daan Sei (Dansi) 丹四.

Hence, each established their separate homes, some stayed put, others moved to Che Ging Chyun (Chejing Cun) (Che Ging Village) 車逕村, Leuhng Hau Tihn (Liangkou Tian) 良口田 and other places or to Sahn Gong (Shengang) 神岡or to other counties but there is no way to find out or verify the facts.

Our Patriarch Daan Chat (Danqi) 丹七 moved to Liuh Choi Chyun (Liaocai Cun) 蓼菜村 in Si Juk Liu Bou (Sizhuliao Bao) (Si Juk Liu

Walled Village) 司竹料堡 in Mouh Dak Leih (Mudeli) 慕德里 in Pun Yuh Yuhn (Panyuxian) 番禺縣 (Pun Yuh County) to live.

The sons and grandsons in Liu Choi Chyun acknowledged him as the primogenitor. Each succeeding descendent then lived there one after the other.

Whether they became scholars (civil servants), farmers, businessmen or artisans, one can see slight improvements in their endeavors. But, if it were not for the skill of the founding father in establishing the family and their accumulation of virtues, how would it be possible for their obtaining these good results? This is what is meant when we say that a strong root will make the branches luxuriant, a river that is deep at its origin will flow a much longer distance. Isn't this saying so true? Therefore, at the present time, with every spring and autumn, offerings and sacrifices are made, and planting is carried out successfully.

These are just the meager efforts that the sons and grandsons had endeavored to repay what their ancestors had done. However, if sons and grandsons were diligent in their studies and had success in passing the civil examinations and bringing honor to the family's reputation, then the work and blessing of those ancestors who went before us and their aspirations would become our clan's great fortune.

To know that this will be passed on not only for one to two generations but possibly to thousands and thousands of generations is the reason this preface is written.

III

From the Beginning to the 75th Year of the Sung Dynasty

During the time of our Primogenitor Sing Yuet Gung (Shengyue Gong) 聖悅公, Emperor Sung Nihng Jung (Song Ningzong) 宋寧宗 (1194-1224), the fourth Emperor of the Southern Sung Dynasty, had a concubine named Sou Sih (Su Shi) 蘇氏, who was very beautiful but rather promiscuous and self-indulgent, and did not fear anything or anyone.

One evening, the Emperor entered her palace. Feeling ill-at-ease and ill-disposed, he, half-heartedly yet stubbornly, tried to indulge in some pleasure but he was not successful. This resulted in the Emperor's displeasure and Sou Sih (Su Shi) was reprimanded on the spot and immediately banished to the "cold palace." But Sou Sih's libido was not abated and was so intense that she decided to flee the palace. She survived by begging during the day and hiding during the night.

At about this time, a wealthy merchant by the name of Wohng Chyuh Maahn (Huang Zhuwan) 黃貯萬 of Ngauh Tihn Fong (Niutian Fang) 牛田坊, Chi Hing Yuhn (Shixing Xian) 始興縣 in Naahm Huhng Fu (Nanxiong Fu) 南雄府, had just transported a shipment of goods to the Capital and was now ready to return home. He was berthed in the bay by the city market. He had just slaughtered a pig to thank his gods for his good fortune and was just about to enjoy his repast when a young woman came to beg for food. This woman was none other than Concubine Sou Sih. It was obvious that Wong Chyuh Maahn did not

8

know who she was. However, he could see that, though her clothes were dirty and torn, she was still quite beautiful.

He was suddenly consumed with lust for her in his heart. He began to cajole her with enticing words, and with the use of innuendo and double-entendre, convinced her to stay and remain hidden in the boat. He then secretly abducted her to his home.

Meanwhile, the Emperor issued a decree and an imperial order to search for and bring Concubine Sou back. Little did he know that his concubine had been gone for a long time and no one had any idea where she could be found. She had disappeared without a trace for quite an extended period. The Emperor became even angrier and gave an imperial order to the Chief of Staff of the Imperial Army, Jeung Ying Jik (Zhang Yingji) 張英績, that he should in turn issue the decree to every local ministry, every prefecture, every province, and every county to seriously investigate to find the missing concubine. However, after many years of fruitless search without any success of finding any traces of the concubine, the minister petitioned the Emperor to permit them to resume and continue the search but this permission was refused by His Majesty.

In the meantime, Wong Chyuh Maahn and Concubine Sou had been home for a number of years, and had reliable information that the coast was not completely clear. Thereupon, the decision was made promptly to change Concubine Sou's name to Mrs. Jeung and to set her up as his secret mistress and paramour. They managed to keep this a secret and no one was able to detect the charade. Unfortunately, one of Mr. Wong's servants, a man by the name of Lahu Jong (Liu Zhuang) 劉壯, rebelled against his master and ran away. He very readily broadcasted the misdemeanor of his master and news of it soon arrived at the Capital.

The aforementioned Chief of Staff of the Imperial Army, Jeung Ying Jik, heard about this crafty and cunning servant and was afraid that this revelation of the secret would eventually get to the Emperor's ears, which would result in a lot of trouble and might cost him his position and even his life.

Therefore, he notified each and every government official, irrespective of their rank, to cover up this misstep. He conceived a secret plan to absolve him of any involvement in the disappearance of Concubine Sou by falsely claiming that he had information of the presence of a nest of robbers in Ngauh Tihn Fong in Guangdong province, and that they were causing a lot of disturbance to the peaceful livelihood of the people there. He, therefore, took up courage to petition the Emperor to allow him to secure some land in the vicinity to construct a facility to station his troops for the purpose of securing peace and apprehending the miscreants in the area.

Coincidentally, a gentleman by the name of Leuhng Kiuh Fai (Liang Qiaohui) 梁喬輝, a son-in-law of Luhng Gun Tin, who was employed as a supervisor in a business in the Capital, heard of the unpleasant news, and fearing this would bode evil, dispatched a family servant to relay this unpleasant news. It did not take too many days before the document approving the forced removal of the tens of thousands of villagers residing in the fifty-eight villages in Ngauh Tihn Fong in Chi Hing Yuhn took effect. Every villager of the tens of thousands in the villages was distressed at the news and many were wailing and crying because of the catastrophe.

The ninety nine families in Jyu Gei Hohng got together and planned on what and how they were to deal with the situation. They heard rumors of the probability of the profitability of migrating south, because the land was wide and sparsely populated. The still undeveloped and unexplored land was suitable for them to migrate to and start their lives anew. At the end of their discussion, they reminisced that what happened to them was not right, and far from fair, but when the master is not righteous and lacks discipline, his ministers will be corrupt. If the ruler is not upright, then ministers will fail to heed advice. Crooked laws will lead to incorrect administration and citizens will bear the brunt, with no recourse for relief.

Thereupon, the group gathered to submit a petition to the provincial authorities to allow them to migrate south. This was refused, and it was therefore decided to resubmit the petition to the Prefecture for their permission, so that they could continue on their journey south. The next chapter is a copy of the petition.

IV

PETITION TO THE PROVINCIAL GOVERNMENT RE: EMIGRATION

We, the petitioners, Luhng Gahn Tin, Loh Gwai, Mahk Sau et al, being residents of Ngaau Tihn Fong, fourteenth Touh 十四圖, Jyu Gei Hohng, wishing to escape from the catastrophe, do hereby plead permission to obtain a timely deliverance from this disaster.

Luhng Gahn Tin and his fellow petitioners have been residents of Jyu Gei Hohng (Zhuji xiang) for generations and have lived in our separate houses. We have always paid our tribute and our farm taxes; have always been law-abiding citizens; have never infringed on any of the laws nor have we owed anyone anything. We have always abhorred anyone who contravened the law. Presently, because of the natural catastrophe which could endanger our lives and home and fearing any unforeseen disaster, and not knowing whether we will have four or five survivors out of every ten if the disaster should strike us, we, therefore, respectfully submit this petition to allow us to migrate.

We pray that permission would be given to us to gather building materials and find land to build our residences. We would respect whatever restrictions decreed and we would not presume to disobey any and all regulations. We are acutely aware that there is no available land close-by to which we can move, but we have heard that land in the south is spacious, sparsely populated, and very suitable for settlement. We dare not presume to make the move without permission.

Herewith, are the signatures of the ninety-nine persons who are begging Your Excellency to approve our petition and grant us the necessary document for passage through different sea and land custom houses. We thank Your Excellency for your indulgence to allow us to go on our way as early as possible so we can build our safe homes to live in.

On this fifth day of the first month of the New Year, in response to the petition to the Provincial Ministry, herewith is the decision of the Minister of Chi Hihng Yuhn (Chi Hihng Province) 始興縣, Minister Yihm Tung Fa (Yan Tonghua) 嚴統化, that permission is granted to the petition.

The petition is a repetition of what has been laid out previously and will not be repeated here.

V

PROCLAMATION OF THANKS

On this tenth day of the first month of the New Year we, the undersigned, hereby proclaim our thanks to Your Excellency for your condescension to decree this document to allow us free passage through all the customhouses whether on land or seaports, thus permitting us peasants the timely opportunity and a clear path to migrate to a safe place to rebuild our lives. We, the following, gratefully submit this petition.

Luhng Gahn Tin	(Long Jintian)	龍近天
Loh Gwai	(Luo Gui)	羅貴
Mahk Sau	(Mai Xiu)	麥秀
Siu Sing Yuet	(Xiao Shengyue)	蕭聖悅
Leih Fuk Wihng	(Li Furong)	李福榮
Wohng Fuk Yuh	(Huang Fuyu)	黃福逾
Leih Ying Yuhn	(Li Yingyuan)	李應元
Luhk Yih Seun	(Lu Yixin)	陸以信
Ngh Yuet	(Wu Yue)	伍悅
Chouh Yat Seuhng	(Cao Yichang)	曹一常
Ngh Maahng Fui	(Wu Mengkui)	吳孟
Jehng Yat Yuhn	(Zheng Yiyuan)	鄭一元
Taahm Gwan Ho	(Tan Junke)	譚君可
Jau Yihn Choih	(Zhou Yancai)	周彥才
Jeung Yuh Hohk	(Zhang Ruxue)	張汝學
Fuhng Yuhn Cheung	(Feng Yuanchang)	馮元昌
Laih Yuhn Muhn	(Li Yuanman)	黎元滿

Louh Yuhn	(Lu Yuan)	盧遠
Fuhng Saam Choih	(Feng Sancai)	馮三才
Wuh Hon Seuih	(Hu Hanrui)	胡漢瑞
Luhk Douh Si	(Lu Daosi)	陸道思
Gou Yuh Si	(Gao Yusi)	高裕思
Leuhng Waih Gou	(Liang Weigao)	梁維高
Yihk Si	(Yi Si)	易思
Mahk Seun Ho	(Mai Xinke)	麥信可
Wohng Yih	(Huang Yi)	黃義
Laih Hung Chiu	(Li Kongzhao)	黎孔昭
Hoh Daaih Sam	(He Dashen)	何大參
Ngh Juhng Yihn	(Wu Zhongxian)	吳仲賢
Chahn Sai Hing	(Chen Shiqing)	陳世卿
Wohng Hoh Yeuhn	(Huang Herun)	黃河潤
Mahn Ho Daaih	(Wen Keda)	文可大
Jau Gun Daaht	(Zhou Guanda)	周觀達
Wohng Juhng Gwai	(Huang Zhonggui)	黃仲貴
Taahm Mahn Gwong	(Tan Wenguang)	譚文廣
Leuhng Wahn Yik	(Liang Hongyi)	梁宏益
Laih Yahn Giht	(Li Renjie)	黎仁傑
Jau Gwan Meih	(Zhou Junmei)	周君美
Leih Baak Jung	(Li Bozong)	李伯宗
Luhk Sing Yuhn	(Lu Shengyuan)	陸聖遠
Leih Dak Yuh	(Li Deyu)	李德裕
Sou Yuh Hing	(Su Ruqing)	蘇汝卿
Jaam Ying Keih	(Zhan Yingqi)	湛英奇
Ngh Gwok Laih	(Wu Guoli)	吳國禮
Wohng Mahn Fu	(Huang Wenfu)	黃文富
Ngau Yih Seun	(Ou Yixin)	區以信
Yihp Saam Chaih	(Ye Sanqi)	葉三齊
Luhk Yeuhn Sihng	(Lu Runcheng)	陸潤成
Fuhng Mahn Jaahk	(Feng Wenze)	馮文澤
Leih Seuhng Luhng	(Li Shanglong)	李上龍
Loh Mahn Yi	(Luo Wenqi)	羅文綺
Wohng Tin Tihng	(Huang Tianting)	黃天挺

Laih Sing Jeun	(Li Shengjun)	黎聖俊
Leuhng Seuhn Fa	(Liang Chunhua)	梁淳化
Hor Yuh Cheuhng	(He Rusiang)	何汝祥
Fuhng Yuhn Jaahk	(Feng Yuanze)	馮元澤
Wong Yuht Jung	(Huang Yuezhong)	黃悅中
Loh Yuhn Buht	(Luo Yuanbi)	羅元弼
Ngh Yuhn Louh	(Wu Yuanlu)	伍元路
Taahm Mahn Fu	(Tan Wenfu)	譚文富
Lauh Mihng Yuhn	(Liu Mingyuan)	劉明遠
Jau Baak Tung	(Zhou Botong)	周伯通
Gwok Ji Gou	(Guo Zigao)	郭子高
Luhk Sai Hing	(Lu Shiqing)	陸世卿
Wohng Haau Haih	(Huang Kaoxi)	黃考系
Jeh Jung Hing	(Xie Zhongqing)	謝中卿
Yun Ho Yik	(Ruan Keyi)	阮可益
Wohng Sing Wihng	(Huang Shengyong)	黃勝永
Ngau Hung Douh	(Ou Kongdao)	區孔道
Lukh Wihng Jaahk	(Lu Rongze)	陸榮澤
Wohng Mahn Laih	(Huang Wenli)	黃文禮
Tong Jo	(Tang Zuo)	湯佐
Laih Mahn Daaht	(Li Wenda)	黎文達
Hoh Mihng Yuh	(He Mingyu)	何明羽
Chahn Sai Douh	(Chen Shidao)	陳世道
Liuh Dak Geui	(Liao Deju)	廖德舉
Leih Ji Choih	(Li Zicai)	李子才
Ngh Sih Laih	(Wu Shili)	吳士禮
Fuhng Yuhn Yuh	(Feng Yuanyu)	馮元俞
Wohng Seuhng	(Huang Chang)	黃裳
Loh Yuet Sau	(Luo Yuexiu)	羅悅秀
Mahk Chyuhn	(Mai Quan)	麥全
Ngh Hin Choih	(Wu Xiancai)	伍顯才
Fuhng Dak Si	(Feng Desi)	馮德思
Tong Daaih Fa	(Tang Dahua)	湯大化
Jau Ji Daaht	(Zhou Zida)	周子達
Wan Juhng Keih	(Yin Zhingqi)	尹仲奇

15

Wohng Yuet Sang	(Huang Yuesheng)	黃悅生
Chouh Yuh Dyun	(Cao Ruduan)	曹汝端
Jung Douh Tuhng	(Zhong Daotong)	鍾道同
Taahm Gwong Seun	(Tan Guangxin)	譚廣信
Jiuh Sai Seuhng	(Zhao Shichang)	趙世常

Herewith is the adjudication of Minister Jung Mahn Daaht (Zhong Wenda) 鍾文達, Minister of Naahm Hung Fu Municipality (Nan Xiong Fu) 南雄府:

Investigation revealed that Luhng Gahn Tin (Long Jintian) and the ninety-nine other persons were originally citizens residing in Jyu Gei Hohng (Zhu Ji Xiang). In their petition, they stated that the reason for their petitioning to move their residences was their concern over the disaster caused by the garrisoning of the military forces in the vicinity and not because of any law or edict that prohibited or enforced them to move. They were petitioning for a permit to allow them free passage to their place of destination. At this point in time, we found no official reason to delay this permission any further.

VI

Official Municipal Proclamation

With respect to the preservation of lives in the refugee problem, Naahm Hung Fu, on this tenth day of the first month of this year, with regards to the petition submitted by Luhng Gahn Tin, et al., concerning the catastrophe and disaster that endangered the lives of five or six out of ten people, we, therefore, upon the issuance of His Majesty's decree, hereby, allow the petitioners to migrate and to construct their residences. It is now decreed that the aforementioned petitioner Luhng Gahn Tin and the ninety-nine others are not unlawful citizens, and that their petition to migrate and build their residences is hereby approved.

It is further instructed that all customhouses, whether on land or sea, will allow them free passage without hindrance, until they have reached their destination. This proclamation will be issued to Luhng Gahn Tin and the ninety-nine other petitioners as a certificate of their approval.

At the beginning of this wonderful year, on the fifteenth day of the first month, the Honorable Secretary Wohng Ying Mauh (Huang Yingmao) 黄鷹茂 carried out the instruction of the Administrative Magistrate of the Prefecture and issued the following certificate. Thereupon, the families of the ninety-nine petitioners began their journey southward from Jyu Gei Hong on the sixteenth day of the third month. On the fifteenth day of the fourth month they reached Lohng Dai Chyun (Langdicun) 蓢底村 in Gu Jit Leih (Gujieli) 古節里 in Dai Leuhng Dou (Daliangdu) 大良都 Gang Jau (Gangzhu) 崗州 in San Wuih Yuhn (Xinhuixian) 新會縣. When they arrived there, they were very fortunate to meet a local person named Fuhng Yuhn Sihng

(Feng Yuancheng) 馮元成, who showed them hospitality by allowing them to rest a few days in his home. Later, Mr. Fuhng took them to the County Prefecture to register their arrival and establish their residencies after paying the necessary tribute. Mr. Fuhng also introduced them to another local person Gong Ying Daaht (Gong Yingda) 龔應達 who acted as their guarantor.

I have decided not to translate the next four documents as they are repetitions of the petition and their subsequent approval:

1. Petition to San Wuih Yuhn to register and establish residencies.
2. Permission granted to reside in San Wuih Yuhn.
3. Petition to Pun Yuh Yuhn (Panyuxian) 番禺縣 to register and establish residencies.
4. Permission granted to reside in Pun Yuh Yuhn.

VII

GENEALOGY

First Generation
   Primogenitor: Daan Chat Gung (Danqi Gong) 丹七公
        Concealed name 諱: Wihng Taai (Yongtai) 永泰
        Manhood name 字: Nihm Yat (Nianyi) 念一
        Eldest son of Syun Yih Gung (Xuanyi Gong) 宣儀公
        Buried: Daai Jou Yuen (Dazu Yuan) 大祖苑
   Spouse 妣: Wuhn Sih (Yun Shi) 運氏
   Sons: Jou Wihng (Zurong) 祖榮
        Jou Fuk (Zufu) 祖福
        Jou Wah (Zuhua) 祖華

Second Generation
   Patriarch: Jou Fuk Gung (Zufu Gong) 祖福公
        Second son of Daan Chat Gung (Danqi Gong) 丹七公
        Buried: Fa Yap (Huayi) Flower City 花邑, Ngaau Minh Deih
        (Niumiandi) "Cow Sleeping Pasture" 牛眠地 cemetery.
   Spouse: Luhk Sih (Lu Shi) 陸氏
        Buried: Fa Yap (Huayi) 花邑Wu Nga Lohk Deih (Wuyaluodi)
        "Raven landing" 烏雅落地cemetery.
   Son: Mihng Daaht (Mingda) 明達
        Home village, Pine Garden Village 本村。松園庄

Third Generation
   Patriarch: Mihng Daaht Gung (Mingda Gong) 明達公
        Son of Jou Fuk Gung (Zufu Gong) 祖福公

Buried: Daaih Jou Yuen (Dazu Yuan) 大祖苑

Spouse: Jeh Sih (Xie Shi) 謝氏

Buried: Daaih Jou Yuen (Dazu Yuan) 大祖苑

Sons: Dai Wuh (Dihu) 帝護

Sing Wuh (Shenghu) 聖護

Home village本村

Fourth Generation

Patriarch: Dai Wuh Gung (Dihu Gong) 帝護公

Eldest son of Mihng Daaht Gung (Mingda Gong) 明達公

Spouse: Douh Sih (Du Shi) 杜氏

Born: Gang Sahn (Gengchen) year 庚辰年, tenth month 十
月ninth day 初九日yauh (you) hour 酉時. Lived 66 years.

Buried: On the seventeenth day of the twelfth month of the
tenth year of the reign of Emperor Wahng Jih (Hongzhi) 弘
治of the Ming Dynasty 明朝.

Re-interred: On the twelfth month of Mouh San (Wushen)
year 戊申, during the reign of Emperor Douh Gwong
(Daoguang) 道光of the Ching (Qing) Dynasty 清朝,
Fortune Master Fuhng (Feng) foretold that on the eleventh
day at the Jih (Si) hour巳時 to repair the grave and to bury
Dai Wuh Gung 帝護公with her.

Sons: Fuk Cheung (Fuchang) 謳昌

Pihng Jou (Pingju) 平祖

Pihng Cheung (Pinchang) 平昌

Gwong Yihn (Guanxian) 廣賢

Home village本村

Fifth Generation

Patriarch: Gwong Yihn Gung (Guanxian Gong) 廣賢公

Fourth son of Dai Wuh Gung (Dihu Gong) 帝護公

Buried: Ravens Landing Cemetery

Spouse: Luhng Sih (Long Shi) 龍氏

Sons: Mauh Ching (Maoqing) 茂青

Ging Chaih (Jingqi) 敬齊

Home village本村
Sixth Generation
    Patriarch: Ging Chaih Gung (Jingqi Gong) 敬齊公
             Second son of Gwong Yihn Gung (Guanxian Gong) 廣賢公
    Spouse: Luhng Sih (Long Shi) 龍氏
    Sons: Ging Mihng (Jingming) 景明
            Wah Saan (Huashan) 華山

Home village本村
Seventh Generation
    Patriarch: Ging Mihng Gung (Jingming Gong) 景明公
             Son of Ging Chaih Gung (Jingqi Gong) 敬齊公
             Buried: On the bank of the Leih (Li) Stream 李溪陂 in the
             Crane Beak Mountain Range 鶴嘴嶺in Flower City 花 邑.
    Spouse: Yuh Sih (Yu Shi) 庾氏
             Buried: Dai Jou Yuen
    Sons: at So (Yisuo) 一所
            Yat Waan (Yiwan) 一灣
            Kiuh Chuhng (Qiaosong) 喬松

Home Village本村
Eighth Generation
Patriarch: Yat So Gung (Yisuo Gong) 一所公
             Eldest son of Ging Mihng Gung (Jingming Gong) 景明公
    Spouse: Jang Sih (Zeng Shi) 曾氏
    Son: Sing Sam (Xingxin) 省心

Pine Garden Village松園庄
Ninth Generation
    Patriarch: Sing Sam Gung (Xingxin Gong) 省心公
             Son of Yat So Gung (Yisuo Gong) 一所公
             Born: Bing Ngh Nihn (Bingwu Nian) 丙午年, ninth month,
    seventeenth day hoih (hai) hour 亥時
             Died: Gaap Yahn Nihn (Jiayin Nian) 甲寅年, sixth month,
    twenty-eighth day
    Spouse: Fuhng Sih (Feng Shi) 馮氏

Born: Ding Mei Nihn (Dingwei Nian) 丁未年, seventh month, ninth day, yauh (you) hour 酉時

Died: Unknown year eighth month, second day.

Buried: Both buried at Dai Jou Yuen

Sons: Jan Hoh (Zehnhe) 振河

Yeuhn Hoh (Runhe) 潤河

Pine Garden Village松園庄

Tenth Generation

Patriarch: Jan Hoh Gung (Zehnhe Gong) 振河公

Son of Sing Sam Gung (Xingxin Gong) 省心公

Spouse: Lauh Sih (Liu Shi) 劉氏.

Married in Leuhng Tihn Chyun (Liangtian Cun) 良田村 (Good Rice Field Village)

Born:Mouh Ji Nihn (Wuzi Nian) 戊子年, twelfth month, twentieth day, Seut (Xu) 戌 hour

Died: Mouh Ji Nihn second month, second day, San (Shen) 申 hour

Sons: Lauh Gwong (Liuguan) 流光

Seuih Gwong (Ruiguan) 瑞光

Gahn Naahm (Jinnan) 近南

Pine Garden Village松園庄

Eleventh Generation

Patriarch: Seuih Gwong Gung (Ruiguan Gong) 瑞光公

Second son of Jan Hoh Gung (Zehnhe Gong) 振河公

Designated name 號: Yuhk Toih (Yutai) 玉臺

Born: Bing Ngh (Bingwu) year 丙午年, eighth month, sixth day, San (Shen) hour 申時

Died: Seuhn Jih (Shunzhi) 順治 Ding Yauh (Dingyou) year 丁酉年, tenth month, twenty-eighth day

Spouse: Hoh Sih (He Shi) 何氏

Born: Gang Seut (Gengxu) year 庚戌年, ninth month, twenty-ninth day, Meih (Wei) hour未時

Died: Hong Hei (Kangxi) 康熙Gei Meih (Jiwei) year 己未年, eleventh month, third day

22

Buried: Both buried at Dai Jou Yuen
Son: Yaht Luhng (Yilong) 逸龍

Pine Garden Village松園庄
Twelfth Generation
Patriarch: Yaht Luhng Gung (Yilong Gong) 逸龍公
Son of Seuih Gwong Gung (Rui Guan Gong) 瑞光公
Designated name 號: Taamh Yan (Tanyin) 潭隱
Born: Seuhn Jih (Shunzhi) 順治 Bing Seut (Bingxu) year 丙戌年, first month, ninth day, Seut hour 戌時
Died: Hong Hei (Kang Xi) 康熙Yuht Meih (Yi Wei) year乙未年 first month, eighth day
Spouse: Fuhng Sih (Feng Shi) 馮氏
Born: Seuhn Jih (Shunzhi) 順治 Bing Gaap (Bingjia) 丙甲年 year, fourth month, twenty-fourth day, Ngh (Wu) hour 午時
Died: Hong Hei (Kangxi) 康熙San Gei (Xinji) 辛己 year, tenth month, twenty-ninth day
Buried: Ox Sleeping pasture, Flower City cemetery
Spouse: Yeuhng Sih (Yang Shi) 揚氏
Born: Hong Hei (Kangxi) 康熙 Yam Yan (Renyin) 壬寅year, eighth month, twenty-third day
Died: Kihn Luhng (Qianlong) 乾隆 Bing Sahn (Bingchen) 丙辰year, eleventh month, fifteenth day
Sons: Jung Wahn (Zongyin) 宗尹
Jung Yih (Zongyi) 宗夷
Jung Lyuhn (Zonglian) 宗聯
Jung Louh (Zonglu) 宗魯
Jung Yahm (Zongren) 宗任
Daughters: Two 二女

Pine Garden Village 松園庄
Thirteenth Generation
Patriarch: Jung Yahm Gung (Zongren Gong) 宗任公
Fifth son of Yaht Luhng Gung (Yilong Gong) 逸龍公
Born: Hong Hei (Kangxi) 康熙Yuet Hoih (Yihai) 乙亥 year, third month, twenty fourth day, Chau (Chou) 丑hour

Died: Kihn Luhng (Qianlong) 乾隆 Gei Maauh (Jimao) year 己卯, eleventh month, twenty-fourth day, Jih (Si) 巳 hour in Maih Gong (Migang) ridge 米岡嶺

Spouse: Gou Sih (Gao Shi) 高氏

Born: Hong Hei (Kangxi) 康熙 Yuht Hoih (Yihai) 乙亥 Year, eleventh month, eleventh day, Mei (Wei) 未 hour

Died: Kihn Luhng (Qianlong) 乾隆 Ding Mei (Dingwei) 丁未 year, ninth month, fourteenth day, Hoih (Hai) 亥 hour

Spouse: Leuhng Sih (Liang Shi) 梁氏

Born: Hong Hei (Kangxi) 康熙 Gei Yauh (Jiyou) 己酉 year, fourth month, twenty second day, San (Shen) 申 hour

Died: Kihn Luhng (Qianlong) 乾隆 Yuht Mei (Yiwei) year, twelfth month, twenty ninth day, Yahn (Yin) 寅 hour

Sons: Lihn Sung (Liansong) 連嵩
Wahn Sung (Yunsong) 雲嵩

Pine Garden Village 松園庄
Fourteenth Generation

Patriarch: Lihn Sung Gung (Liansong Gong) 連嵩公

Eldest son of Jung Yahm Gung (Zongren Gong) 宗任公

Born: Yung Jing (Yongzheng) 雍正 Gang Seut (Gangxu) 庚戌 year, seventh month, fourteenth day, San (Shen) 申 hour

Died: Kihn Luhng (Qianlong) 乾隆 Gaap Ngh (Jiawu) 甲午 year, twelfth month, fifteenth day, Gei (Ji) 巳 hour

Spouse: Gong Sih (Jiang Shi) 江氏

Born: Yung Jing (Yongzheng) 雍正 Yuht Maauh (Yimao) 乙卯 year, fifth month, fifteenth day, Sahn (Chen) 辰 hour

Died: Ga Hing (Jiaqing) 嘉慶 Gei Meih (Jiwei) 己未 year, eleventh month, fourteenth day, Yahn (Yin) 寅 hour

Son: Bing You (Bingyao) 秉耀

Daughter: Married Fuhng (Feng) 馮 of Daaih Mohng Lihng (Dawangling) 大罔嶺 The Great Deceiver Mountain Village.

In the year of Gang Yahn (Geng Yin) 庚寅, during the reign of Emperor Douh Gwong (Daoguang) 道光, on the eleventh month, they were buried in Cheuhn Si Lihng (Xun Shi Ling) 巡獅嶺, which the locals called Cheuhn Sei Lihng (Xun Si Ling) 巡四嶺, in the mountain range behind Mah Nah Tong (Ma Na Tang) Pond 蟆姆塘in the village of Leuhng Tihn (Liantian) 良田. This site was considered unfavorable and a new fortune teller was consulted. In the year of Gwai Mauh (Guimao) 癸卯, a new site was chosen. However, the family decided not to believe in these fortune tellers.

Gong Sih (Gongshi) gave birth to a daughter when she was 27 and a son when she was 35. She became a widow at the age of 39 and her mother-in-law died when she was 43. Her daughter was married when she was 43 and her son was married when she was 50. She lived to see four grandchildren and died at the good age of 65.

Pine Garden Village 松園庄
Fifteenth Generation
Patriarch: Bing You Gung (Bingyao Gong) 秉耀公
Son of Lihn Sung Gung (Liansong Gong) 連嵩公
Pet name 乳名: Saam Gwong (Sanguang) 三光
Second name 別字: Mihng Chaih (Mingqi)　　　　明齊
Designated name 號: Hahng Lohng (Henglang)恒朗
Born: Kihn Luhng (Qianlong) Gei Chau (Jichou) 己丑year, second month, first day, Yau (Yiu) 酉hour
Left for the foreign land Dou Gwong (Dowguang) Gang Sahn (Gangchen) 庚辰year
Died: Haam Fung (Xianfeng) 咸豐Yam Ji (Jenji) 壬子year Fourth month, fourth day, Yan (Yen) 寅hour
Moved to reside in Pine Garden Village 松園庄

Bing Yiu Gung (Bingyao Gong) had chosen an auspicious date to start his business and became well known far and wide. He contracted with Jang Bing Jiu (Zengbingzhao) 曾丙照of Luhng Gong (Longgang) 龍岡and chose a date to build his new house. Rather unexpectedly, and for some unknown reason, Bing Jiu (Bingzhao) claimed that the date was not propitious and intended to break the contract. A lawsuit was filed and when the judgment came Bing Jiu (Bingzhao) was adjudicated to compensate Bing Yiu (Bingyao) 4 vats of Fa Gong (Huagang) wine. Bing Jiu (Bing Zhao) could not fulfill the obligation. Bing Jiu instead went to Bing Yiu's home and killed himself. Bing Yiu decided to flee to a foreign country to avoid the consequences.

Spouse: Chan Sih (Chen Shi) 陳氏
> Born: Kihn Luhng (Qianlong) Ding Hoi (Dinghai) 丁亥 year, seventh month, third day, Gei (Ji) 己hour
> Died: Dou Gwong (Duguang) San Gei (Shenji) 辛己year, eleventh month, seventh day, Mei (Wei) 未hour

Sons: Hor Pahng (Kerpeng) 可
> Nga Gwaih (Yakui) 亞匱 Died in infancy
> Hor Gui (Keju) 可居
> Hor Daht (Keda) 可達
> Hor Chuhng (Kecong) 可從

Concubine: Hauh Sih (Hau Shi) 侯氏
> Born: Kihn Luhng (Qianlong) Yuht Gei (Yiji) 乙己 year, fifth month, nineteenth day, Gei (Ji) 己 hour
> Died: Gar Hing (Jiaqing) Gang Ngh (Gengwu) 庚午, eighth month, eleventh day. She drowned herself in a well.

Sons: Nga Leuih (Yalei) 亞壘 Died in infancy
> Hor Cheuhng (Kexiang) 可翔

Concubine: Foreigner

Sons: Nga Duhng (Yagong) 亞動
> Nga Sok (Yashuo) 亞朔

Pine Garden Village 松園庄
Sixteenth Generation
Patriarch: Hor Sou Gung (Kesu Gong) 可酥公
> Seventh son of Bing You Gung (Binyau Gong) 秉耀公
> Name: Nga Sok (Yashuo) 亞朔
> Born: In foreign land on Suet Ji (Xuzi) 戌子 year, eighth month, first day, Maauh (Mao) 卯 hour
> Died: Gwong Seuih (Guangxu) Gang Yahn (Gengyin) 庚 year, leap second month, fourteenth day

Spouse: Dou Sih (Du Shi) 杜氏
> Born: Gaap Ngh (Jiawu) 甲午year, sixth month, fourteenth day, Yauh (You) 酉hour

Died: Seut Ji (Xuzi) year, seventh month, twenty-fourth day
Son: Chyuhn Sing (Chuansheng) 傳勝

Pine Garden Village松園庄
Seventeenth Generation
Patriarch: Jan Cheung Gung (Zengchang Gong) 振昌公
Son of Hor Sou Gung (Kesu Gong) 可酥公
Name: Chyuhn Sing (Chuansheng) 傳勝
Manhood name: Yauh Kahm (Youqin) 友琴
Spouse: Jeung Sih (Zhang Shi) 張氏
Married: Surabaya, Java (Indonesia)
Sons: Yin Hing (Yanxing) 燕興
Yam Cheuhng (Renxiang) 任祥
Wan Nam (Yunnan) 雲南
Daughters: Two
Spouse: Jong Sih (Zhuang Shi) 莊氏
Married: Swatow
Sons: Kihng Choih (Qiongcai) 瓊材
Lahm Choih (Lincai) 林材
Leuhng Choih (Liangcai) 良材
Ga Choih (Jiacai) 嘉材
Daughters: Meih Laahn (Meilan) 美蘭
Spouse: Mr. Heui [Hui] (Xu) 許
Meih Ching (Meiqing) 美清
Spouse: Mr. Choi (Cai) 蔡

Pine Garden Village松園庄
Eighteenth Generation
Patriarch: Kihng Choih Gung (Qiong Cai Gong) 瓊材公
First son of Jan Cheung Gung (Zengchang Gong) 振昌公
Manhood name: **Hon Giht** [Hon Kit] (Hanjie) 漢傑
Date of Birth: May 15, 1900
Place of Birth: Swatow
Buried: February 18, 1972, Windsor, Ontario, Canada
Spouse: Choi Sih (Cai Shi) 蔡氏

27

Name: **Choi Gam Jing** [Choy Kam Ching]
(CaiJinzhen) 蔡錦貞
Christian name: **Helen**
Date of Birth: July 15, 1901
Place of Birth: Swatow
Married: Swatow
Date of Marriage: 1924
Buried: May 10, 1962 Hong Kong
Sons: Gwong Jou [Kwong Tso] (Guangzu) **Fred** 光祖
Date of Birth: November 25, 1925
Gwong Ji [Kwong Chee] (Guangzhi) **Kenneth**光祉
Date of Birth: September 7, 1928
Daughters: Bik Ji [Pek Che] (Bizhi) **Patsy** 碧芝
Date of Birth: July 4, 1930
Spouse: San Hon Kyuhn [Sun Hon Kuen] (Xin Hanquan)
辛漢權 **Jeffrey**
Bik Chyuhn [Pek Cheun] (Biquan) **Margaret**碧荃
Date of Birth: October 18, 1932
Spouse: Chahn Yat Keui [Chan Yit Kiu] (Chen Yiju) 陳一
駒 **Kenneth**

Patriarch: Ga Choih Gung (Jiacai Gong) 嘉材公
Fourth son of Jan Cheung Gung (Zengchang Gong) 振昌公
Manhood name: **Hon Liht** [Hon Lit] (Hanlie) 漢烈
Christian name: **Henry**
Date of Birth: August 18, 1910
Place of Birth: Swatow
Buried: Vancouver, B.C., Canada
Spouse: Gou Sih (Gao Shi) 高氏
Name: **Gou GamWahn** [Go Kam Wan] (Gao Jinyun) 高錦雲
Christian name: **Kitty**
Married: Canton
Date: October 11, 1936
Son: Gwong Junh [Kwong Chung] (Guangzhong) **John**光中
Date of Birth: January 16, 1948
Place of Birth: Hong Kong

28

Daughters: Waih [Wai] (Hui) **Eileen** 慧

Spouse: Yeuhng Si Houh [Yeung Si Ho] (Yang Sihao) 揚思豪 **Francis Mahn** [Man] (Min)

Gloria 敏

Spouse: Dahng Yan [Tang Yan] (Deng En) 鄧恩 **Meih** [Mei] (Mei)

Connie 美

Spouse: Yu Yahn [Yu Yan] (Yu Ren) **William** 於仁

Pine Garden Village松園庄

Nineteenth Generation:

Gwong Jou Gung [Kwong Tso] (Guangzu Gong) **Fred** 光祖公
Eldest son of Kihng Choih Gung (Qiongcai Gong) 瓊材公
Born: November 25, 1925

Spouse: Wohng Hah Lihng [Wong Ha Ling] (Huang Xialing) 黃霞齡
Christian name: **Helen**
Born: June 7, 1932

Married: St. Paul's Church, Hong Kong
Date: December 1, 1956

Daughter: Juhng Yih [Chung Yee] (Zhongyi) **Leslie** 仲儀
Date of Birth: January 2, 1958

Spouse: Giovanni Ferrazzo

Sons: Gihn Fan [Kin Fan] (Jianxun) **Rory James** 健勳
Date of Birth: April 22, 1959

Yauh Fan [Yau Fan] (Youxun) **Al Norman** 佑勳
Date of Birth: August 25, 1962

Gwong Ji Gung [Kwong Chee] (Guangzhi Gong) **Kenneth** 光祉公
Second son of Kihng Choih Gung (Qiong Cai Gong) 瓊材公
Born: September 7, 1928
Place of Birth: Hong Kong

Spouse: Mary Elizabeth Faber 費妙齡
Born: June 7, 1937
Place of Birth: Martins Ferry, Ohio, USA
Married: Mount Vernon Place Methodist Church, Baltimore, Maryland, USA

Date: August 22, 1956

Son: **Sih Fan** (Shixun) 仕勳 **Stephen Marcus**
Date of Birth: December 5, 1959
Place of Birth: Queen Mary Hospital, Hong Kong

Daughters: Gaai Yih [Kai Yee] (Jiayi) 佳儀 **Ravenna Kay**
Date of Birth: February 18, 1958
Place of Birth: Maryland General Hospital, Baltimore, Maryland, USA
Spouse: Steven Howard Dinolfo

Dak Yih [Tak Yee] (Deyi) 德儀 **Deborah Jean**
Date of Birth: January 30, 1962
Place of Birth: Maryland General Hospital, Baltimore, Maryland, USA
Spouse: Bruce Wayne Brosch

Bik Yih [Bik Yee] (Biyi) 碧儀 **Rebecca Mary**
Date of Birth: July 4, 1963
Place of Birth: Bon Secour Hospital, Baltimore, Maryland, USA
Spouse: Marc William Romine

Yi Yih [Yi Yee] (Yiyi) 漪儀 **Yvette Elizabeth**
Date of Birth: October 17, 1967
Place of Birth: Nethersole Hospital, Hong Kong
Spouse: Andrew Lawrence McMullen

Bik Ji [Pek Che] (Bizhi) 碧芝 **Patsy**
Third child of Kihng Choih Gung (Qiong Cai Gong) 瓊材公
Date of Birth: July 4, 1930
Place of Birth: Hong Kong
Spouse: Jeffrey Hon Kuen Sun
Date of Birth: October 27, 1931
Place of Birth: Hong Kong
Married: St. Paul's Church, Hong Kong
Date: June 11, 1958

Son: San Dihng Wah [Sun Ding Wah] (Xin Dinghua) 辛定華
Patrick
Date of Birth: December 21, 1958

Place of Birth: Nethersole Hospital, Hong Kong
Daughter: San Ging Chih [Sun King Chi] (Xin Jingci) 辛敬慈 **Petrina**
Date of Birth: February 9, 1961
Place of Birth: Kowloon Hospital, Kowloon, Hong Kong
Spouse: Steve Hung

Bik Chyuhn [Pek Cheun] (Biquan) 碧荃 **Margaret**
Fourth child of Kihng Choih Gung (Qiong Cai Gong) 瓊材公
Date of Birth: October 18, 1932
Place of Birth: Hong Kong
Spouse: Chahn Yat Keui [Chan Yit Kiu] (Chen Yiju) 陳一駒 **Kenneth**
Date of Birth: August 18, 1930
Place of Birth: Suzhou, China
Married: St. John's Cathedral, Hong Kong
Date: December 8, 1962
Son: Chahn Gei Leuht [Chan Kai Lek] (Chen Jilu) 陳紀律 **Derek**
Date of Birth: November 9, 1970
Place of Birth: Hotel Dieu, Windsor, Ontario, Canada
Daughters: Chahn Gei Yin [Chan Kai Yin] 陳紀賢 **Renee Sarah Chan**
Date of Birth: July 26, 1963
Place of Birth: Hong Kong
Spouse: Jeff Clark
Chahn Gei Hang [Chan Kai Hang] 陳紀衡 **Elaine Chan**
Date of birth: November 11, 1965
Place of Birth: Hong Kong
Spouse: Mario Fabiano

Waih [Wai] (Hui) 慧 **Eileen**
Eldest child of Ga Choih Gung (Jiacai Gong) 嘉材公
Place of Birth: Hong Kong
Spouse: Yeung Si Houh [Yeung Sze Ho] (Yang Sihao) 揚思豪 **Francis**
Married: St. Teresa's Church, Hong Kong

Date: September 23, 1961
Daughter: Claire Yeung
Place of Birth: Kowloon Hospital, Kowloon, Hong Kong

Mahn [Man] (Min) 敏 **Gloria**
Second child of Ga Choih Gung (Jiacai Gong) 嘉材公
Place of Birth: Hong Kong
Spouse: Dahng Yan [Tang Yan] (Deng En) 鄧恩
Married: St. Thomas' Church, Corstorphine, Edinburgh, Scotland, UK
Date: June 10, 1965
Son: Hugh Tang
Date of birth: June 28, 1966
Place of Birth: Queen Mary Hospital, Hong Kong
Daughter: Genevieve Tang
Date of Birth: January 12, 1968
Place of Birth: Nethersole Hospital, Hong Kong

Meih [Mei] (Mei) 美 **Connie**
Third child of Ga Choih Gung (Jiacai Gong) 嘉材公
Date of Birth: February 14, 1944
Place of birth: Hong Kong
Spouse: Yu Yahn [Yu Yan] (Yu Ren) 於仁
Married: Holy Name, Vancouver, BC, Canada
Date: July 27, 1968
Daughter: Carol Yu
Date of Birth: April 16, 1969
Place of Birth: Vancouver General Hospital Willow Pavilion, Vancouver, BC, Canada
Son: **Ian Yu**
Date of Birth: March 26, 1970
Place of Birth: Vancouver General Hospital Willow Pavilion, Vancouver, BC, Canada

Gwong Jung Gung (Guangzhong Gong) 光中公 **John**
Fourth child of Ga Choih Gung (Jiacai Gong) 嘉材公

Date of Birth: January 16, 1948
Place of Birth: Hong Kong
Spouse: Susan Chang Siu 張學諄
Date of Birth: April 2, 1947
Place of Birth: Hangchow, 杭州 China
Married: St. Matthias Anglican Church, Vancouver, BC, Canada
Date: August 4, 1973

Son: **Jin Bong** [Chin Bong] (Zhanbang) 展邦
Date of Birth: June 3, 1975
Place of Birth: Ottawa, Ontario, Canada

Daughter: Jin Mihng [Chin Ming] (Zhanming) 展明
Date of Birth: December 9, 1978
Place of Birth: Ottawa, Ontario, Canada

Twentieth Generation:
Leslie Ann (Siu) Ferrazzo
Eldest child of **Fred & Helen (Wong) Siu**
Date of birth: January 2, 1958
Place of Birth: St. Francis Hospital, Kowloon, Hong Kong

Spouse: Giovanni Ferrazzo
Date of Birth: September 9, 1954
Place of Birth: Mesoraca, Italy
Married: St. Francis of Assisi, Assisi, Italy
Date: April 11, 2000

Son: **Domenico Ferrazzo**
Date of Birth: August 28, 2004
Place of Birth: Windsor Regional Hospital Metropolitan Campus, Windsor, ON, Canada

Daughter: Maria Rosaria Ferrazzo
Date of Birth: August 28, 2004
Place of Birth: Windsor Regional Hospital Metropolitan Campus, Windsor, ON, Canada

Rory James Siu
Second child of **Fred & Helen (Wong) Siu**

Date of Birth: April 22, 1959
Place of Birth: St. Francis Hospital, Hong Kong

Spouse: Catherine Lyn Ball

Date of Birth: July 24, 1961
Place of Birth:
Married: St. Mark by the Lake Anglican Church, St. Clair Beach, Windsor, ON, Canada
Date: May 23, 1988

Daughters: Caitlin Rae Siu

Date of Birth: June 7, 1989
Place of Birth: Windsor Regional Hospital Metropolitan Campus, Windsor, ON, Canada
Kirstin Alyssa Siu
Date of Birth: September 15, 1990
Place of Birth: Windsor Regional Hospital Metropolitan Campus, Windsor, ON, Canada
Jillian Rose Siu
Date of Birth: September 28, 1994
Place of Birth: Windsor Regional Hospital Metropolitan Campus, Windsor, ON, Canada

Alfred Norman Siu

Third child of **Fred & Helen (Wong) Siu**
Date of Birth: August 25, 1962
Place of Birth: Nethersole Hospital, Hong Kong

Spouse: Irene Mary Kenney

Date of Birth: September 20, 1956
Place of Birth:
Married: St. Paul's United Church, Windsor, Ontario, Canada
Date: October 1, 1991

Daughter: Leah Mary Siu

Date of Birth: December 21, 1995
Place of Birth: Windsor Regional Hospital, Windsor, Ontario, Canada

Ravenna Kay (Siu) Dinolfo

Eldest Child of **Kenneth & Mary Elizabeth, Betty (Faber) Siu**

Date of Birth: February 18, 1958

Place of Birth: Maryland General Hospital, Baltimore, Maryland, USA

Spouse: Steven Howard Dinolfo

Date of Birth: January 9, 1954

Place of Birth: Saint Louis, Missouri, USA

Married: First United Methodist Church, Jefferson City, Missouri, USA

Date: December 28, 1979

Sons: Anthony Kenneth Dinolfo

Date of Birth: March 2, 1984

Place of Birth: St. Mary's Hospital, Jefferson City, Missouri, USA

Died: February 8, 2000

Buried: February 10, 2000, Jefferson City, Missouri, USA

Joseph Ambrose Dinolfo

Date of Birth: May 6, 1986

Place of Birth: St. Mary's Hospital, Jefferson City, Missouri, USA

Daughters: Kathleen Elizabeth Dinolfo

Date of Birth: August 5, 1988

Place of Birth: St. Mary's Hospital, Jefferson City, Missouri, USA

Died: November 6, 2012

Buried: November 10, 2012, Jefferson City, Missouri, USA

Janis Rae Dinolfo

Date of Birth: February 22, 1991

Place of Birth: St. Mary's Hospital, Jefferson City, Missouri, USA

Stephen Marcus Siu

Second child of **Kenneth & Mary Elizabeth, Betty (Faber) Siu**

Date of Birth: December 5, 1959
Place of Birth: Queen Mary Hospital, Hong Kong
Spouse: Jennifer Marie Scott
Date of Birth: January 12, 1971
Place of Birth: University Hospital, Iowa City, Iowa
Married: Oakwood Baptist Church, Lees Summit, Missouri, USA
Date: July 19, 1997

Deborah Jean (Siu) Brosch
Third child of **Kenneth & Mary Elizabeth, Betty (Faber) Siu**
Date of Birth: January 30, 1962
Place of Birth: Maryland General Hospital, Baltimore, Maryland, USA
Spouse: Bruce Wayne Brosch
Date of Birth: October 10, 1963
Place of Birth: San Antonio, Texas, USA
Married: First Baptist Church, Jefferson City, Missouri
Date: April 3, 1993

Rebecca Mary (Siu) Romine
Fourth child of **Kenneth & Mary Elizabeth, Betty (Faber) Siu**
Date of Birth: July 4, 1963
Place of Birth: Bon Secours Hospital, Baltimore, Maryland, USA
Spouse: Marc William Romine
Date of Birth: December 2, 1954
Place of Birth: Sigourney, Iowa, USA
Married: First Baptist Church, Jefferson City, Missouri, USA
Date: March 23, 1991
Son: Austin Morris Romine
Date of Birth: April 18, 1997
Place of Birth: St. Mary's Hospital, Jefferson City, Missouri, USA

Yvette Elizabeth (Siu) McMullen
>Fifth child of **Kenneth & Mary Elizabeth, Betty (Faber) Siu**
>Date of Birth: October 17, 1967
>Place of Birth: Nethersole Hospital, Hong Kong

Spouse: Andrew Lawrence McMullen
>Date of Birth: June 5, 1964
>Place of Birth: Kansas City, Missouri
>**Married:** Grace and Holy Trinity Cathedral, Kansas City, Missouri,
>USA
>Date: August 10, 1991

Daughters: Hannah Lacey McMullen
>Date of Birth: December 20, 1994
>Place of Birth: St. Luke's Hospital, Kansas City, Missouri, USA

Rachel Elizabeth McMullen
>Date of Birth: July 18, 1997
>Place of Birth: St. Luke's Hospital, Kansas City, Missouri, USA

Natalie Day McMullen
>Date of Birth: October 13, 1999
>Place of birth: St. Luke's Hospital, Kansas City, Missouri, USA
>Died: October 13, 1999 Buried: October 18, 1999, Leavenworth, Kansas, USA

Abigail Grace McMullen
>Date of Birth: October 1, 2001
>Place of Birth: St. Luke's Hospital, Kansas City, Missouri, USA

Sophia Hope McMullen
>Date of Birth: December 21, 2004
>Place of Birth: St. Luke's Hospital, Kansas City, Missouri, USA

Patrick Sun
>Eldest child of **Jeffery & Patsy (Siu) Sun**
>Date of Birth: December 21, 1958
>Place of Birth: Nethersole Hospital, Hong Kong

Spouse: Cynthia Mong [Mong Sien Yee] 蒙情兒
>Date of Birth: August 8, 1959
>Place of Birth: Hong Kong

Married: St. Margaret's Church, Hong Kong
    Date: June 19, 1989
Son: **Jeremy Sun [Sun Hien Kwan]** 辛衍君
    Date of Birth: October 8, 1994
    Place of birth: Adventist Hospital, Hong Kong
Daughters: Lauren Sun [Sun Waih Kwan] 辛蕙君
    Date of Birth: October 26, 1995
    Place of Birth: Hong Kong Sanatorium & Hospital, Hong Kong
Kristen Sun [Sun Yin Kwan] 辛妍君
    Date of Birth: July 23, 1998
    Place of Birth: Hong Kong Sanatorium & Hospital, Hong Kong

Petrina (Sun) Hung
    Second child of **Jeffrey & Patsy (Siu) Sun**
    Date of Birth: February 9, 1961
    Place of Birth: Kowloon Hospital, Kowloon, Hong Kong
Spouse: Steve Hung
    Date of Birth: August 25, 1956
    Place of Birth: Hong Kong
Married: Christ Church, Kowloon Tong, Hong Kong
    Date: February 25, 1989
Sons: **Sean Hung [Hung Jaak Lai]** 洪澤禮
    Date of Birth: March 5, 1991
    Place of Birth: Adventist Hospital, Hong Kong
Ivan Hung [Hung Jaap Tso] 洪澤祖
    Date of Birth: October 8, 1996
    Place of Birth: Hong Kong Sanatorium & Hospital, Hong Kong

Renee Sarah Chan
    Eldest child of **Kenneth & Margaret (Siu) Chan**
    Date of Birth: July 26, 1963
    Place of Birth: Hong Kong

Spouse: Jeff Clark
Date of Birth: October 3, 1963
Place of Birth: Toronto, Ontario, Canada
Married: Toronto, Ontario, Canada
Date: August 20, 1988
Daughters: Frances Clark
Date of Birth: April 16, 1991
Place of Birth: Halifax, Nova Scotia, Canada
Valerie Clark
Date of birth: April 6, 1993
Place of birth: Halifax, Nova Scotia, Canada
Laura Clark
Date of Birth: August 20, 1997
Place of birth: Halifax, Nova Scotia, Canada

Elaine Chan
Second child of **Kenneth & Margaret (Siu) Chan**
Date of Birth: November 11, 1965
Place of Birth: Hong Kong
Spouse: Mario Fabiano
Date of Birth: October 24, 1966
Place of Birth: Italy
Married: Toronto, Ontario, Canada
Date: June 18, 1994
Son: Joey Fabiano
Date of Birth: May 26, 1996
Place of Birth: Toronto, Ontario, Canada
Daughters: Claire Fabiano
Date of Birth: September 24, 2004
Place of Birth: Toronto, Ontario, Canada
Elizabeth Fabiano
Date of Birth: April 11, 2006
Place of Birth: Toronto, Ontario, Canada

Derek Chan
Third child of **Kenneth & Margaret (Siu) Chan**

Date of Birth: November 9, 1970

Place of Birth: Hotel Dieu, Windsor, Ontario, Canada

Spouse: Sharon Lai Fan Lau

Date of Birth: July 18, 1970

Place of Birth: Li Kee Hospital, Kowloon, Hong Kong

Married: Cotton Tree Drive Marriage Registry, Hong Kong

Date: May 10, 1996

Daughters: Hailey Chan

Date of Birth: November 8, 1996

Place of Birth: St. Teresa's Hospital, Kowloon, Hong Kong

Krista Chan

Date of Birth: October 26, 2002

Place of Birth: North York Hospital, Toronto, Ontario, Canada

Claire Yeung

Eldest daughter of **Francis & Eileen (Siu) Yeung**

Place of birth: Kowloon Hospital, Hong Kong

Spouse: Vivienne Stewart

Married: Supreme Court, Vancouver, BC, Canada

Date: June 11, 2005

Hugh Tang [Ho Yin] 浩然

Eldest child of **Yan & Gloria (Siu) Tang**

Date of Birth: June 28, 1966

Place of Birth: Queen Mary Hospital, Hong Kong

Spouse: Ivy Chan[Chahn On Ming] 陳安明

Married: Cotton Tree Drive Marriage Registry, Hong Kong

Date: August 17, 2001

Son: **Ernest Tang** 子

Date of Birth: February 15, 2002

Place of birth: Adventist Hospital, Hong Kong

Genevieve Tang [Tse Wai] 之慧

Second child of **Yan & Gloria (Siu) Tang**

Date of birth: January 12, 1968

Place of birth: Alice Ho Miu Ling Nethersole Hospital, Hong Kong

Carol Yu[Ka Hei] 加曦
Eldest child of **Yan & Connie (Siu) Yu**
Date of birth: April 16, 1969
Place of birth: Vancouver General Hospital Willow Pavilion, Vancouver, BC, Canada
Spouse: Maury Kolof
Married: Beth Israel Synagogue. Vancouver, BC, Canada
Date: August 8, 1999
Daughter: Hanna Samantha Kolof [Mei] 美
Date of birth: September 17, 2001
Place of birth: BC Women's Hospital, Vancouver, BC, Canada
Son: Aidan Marcus Kolof [Yan] 仁
Date of birth: July 7, 2003
Place of birth: BC Women's Hospital, Vancouver, BC, Canada

Ian Yu [Ga Wahng] 加弘
Second child of **Yan & Connie (Siu) Yu**
Date of birth: March 26, 1970
Place of birth: Vancouver General Hospital Willow Pavilion, Vancouver, BC, Canada
Spouse: Heather [Mui Si] 梅氏
Married: Holy Name, Vancouver, BC, Canada
Date: September 11, 1999
Sons: **Logan Yu [Tsi Yan]** 智仁
Date of birth: September 3, 2003
Place of birth: BC Women's Hospital, Vancouver, BC, Canada
Liam Michael Yu [Tsi Hang] 智恆
Date of birth: December 4, 2005
Place of birth: BC Women's Hospital, Vancouver, BC, Canada

Linden Edward Yu [Tsi Geen] 智堅
>Date of birth: December 4, 2005
>Place of birth: BC Women's Hospital, Vancouver, BC, Canada

Henry Eugene Siu [Tsien Bong] 展邦
>Eldest child of **John & Susan (Chang) Siu**
>Date of Birth: June 3, 1975
>Place of Birth: Ottawa, Ontario, Canada

Spouse: Jodie Lee Thompson [Tong Siu Yee] 湯兆宜
>Date of Birth: July 21, 1973
>Place of Birth: Medicine Hat, Alberta, Canada

Married: Cecil Green House, Vancouver, BC, Canada
>Date: July 3, 1999.

Son: **Holden Thompson Siu [King Dou]** 敬道
>Date of Birth: April 4, 2008
>Place of Birth: Vancouver, BC, Canada.

Lindsay Lorraine (Siu) Raedcher [Tsien Ming] 展明
>Second child of **John & Susan (Chang) Siu**
>Date of Birth: December 9, 1978
>Place of Birth: Ottawa, Ontario, Canada

Spouse: Chris Raedcher 芮
>Date of Birth: November 26, 1971
>Place of Birth: Canada

Married: Vancouver, BC, Canada.
>Date: May 9, 2009

Son: Rivers Raedcher [Yan Hor] 恩河
>Date of birth: November 21, 2010
>Place of birth: Vancouver, BC, Canada

Twenty First Generation:
Domenico Ferrazzo
>Eldest child of **Giovanni & Leslie Ann (Siu) Ferrazzo**
>Date of Birth: August 28, 2004

TOTAL TRANSFORMATION

Place of Birth: Windsor Regional Hospital, Metropolitan Campus, Windsor, ON, Canada

Maria Rosaria Ferrazzo
Second child of **Giovanni & Leslie Ann (Siu) Ferrazzo**
Date of Birth: August 28, 2004
Place of Birth: Windsor Regional Hospital, Metropolitan Campus, Windsor, ON, Canada

Caitlin Rae Siu
Eldest child of **Rory & Catherine (Ball) Siu**
Date of Birth: June 7, 1989
Place of Birth: Windsor Regional Hospital, Windsor, ON, Canada

Kirstin Alyssa Siu
Second child of **Rory & Catherine (Ball) Siu**
Date of Birth: September 15, 1990
Place of Birth: Windsor Regional Hospital, Windsor, ON, Canada

Jillian Rose Siu
Third child of **Rory & Catherine (Ball) Siu**
Date of Birth: September 28, 1994
Place of Birth: Windsor Regional Hospital, Windsor, ON, Canada

Leah Mary Siu
Eldest child of **Al & Irene (Kenney) Siu**
Date of Birth: December 21, 1995
Place of Birth: Windsor Regional Hospital, Windsor, ON, Canada

Anthony Kenneth Dinolfo
Eldest child of **Steven & Kay (Siu) Dinolfo**
Date of Birth: March 2, 1984

43

Place of Birth: St. Mary's Hospital, Jefferson City, Missouri, USA
Died: February 8, 2000
Buried: February 10, 2000, Jefferson City, Missouri, USA

Joseph Ambrose Dinolfo

Second Child of **Steven & Kay (Siu) Dinolfo**
Date of Birth: May 6, 1986
Place of Birth: St. Mary's Hospital, Jefferson City, Missouri, USA
Spouse: Jules Brogan Moore
Date of Birth: December 4,1986
Place of Birth: Charles E. Still Hospital, Jefferson City, Missouri, USA
Married: October 16, 2014, Jacksonville Beach, Florida, USA
Sons: **Brooks Anthony Dinolfo**
Date of Birth: July 7, 2010
Place of Birth: Capital Regional Medical Center, Jefferson City, Missouri, USA

Milo Kene Dinolfo

Date of Birth: August 5, 2013
Place of Birth: Capital Regional Medical Center, Jefferson City, Missouri, USA
Daughter: Morrison Michaele Dinolfo
Date of Birth: January 20, 2012
Place of Birth: Capital Regional Medical Center, Jefferson City, Missouri, USA

Kathleen Elizabeth Dinolfo

Third child of **Steven & Kay (Siu) Dinolfo**
Date of Birth: August 5, 1988
Place of Birth: St. Mary's Hospital, Jefferson City, Missouri, USA
Died: November 6, 2012
Buried: November 10, 2012, Jefferson City, Missouri, USA

Janis Rae Dinolfo
> Fourth child of **Steven & Kay (Siu) Dinolfo**
> Date of Birth: February 22, 1991
> Place of Birth: St. Mary's Hospital, Jefferson City, Missouri, USA

Austin Morris Romine
> Child of **Marc & Becky (Siu) Romine**
> Date of Birth: April 18, 1997
> Place of Birth: St. Mary's Hospital, Jefferson City, Missouri, USA

Hannah Lacey McMullen
> Eldest child of **Andrew & Yvette (Siu) McMullen**
> Date of Birth: December 20, 1994
> Place of Birth: St. Luke's Hospital, Kansas City, Missouri, USA

Rachel Elizabeth McMullen
> Second child of **Andrew & Yvette (Siu) McMullen**
> Date of Birth: July 18, 1997
> Place of Birth: St. Luke's Hospital, Kansas City, Missouri, USA

Natalie Day McMullen
> Third child of **Andrew & Yvette (Siu) McMullen**
> Date of Birth: October 13, 1999
> Place of birth: St. Luke's Hospital, Kansas City, Missouri, USA
> Buried: October 13, 1999, Leavenworth, Kansas, USA

Abigail Grace McMullen
> Fourth child of **Andrew & Yvette (Siu) McMullen**
> Date of Birth: October 1, 2001
> Place of Birth: St. Luke's Hospital, Kansas City, Missouri, USA

Sophia Hope McMullen
> Fifth child of **Andrew & Yvette (Siu) McMullen**
> Date of Birth: December 21, 2004
> Place of Birth: St. Luke's Hospital, Kansas City, Missouri, USA

Jeremy Sun

    Eldest Child of **Patrick & Cynthia (Mong) Sun**

    Date of Birth: October 8, 1994

    Place of Birth: Adventist Hospital, Hong Kong

Lauren Sun

    Second child of **Patrick & Cynthia (Mong) Sun**

    Date of Birth: October 26, 19

    Place of Birth: Hong Kong Sanatorium & Hospital, Hong Kong

Kristin Sun

    Third child of **Patrick & Cynthia (Mong) Sun**

    Date of Birth: July 23, 1998

    Place of Birth: Hong Kong Sanatorium & Hospital, Hong Kong

Sean Hung

    Eldest child of **Steve and Petrina (Sun) Hung**

    Date of Birth: March 5, 1991

    Place of Birth: Adventist Hospital, Hong Kong

Ivan Hung

    Second child of **Steve & Petrina (Sun) Hung**

    Date of Birth: October 8, 1996

    Place of Birth: Hong Kong Sanatorium & Hospital, Hong Kong

Frances Clark

    Eldest child of **Jeff & Renee (Chan) Clark**

    Date of Birth: April 16, 1991

    Place of Birth: Halifax, Nova Scotia Canada

Valerie Clark

    Second child of **Jeff & Renee (Chan) Clark**

    Date of Birth: April 6, 1993

    Place of Birth: Halifax, Nova Scotia Canada

Laura Clark
>Third child of **Jeff & Renee (Chan) Clark**
>Date of Birth: April 20, 1997
>Place of Birth: Halifax, Nova Scotia Canada

Joey Fabiano
>Eldest child of **Mario & Elaine (Chan) Fabiano**
>Date of Birth: May 26, 1996
>Place of Birth: Toronto, Ontario, Canada

Claire Fabiano
>Second child of **Mario & Elaine (Chan) Fabiano**
>Date of Birth: September 24, 2004
>Place of Birth: Toronto, Ontario, Canada

Elizabeth Fabiano
>Third child of **Mario & Elaine (Chan) Fabiano**
>Date of Birth: April 11, 2006
>Place of Birth: Toronto, Ontario, Canada

Hailey Chan
>Eldest child of **Derek & Sharon (Lau) Chan**
>Date of Birth: November 8, 1996
>Place of Birth: St. Teresa's Hospital, Kowloon, Hong Kong

Kristen Chan
>Second child of **Derek & Sharon (Lau) Chan**
>Date of Birth: October 26, 2002
>Place of Birth: North York Hospital, Toronto, ON, Canada

Ernest Tang
>Eldest child of **Hugh & Ivy (Chan) Tang**
>Date of Birth: February 15, 2002
>Place of Birth: Adventist Hospital, Hong Kong

Hanna Samantha Kolof
>Eldest child of **Maury & Carol (Yu) Kolof**

Date of Birth: September 17, 2001
Place of Birth: B.C. Women's Hospital, Vancouver, BC, Canada

Aidan Marcus Kolof

Second child of **Maury & Carol (Yu) Kolof**
Date of Birth: July 7, 2003
Place of Birth: B.C. Women's Hospital, Vancouver, BC, Canada

Logan Yu

Eldest child of **Ian & Heather (Bui) Yu**
Date of Birth: September 3, 2003
Place of Birth: B.C. Women's Hospital, Vancouver, BC, Canada

Liam Michael Yu

Second child of **Ian & Heather (Bui) Yu**
Date of Birth: December 4, 2005
Place of birth: B.C. Women's Hospital, Vancouver, BC, Canada

Linden Edward Yu

Third child of **Ian & Heather (Bui) Yu**
Date of Birth: December 4, 2005
Place of birth: B.C. Women's Hospital, Vancouver, BC, Canada

Holden Thompson Siu

Eldest child of **Henry Eugene & Jodie Lee (Thompson) Siu**
Date of Birth: April 4, 2008
Place of Birth: B.C. Women's Hospital, Vancouver, BC, Canada

Rivers Raedcher

Eldest child of **Chris and Lindsay (Siu) Raedcher**
Date of Birth: November 21, 2010
Place of Birth: B.C. Women's Hospital, Vancouver, BC, Canada

VIII

INTERLUDE

I've just finished documenting what was purported to be the beginning of our family tree and the subsequent generations of the Siu Clan. I've also tried to trace, as much as possible, the facts as recorded in the transcribed copy of our Juhk Pou, which my second uncle, Lahm Choy obtained from the temple in Pun Yuh (Panyu) county.

Just as the genealogy book intimated in the first sentence that a tree looks to its root and a river to its origin, so *Homo sapiens* have an affinity to search for their beginnings. Is it any wonder, then, that the first sentence of the first chapter of the first book, i.e., Genesis 1:1, of the Holy Bible reads, [1]" *In the beginning God created the heavens and the earth?"* [24] The Holy Bible is the Inspired Word of God, the Book which all "true followers" of Jesus Christ believe in, the Book that contains the authoritative truths about God, His sovereignty, His preexistence and eternality, and His creation of the whole universe with neither the assistance from anyone nor the use of any preexistent matter! The point I want to make is that I believe that God was alone when this event took place at the beginning and He created the universe out of nothing (*creation ex nihilo*). In His creation He created light and separated it from darkness, and then he caused the land to rise out of the waters. In effect, God was responsible for the creation of time and space. This, to me, is the most significant event of the Creation account apart from His creation of Adam and Eve.

Talking about time and space reminds me of the story of our

---

[24] *The Holy Bible: New International Version.* 1996, c1984 (electronic ed.) (Ge 1:1). Grand Rapids: Zondervan.

designated Primogenitor **Siu Sing Yuet Gung** in our genealogy story. You will recall from the Sou Concubine incident at the beginning of the story that this took place in Hsuchou in Jiangsu Province during the reign of the Emperor Sung Ningzong (1194-1224). It is my assumption from the information given that the date of the Sou incident was in the year 1208 AD. **Holden Thompson Siu** was born in 2008, which would mean that his date of birth would be 800 years from the time the infamous Sou Concubine incident took place. In other words, the time span from our designated Primogenitor, Siu Sing Yuet Gung up to and including our newest member of the family, Holden Thompson Siu, is 800 years and runs through twenty generations. At that time our Primogenitor Siu Sing Yuet was probably about 40 - 50 years old and I will agree arbitrarily that a generation is reckoned to occur or recur on an average of a forty year cycle. Since Holden is designated as the twenty-first generation, it would be exactly correct according to this reckoning of 40 years to a generation making a total of 800 years, which is exactly the time span between Siu Sing Yuet Gung's move southward toward PunYuh and the time of Holden's birth.

I am enclosing an interesting history of the Southern Sung Dynasty and its relation to Hong Kong and the Chinese Emperors' timeline just for your curiosity. Enjoy.

IX

EMPEROR SONG NINGZONG

The **Song Dynasty** (宋朝 960-1279) is divided into **Northern Song** (960-1127) in which Song controlled both Northern and Southern China and when the capital was in Kaifeng, and **Southern Song** (1127-1279) in which Song lost control of Northern China to the Liao Dynasty, later replaced by the Jin Dynasty (1115-1234) and retreated south of the Yangtze River to form its capital at Hangzhou.

In 1276, the Southern Song Dynasty court fled to Guangdong by boat, fleeing Mongol invaders, and leaving Emperor Gong of Song China behind. Any hope of resistance centered on two young princes, Emperor Gong's brothers. The older boy, Zhao Shi, aged nine, was declared emperor, and, in 1277, the imperial court sought refuge first in Silvermine Bay (Mui Wo) on Lantau Island and later in today's Kowloon City, Hong Kong (see also Sung Wong Toi). The older brother became ill and died, and was succeeded by the younger, Zhao Bing, aged seven.

When in 1279 the Song army was defeated in its last battle, the Battle of Yamen, against the Mongols in the Pearl River Delta, a high official is said to have taken the boy emperor in his arms and jumped from a cliff top into the sea, drowning both of them. These emperors are also believed to have held court in the Tung Chung valley, which takes its name from a local hero who gave up his life for the emperor. Hau Wong, an official from this court, is still revered as a god in Hong Kong.

X

Chinese Dynasties
中國朝代

Five Rulers 黃帝至舜	ca. 27-22 cent. BC
Xia Dynasty 夏	a. 22-16 cent. BC
Shang Dynasty 商	16 cent. BC – 1066 BC
Zhou Dynasty 周	
Western Zhou 西周	1066 BC – 771 BC
Eastern Zhou 東周	
Spring and Autumn 春秋時代	ca. 8-3 cent. BC
Warring States 戰國時代	770 BC – 221 BC
Qin Dynasty 秦	221 BC – 206 BC
Han Dynasty 漢	
Western Han 西漢	206 BC – 8 AD
Eastern Han 東漢	25 – 220
Three Kingdoms 三國	
Wei 魏	220 – 265
Shu 蜀	221 – 263
Wu 吳	
Six Dynasties 六朝	
Jin 晉	
Western Jin 西晉	265 – 316
Eastern Jin 東晉	317 – 420
Southern and Northern Dynasty 南北朝	
Southern Dynasty 南朝	420 – 589

Northern Dynasty 北朝	386 – 581
Sui Dynasty 隋	581 – 618
Tang Dynasty 唐	618 – 907
Five Dynasties 五代	907 – 960
Song Dynasty 宋	
Northern Song 北宋	960 – 1127
Southern Song 南宋	1127 -1279
Liao Dynasty 遼	907 -1125
Western Xia Dynasty 西夏	1032 - 1227
Jin Dynasty 金	1115 – 1234
Yuan Dynasty 元	1279 -1368
Ming Dynasty 明	1368 – 1644
Qing Dynasty 清	1644 – 1911
Republic of China 中華民國	1912 -
People's Republic of China 中華人民共和國	1949 -

Events Outside of China at the Same Time

Outside	Dynasty
Egypt	Neolithic
	Shang
Assyria	Zhou
Greece	Qin
Roman Empire	Han
Dark Ages	Three Kingdoms
	Jin
	Sui
Charlemagne	Tang
Five Dynasties	
Feudalism in Europe	Song
	Yuan
Renaissance	Ming
Industrial Revolution	Qing

XI

MY GRANDFATHER: SIU YAU KAM

Figure 2. Siu Yau Kam (Xiao Youqin) 蕭友琴, my grandfather

According to our genealogy book, my grandfather was born in Surabaya, Indonesia. There was no notation of his date of birth or any other details except that he married a woman surnamed Cheung and had three sons and two daughters in Surabaya.

The next entry showed that he married my grandmother, surnamed Jong in Swatow (Shantou) who gave birth to two daughters and four sons, my father being the oldest son and the third child of my grandparents.

I know that my grandfather was alive when I was born in 1928 and that he was bed-ridden for about seven years, most probably from a stroke, before he died. I do not have the date of his death nor do I remember any of the details of the funeral. I remember vaguely that our family went to Swatow on a steamer from Hong Kong for his funeral. I was perhaps five or six at the time, but I am only guessing. He was buried in Song Tin (Sangtian). Checking with Uncle Henry's widow, Aunt Kitty, who is now 94 years old and still lucid, I found out that Grandfather died in early 1937. Aunt Kitty married Uncle Henry in 1936 and Grandfather passed away the following year.

Figure 3. Siu Clan migration map.
Siu Clan migrated in Sung Dynasty from Hsu Chow (A) to Pun Yuh (B). Later generations migrated to Surabaya, Indonesia (C). Grandfather Siu migrated from Surabaya to Swatow (Shantou) (D).

Recently, I found out from a distant relative who was a resident of Song Tin that my grandfather was the "mayor" of the village of Song Tin. However, I have not been able to find out how and when he got there from Surabaya, nor when he retired and how he got to Swatow. I regret very much that I did not have the opportunity to go there for a visit with this relative of mine. I could have found out some interesting facts, but I'm afraid this will remain an enigma this side of eternity.

While reading through the genealogy, I came across an interesting alteration in my great-great-grandmother's surname. It looks as if my grandfather was responsible for making the alteration. We surmise that he wanted to hide the fact that his father was half Chinese and half Indonesian. Let me explain.

The original entry for his grandmother's surname was the word that designated she was a foreigner, 番氏, and not a Chinese. As you look closely at the word in the genealogy book, you can see that a radical for water has been added to the left side of the word, which altered the word into the word for Poon (Pan), a common Chinese surname 潘氏.

I bring this interesting addendum to point out the fact that we now understand fully why one of my sisters and one of my cousins, my father's brother's daughter both have a striking resemblance to the beautiful Indonesian girls. This trait also appears in subsequent generations, in one of my daughters and one of my granddaughters.

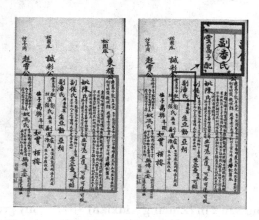

Figure 4. Page from Siu Family Genealogy
On the left is the unmarked page. On the right the
alterations are magnified and highlighted in gray.

XII

MY GRANDMOTHER: JONG SAU YIN

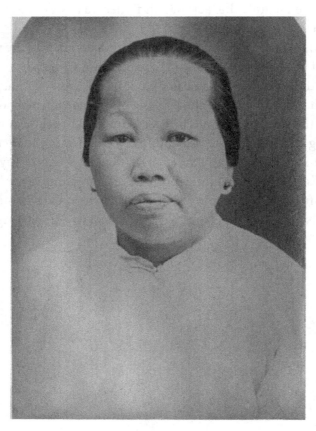

Figure 5. Jong Sau Yin (Zhuang Xiuxian) 莊秀賢**, my grandmother**

I was never told, nor have I ever been aware, when Grandmother came
to live with us in Hong Kong following Grandfather's burial. However,

I would not be too far off the mark if I were to suppose that she could have moved from Swatow to Hong Kong in the late 1930's. One reason for this was the Marco Polo Bridge Incident, which happened on July 7, 1937, when Japan, using the pretense of their search for a missing soldier, invaded China. The result was that Japan invaded a number of port cities in China, including Swatow and Canton, which led to a considerable migration of people from the affected areas to avoid the devastation of war and the Japanese military occupation. There was an influx of thousands of refugees into Hong Kong. In fact, one of my cousins—the eldest daughter of my eldest aunt, that is, my father's eldest sister—came to live with us about the same time, with her son named "Porky", who may be around four or five years younger than I. He used to hang around me a lot. The sad part is that we lost contact with each other with the onset of the Second World War on December 8 (December 7 in the USA), 1941.

My memories of my grandmother, 莊秀賢, are quite vague because I don't think that we were very close any of the time that she lived with us. I do remember that she was very good at sewing and quilting and, during the first few years of her stay with us, she even made the shirts and shorts that I wore every day. She had a special worktable where she laid out the material. Then she would place the paper patterns over it and pin them on the material before cutting the patterns out. Then she would sew the pieces together with the sewing machine or, as often was the case, by hand with needle and thread.

She never told me about herself or her past though I don't think that I could stay still long enough for her to tell me anything that would interest me. I do know that she smoked. She did have one of those fancy metal water pipes that she used to smoke her native tobacco. Sometimes she would roll the tobacco into wedge-shaped cigarettes by hand and smoke them. She kept her hair in a bun which was capped off with a commercially made bun with a net over it. She also used thick gummy "pomade" made from resin that was soaked out of strips of wood shavings shaved with a plane to keep her hair tidy. Finally, she had bound feet up till after the Revolution and the overthrow of the Ching Dynasty. Her feet were quite deformed so she had a very different gait and could not walk fast at all. She used to tell us that when they began to bind her feet, the soles of the feet would rot away and they had to unwrap the binding once in a while to clean her feet and to get rid of the debris from the degenerating skin and soft tissue that was pressed and bound up. She said that she had a lot of pain even when the binding was unwrapped. What a warped sense of beauty!

One very unhappy accident happened to Grandmother one night around 1950. I cannot remember the exact time but it could have been about the time I was a fourth year medical student at the University of Hong Kong. I say that because it was a compulsory requirement to reside at the dormitory in the University for the first three years after which we could live wherever we wanted. Since the accident happened when I was living at home then it stands to reason that it was around 1950.

Grandmother had trouble getting to sleep at night and she would still be up pacing the floor until three or four o'clock in the morning. Meanwhile, I had gone to bed earlier than usual because I had to wake up early the next morning so I could cross the harbor and get to the University in time for an examination at eight o'clock in the morning. Grandmother was getting in and out of bed in her room at the back of the house and she fell and struck her head on the hard concrete floor making a big cut in her scalp. The servant tried to help her and she managed to stop the bleeding by sticking a big wad of tobacco into the wound and wrapping a big towel around her head. It did stop the bleeding.

She quickly went to tell my father and when he saw Grandmother and the bloody bandage, he tried to get back to his room, probably to tell my mother, and promptly fainted on the way. Meanwhile, Mother was up and they got Father back in bed and they decided to wake Fred up to take care of things. Unfortunately, when Fred got back to see Grandmother, he did the exact thing Father did. Soon, they got me up and after I got dressed in a hurry, the servant and I took Grandmother with us to Kowloon Hospital. Needless to say, the nurses and the doctor gave me a lecture on the principles of first aid and how tobacco, especially the locally produced kind, was not the ideal haemostatic agent to use. I am sure they did not know that I was a medical student or at least I did not volunteer that information. It could have been a lot more embarrassing to say the least!

60

Grandmother had to be hospitalized and after the paperwork was finalized, I was informed by the police that I had to report the accident to the Police Substation in Tsim Sha Tsui so off I went to the Police Station. Finally, it was time to go home to get changed and head off to the University. I can't remember whether I passed the exam or not, but I did go on to graduate from the Medical Faculty of the University of Hong Kong at the end of six years and was in the first graduating class of the University Medical Faculty after the end of hostilities of the Second World War.

Grandmother was discharged from hospital and went to stay with Uncle Henry and Aunt Kitty. She apparently had a stroke and sadly was bed-ridden. It had to be a strain on Uncle Henry, Aunt Kitty, and my cousins. According to my cousins, Grandmother never quite recovered from the fall which broke her head and apparently damaged her mind. Grandmother didn't seem to be in her right mind again. She never left her bed. She never recognized anybody. She just kept talking aloud in her native dialect to either herself or some imaginary person non-stop, day and night. She seemed to be at times wailing, at times yelling and at times pleading. She passed away on April 6, 1952. It was the day after Ching Ming, or Tomb-Sweeping Day, a traditional Chinese festival also called Ancestors' Day.

XIII

MY PARENTS: MR. AND MRS. SIU HON KIT

**Figure 6. Mr. & Mrs. Siu Hon Kit, my father
and mother, at their wedding**

My parents were married in Bethel Church in Swatow (Shantou) in 1924. I had no knowledge of how they met and how long they were engaged until Gloria, my cousin, told me a romanticized story of my parents' meeting. It was my second aunt, my father's elder sister, who brought them together. And it was the same Second Aunt who told my cousins the story. Second Aunt met my mother at True Light Middle School. She saw a sweet and gentle girl, educated, from a good family, the right age, a Christian, and, most important of all, a Swatow girl! It was a godsend. Second Aunt immediately thought about her younger brother, i.e., my father, who was probably too shy to approach girls. How could she let this golden opportunity slip! So she played the part of matchmaker, got a figurative big palm-leaf fan (大葵扇), and started fanning and fanning the spark she thought she saw, and kept fanning and fanning until she ignited their fire. The romance story had a happy ending. My parents were married at Bethel Church in Swatow in an elaborate western-style Christian wedding. Mother was a beautiful bride!

The following year, my elder brother was born. They probably left Swatow (Shantou) in 1926 or 1927 to come to Hong Kong, where my father started his business. My mother never told us what my father did except that he was in the export business. It appeared that my father had shipped a shipment of goods on order to the United States but never received any payment for it because of the Great Depression. Mother never elaborated the details to us, except that it devastated my father so much that he almost became a recluse for two years, owing to his depression. Although I was not told the exact date it happened, mother had many times reminded me of the Great Depression and how it had caused my father's business to collapse, just as it happened to a lot of people throughout the world at that particular period. She did not sound bitter even though the two years must have been difficult to endure. I can surmise that my mother's faith in God must have sustained her. She was understanding and supportive all through. She finally convinced my father that he had nothing to be ashamed of. After two years she coaxed him to go under the employ of my maternal grandfather in his store and help manage the export business. My father did become the Export Manager of the Swatow Drawn Work Co., Ltd., and retired around 1970.

It is a joy to know that every friend and acquaintance of my father expressed to us the fact that my father was an honest and honorable man.

XIV

MY FATHER: SIU HON KIT

Figure 7. Siu Hon Kit, my father

My father retired in 1970 and emigrated to Windsor, Ontario in Canada, where my older brother resided. My father visited us in Jefferson City and stayed with us for a while. At that time, I was going through one of the trying times in my life. It was a hiatus in my career where I had to patiently wait for the licensing law in Missouri to change.

We were living in a rented house but because we needed more space my father helped to panel the basement so we could have an extra bedroom and living space.

I was quite surprised that he was quite good at carpentry, especially since I had never seen him take up a hammer or a saw in all my "growing-up" years. We knew he was very good at planting roses and fruit trees. We still think of those delicious peaches he grew in Fred's front yard in Windsor and wish we could have some now.

Figure 8. Father in front yard 108 Belair Dr.

When he was staying with us we learned some healthy habits he had, though at the time we thought they were rather quaint. Betty and I would sometimes reminisce and chuckle to ourselves over his idiosyncrasies. But, he always reminded me of the old time scholar gentlemen, we know as Gwan Ji (Junzi) 君子. Let me give you an example of what I mean. This is a little ditty he wrote one day when he was staying with us in Jefferson City:

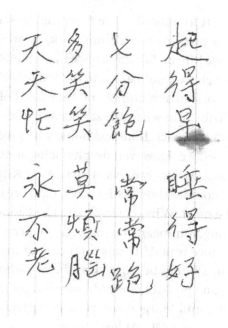

Figure 9. Father's ditty

Early to rise
Do sleep well
Seventy-percent full
Always take walks
Laugh a lot
Do not worry
Be busy every day
Never get old

One of the highlights of my life was that my father was present at the commencement and the reception when I started my surgical practice in Jefferson City in 1972. I sincerely hoped that was one of the proud moments of his life.

As I look back over the years in an attempt to write something about my father, I am struck with the stark realization that I don't know a whole lot about my father. I do remember that he was a man of few words and, besides, we remember that when we were kids we seldom saw him when we were home. In other words, he was seldom around. We often said that when we left for school in the morning, he was usually still in bed and by the time he came home from work, we would be already in bed. We did get to see him on Sundays, once in a while, especially during Christmas time, when we would all go to the Swatow Christian Church in Hong Kong to worship as a family and then head off to a restaurant for Yam Cha and Dim Sum when the service was over.

My father was very strict. If he was home when we were awake, we knew we'd better behave. However, despite being notoriously naughty and mischievous and extremely hyper-active (Aunt Kitty would endorse these epithets and could elaborate on them), I am proud to say that my father loved me the most. Why do I say that? The Chinese have a saying which goes, "Hitting you means loving you, so, because I love you let me hit you a few more times!" If this is true, then my father loved me the most among my siblings because I was the one who got spanked the most by my father, and probably the only one who got spanked. So there, Fred! So there, Patsy and Margaret! (I guess, secretly, we were glad that father was seldom home, LOL. At least I was.)

Things changed a lot during the Second World War because my father had to stay home a great deal of the time, partly for political reasons and partly the result of economic constraints.

Rightly or wrongly...whether I plead guilty or plead the Fifth Amendment...Uncle Harry, my mother's brother, who was ranked sixth in the family, gave me a nickname, which branded me in our family a little, but was certainly a common sentiment in the Choy family which is my mother's family. He called me "Durian." Yet, it really is quite a relatively neutral name. Let me explain. If you are familiar with the fruit, it is a much-prized fruit in Malaysia and Singapore, where a lot of these fruit trees are cultivated. For those who are aficionados of the very pungent fruit, there is nothing on earth that can compare with its smell and taste. To them, it is a heavenly fruit that can send them heavenward once they are able to put their teeth to it. Conversely, if you are among those who can get violently ill if they get too close to the fruit and if they were foolish enough to get coaxed into trying a taste of it, it is hard to imagine what their reaction would be. In case you want a better description of it, Betty said that it tasted like cat excrement! Anyway, there you have it. Uncle Harry who was obviously not a fan of the fruit gave me the nickname, but I like to think that just as the aromatic and smelly fruit can bring screams of delight to the fanatic who would die for the fruit and send the squeamish dissenter who would not want to be caught dead with a bite of the fruit in the mouth for dear life, so it is with me. There are those who have branded me a hopeless brat but then there are those who, like my mother, knew that one day things would be different...that one day I would be transformed.

XV

My Mother: Choy Kam Ching

Figure 10. Choy Kam Ching, my mother

My mother was the eldest child in the family. She had six brothers and four sisters, but the youngest brother died in infancy.

My mother told us that when she was in her high school years she was sent to school in Shanghai with Aunt Bernice and Uncle Geoffrey, the second and third child in the family. There she learned to play the piano and lawn tennis. She said she liked to play tennis a lot but as is often the case, a favorite sport can turn out to be a bugaboo in your life.

She dislocated her shoulder during one of her matches and as a result had to return to Swatow to recuperate. This cut short her ambition of becoming good at her favorite sport though she was able to travel to Canton (Guangzhou) to continue her education. She attended True Light Middle School, an elite Christian school that was, and is still, well-known for its academic standards as well as for being a champion of Christian education for young women. It was while she was attending True Light Middle School that she met my second aunt and, through her, my father. As I reported earlier they had a Christian wedding at Bethel Church.

Speaking of the Christian wedding brings to mind how our family became Christians. One of the most encouraging things I have heard from my mother and my maternal Uncle Ted was the conversion of Great-grandmother Choy and my grandfather Choy Hon Yuen. I shall not go into great detail because this was well documented in my Uncle Ted's Autobiography *"My Dreams and Visions"* Golden Morning Publishing. Winchester, Virginia 22604, USA.

The following excerpt is crystallized from what Uncle Ted wrote in p.12 of his autobiography:

Uncle Ted's father had promised the missionary doctor who treated him for his severe stomach ailment, that should he be healed, he would give serious thought to the Christian faith. Uncle Ted said that God did heal his father, my Grandfather Choy, through the prayers and skill of the Christian doctor. Then Grandfather Choy made a sincere and life-changing decision to worship the True God and believe in Jesus Christ as his Savior.

Tragically, however, an unexpected turn of events occurred when Grandfather Choy found out soon after his conversion, that his mother, my Great-grandmother Choy took exception and immediately ran away from home and starved herself in protest. Grandfather Choy, being a dutiful and filial son, immediately set out and made a diligent search for his mother. He finally found her secluded in an abandoned house and it took a considerable amount of leading and coaxing before she agreed to return home with her son. It took a lot of love and understanding, plus an inordinate amount of fervent prayer, care and concern of the family and Christian friends before Great-grandmother Choy finally accepted

Jesus as her Savior and converted to Christianity. Nevertheless, what follows is even more spectacular and almost beyond belief!

Prior to her most remarkable and praiseworthy conversion to Christianity, Great-grandmother Choy was known to be a serious, no-nonsense worshipper of the spirits with a reputation of having a curt and fierce disposition...in other words, a bad temper. She was very careful about her offerings to her gods and burned her joss sticks regularly to keep up her good graces with the spirits and the gods. It was small wonder that she was angry with Grandfather Choy for becoming a Christian.

The Chinese have this belief that when you die, your spirit will need a son to offer incense and offerings so that the gods will conduct the spirit of the deceased home instead of leaving it to become a wandering spirit, a curse not to be endured. Great-grandmother Choy was angry with Grandfather Choy for not fulfilling his duty as a son, thus depriving her of someone to guide her spirit home when it came time for her to depart from this world. This was one of the reasons why the non-Christian Chinese disowned their children should they become Christians. They believed that the sons were sinning against the laws of filial piety, leaving their spirits wandering in the air with no one to lead them home. But, the most remarkable transformation was that Great-grandmother Choy became quite the "prayer-warrior" after becoming a Christian. She was well-known for her practice of sitting by the front room window each and every morning praying fervently that some of her children, grandchildren and grandchildren's children would become Christians, in spite of the fact that the young children of the neighborhood gathered in front of the house to make fun of the old lady!

Praise God! While I do not have the date of her conversion, Great-grandmother Choy died in 1929 and had one of the biggest Christian burials in Bethel Church in Swatow. It is with profound gratitude and honor to say that eighty years after her death, I can count at least nine of her descendents who had been or are now serving our Lord Jesus Christ as pastors, preachers, ministers or church-workers, scattered over four different countries in three continents, as of this date in 2010. Hallelujah!

What do I say to all of this? Simple! Prayer works. As the Scripture says, "[37]For nothing is impossible with God."[25] (Luke 1:37). This confirms in my mind the faithfulness of God in keeping His Covenant with us and reminds me of my obligation to keep faith at my end with my Covenant with God.

You could have noticed as you read this book the picture of my parents' wedding. They were married in the Bethel Church in Swatow in 1924 and it would have been one of the big Christian weddings in the church because by this time, my mother's father, Grandfather Choy would have been quite successful in his business besides being a faithful Christian and most likely a supporter of the church.

I was told that Grandfather Choy became a successful businessman when he went to Hong Kong to ply his trade on the ever-growing freighter and passenger steamer business between the ports of Hong Kong and those in the United Kingdom, Western Europe, and the United States. What Grandfather Choy and others from Swatow did was to carry their supply of embroidered silk or linen blouses, handkerchiefs, table cloths, pajamas, bed sheets, and pillow cases, get permission to board the ships after they were berthed or docked, spread their wares out on deck and start selling. They were all so successful that they all eventually opened their shops in the Central District of Hong Kong and eventually they all were involved with exporting their goods to Australia, South Africa, Europe, the United States, and Canada.

However, one thing that I feel obligated to tell you is that most pleasing to all of us is that all these businessmen from Swatow did not live and act as competitors, but rather, they remembered that most, if not all, were Christians in Swatow, and they felt the need to unite and start a Swatow-speaking Church in their district so that they could have a church to worship their God together. Anyway, they did what they hoped to do and started a church in Hong Kong.

They, therefore, organized and started the Swatow Christian Church in the Central District of Hong Kong. Originally the church was on the 3rd floor of On Lok Yuen Restaurant and Company on Queen's Road Central. I do not have the date they started the church though I can remember going to the church to celebrate Christmas with the family. It was a necessity then because they called their pastor from Swatow and

---

[25] The NIV Study Bible, Zondervan, Grand Rapids, MI, USA, 1536

it was beneficial to the folks to be able to worship in their own tongue and dialect. The church is still there, though it has moved to Shelly Street and, I am sure, most things are now done in Cantonese since the newer generations that grow up in Hong Kong have difficulty using their mother dialect of Swatow!

Earlier, I said that my parents were married in Bethel Church in Swatow in 1924 in a big Christian church wedding, probably attended by a lot of friends and relatives. The following year Fred was born.

Once again, I can only fall back to my conjecture that my parents decided that it was best for them that they should migrate to Hong Kong in hopes of starting a business that might be as lucrative as the one my grandfather did when he came to Hong Kong. They left Fred in Swatow under the care of Grandmother Choy and made their way to Hong Kong, most probably in 1927. As best I could gather, my father had a business partner and they were engaged in the same business as my Grandfather Choy. It could have been that they were doing more of an export trade as opposed to being in the retail business. Perhaps my father's business was quite auspicious at the beginning seeing that it was at the time of the Roaring Twenties and the Western World was enjoying the bounty of this luxurious cornucopia.

On the 7th day of September, 1928, in the midst of the Year of Dragon, I was brought into the world in our flat on the 1st floor of No. 91 Austin Road, in Kowloon, with the help of a Japanese midwife. On all accounts, the Year of the Dragon according to the Chinese Zodiac is a good year, since the Dragon, in Chinese mythology, is an auspicious animal representing the Emperor. Who would have thought that, within a year of my birth that the whole financial world would collapse from the notorious Great Depression of 1929? Suffice it to say that, as my mother had frequently remarked, my father lost his fortune overnight. His merchandise was shipped overseas but there was no money to pay for the goods. Mother would only recount that Father became a recluse overnight and would not step out of the house for months on end. Being a Chinese "gentleman scholar" or Gwan Ji, he felt ashamed and took it very personally.

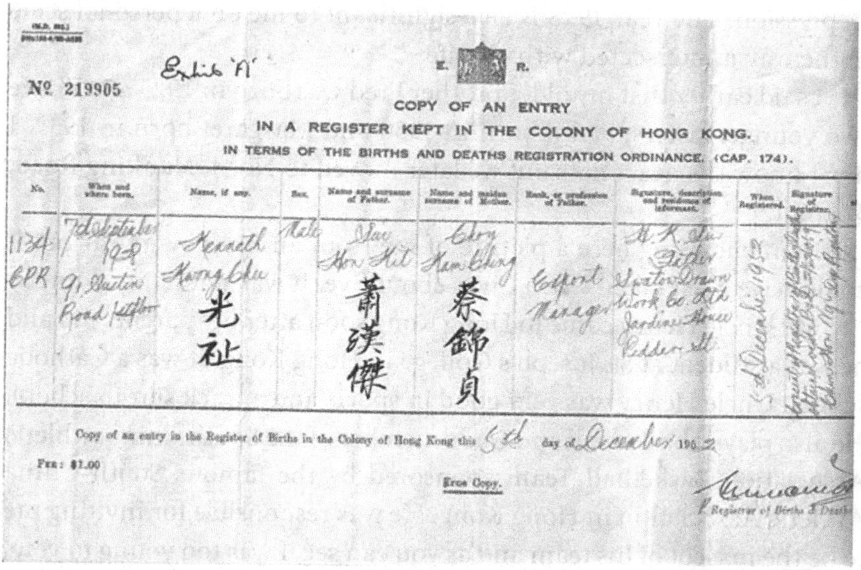

Figure 11. My birth certificate.

My mother said that it took him two years to get out of his depression. My mother consoled him and encouraged him as much as she could. I don't doubt that she spent a lot of time in prayer. In the meantime, she most likely helped the household expenses by taking in embroidery piece-work such as handkerchiefs, blouses, table clothes, and pajamas, from Swatow Drawn Work Company. She would also "hire" girls from the Swatow community to come and join in this enterprise.

Praise God that Mother was patient and loving, and finally Father agreed to take a position in Grandfather Choy's company, and ultimately, he became the Export Manager of the Swatow Drawn Work Company, where he loyally and honorably contributed his abilities for many years of honest and loyal service. I had earlier talked about his retirement and subsequent emigration to Canada.

The year 1928 was a momentous year in more ways than one, but most significantly, the after-effects of what took place were felt worldwide as well as long-lasting and universal. The significant thing about the year 1928, according to Wall Street, the financial world and the banking industry, is that 1928 signals the end of the "Roaring Twenties" with its excesses and the beginning of what we now know as the Great

Depression. The year 1928 is also significant to me on a personal scale in the way it intersected with my life.

I said earlier that my older brother Fred was born in 1925 and I have two younger sisters, Patsy, born in 1930 and Margaret born in 1932. I don't know the exact date but we later moved to No. 4, Nanking Road, 3rd floor.

I am enclosing here a picture of me from an unknown year but it could have been taken when I was about five. It was not of my doing.

My Uncle Henry came to Hong Kong soon after my parents did and he was a student at St. Joseph's College in Hong Kong. It was a Catholic school. Uncle Henry was very good in sports and a track star in school. He also played basketball and was a member of the South China Athletic Association Basketball Team sponsored by the famous South China Athletic Association in Hong Kong. He was responsible for inviting me to be the mascot of his team and as you can see, I was too young to vote, so there I was.

Figure 12. The mascot of SCAA Basketball Team.
Uncle Henry is on front row 3rd from left

South China Athletic Association was for a long time a perennial powerhouse in soccer or association football, though her basketball team was also quite prominent, and so was lawn tennis. I am not sure whether the team won the Championship or not—probably not, because I was not invited to be the mascot the following year. One interesting result of this encounter with the basketball team was that when I studied medicine at the University of Hong Kong in 1952, I got interested in playing basketball. I was not a star but I became involved with being the Hon. Secretary of the Hong Kong University Basketball Association. I was able to invite Mr. Siu Kit Man 蕭傑民 to be our Hon. Coach and was honored that he was willing to serve a second year when I was elected Chairman of the Association.

Mr. Siu is seated on the fourth seat from the left on the front row in the picture. Doubtless, you would easily come to the conclusion that he and my Uncle Henry were very good friends, or you might even say they were like brothers; after all, they have the same surname.

XVI

PRIMARY SCHOOL
1933 to 1937

Kwong Wah Primary School光華小學 was situated on the first floor of
No. 222 Nathan Road, just to the north of the intersection with Jordan
Road, on the west side of Nathan Road. It had four classrooms from
Primary 1 to Primary 4. The headmistress was a Miss Ko 高 and she had
three other teachers helping her. One was her younger sister, while the
other two were two sisters who were also her sisters-in-law. The teachers
and the Headmistress were all Christians and were very friendly and
kind. The teachers were all married except for the Headmistress. It was
a very friendly and personal and personable school. The only drawback
was that it did not have a playground or soccer field.

My brother Fred and I were enrolled at the school in September of
1933. I entered the school system as a Primary One student and Fred was
most likely in Primary Two. The year was 1933 and I was soon to be five.

I do want to tell you about one of my best friends ever. His name
is Tsang Shiu Liang曾紹良. He is a year older than I and he lived with
his family in the flat next door to ours. We were on the 2nd floor of No.
4 Nanking Street and Ah Mak亞目 (Eye, in the Swatow dialect and
duly called Uncle Eye by our kids) Shiu Liang's family lived in No. 6.
His father, Mr. Tsang Gyiap Boon曾業文, was known in his office and
among his friends, as well as the public, as曾師耶. He was the interpreter
at Johnson, Stokes and Masters, Solicitors, a very famous and well-
known law firm in Hong Kong. When my father eventually worked
for Grandfather Choy as the export manager in his company, which he

aptly named The Swatow Drawn Work, Co. Ltd., they had their legal work done by Johnson, Stokes and Masters, probably because of the connection with Mr. Tsang. Mr. Tsang became a very close friend of my father's and naturally his kids also became our friends. Shiu Liang had two elder brothers and an elder sister. The two older siblings became friends with my Uncle Steve and Aunt Lillian, my mother's youngest brother and sister. His second older brother, Shiu Fan紹勳, nicknamed Nose鼻, is the same age as my brother Fred. Ah Mak and I were in the same grade at Kwong Wah Primary School. I had a good education there.

My parents made a decision that we should continue our education in a school where we could learn both English and Chinese, It was quite natural for them to ask Uncle Henry to help us enter La Salle College in Kowloon City. It was a new school and Uncle Henry knew the Christian Brothers who ran the school since he graduated from St. Joseph's College in Hong Kong. I remember my mother talking about how Uncle Henry was able to get the Brothers to give us a discount of HK$1.00 on the school fees. I think it was from HK$4.00 to HK$3.00 a month. I will have more to say about my years in La Salle College later. I am not sure where Shiu Liang went to school after he left Kwong Wah Primary. However, as luck would have it, our families moved out of Nanking Street at the same time and our new homes were in adjoining streets in Tsim Sha Tsui. We moved to the ground floor of No. 11 Cameron Road while Shiu Liang's family moved to No. 16 Granville Road. Our houses were directly back to back across a back alley. It was not at all difficult for us to get together and play all our childhood games together in the streets in front of our houses.

Another unending tie we had was that our families were members and worshippers in the same Swatow Christian Church that my grandfather organized with some of his business friends in Hong Kong, since both our families came originally from Swatow. As time went on, the church found it necessary to have a chapter started in Haiphong Road in the Tsim Sha Tsui section of Kowloon since many of us were living in Kowloon. It was a lot more convenient for us to attend Sunday school and the Sunday morning worship in the佈道所Evangel Hall of the Swatow Christian Church.

Eventually the congregation grew so fast and furious that a new church was finally built on Pratt Avenue where it remains to this day. Sometime around 1950, Ah Mak and I soon gathered about a dozen of the guys who were our friends in church, ranging in age from sixteen to twenty-one and we became fast friends. We were active in our church activities but also gathered often to shoot the breeze, hangout, eat noodles and snack foods and generally had ourselves a lot of good clean fun. We dubbed ourselves the馬浪盪 (literally the horse's waves). More often than not, we really enjoyed the times we had together when we could go to a noodle shop or a dessert shop and enjoy the good food and the camaraderie. Looking back, I can say I am thankful to God that none of us ever got into trouble with the church, the adults, or the parents. Needless to say, we never had any encounters with the law.

Another pleasant memory I had of my pal Shiu Liang was that when we were in our preteen years, we would often take walks together from our homes in Tsim Sha Tsui and we would walk north on Chatham Road, past Hung Hom and end our walk in Kowloon City. We just talked about our happy times, the funny episodes in our lives, our dreams and hopes for the future. We would often be so tired at the end of the walk to Kowloon City that we would ride the bus home. However, more often than not we would be out of any pocket money and would have to grin and bear it and walk home.

This link to our friendship remained strong even through the forced separation of the Second World War, when Ah Mak's family evacuated to the village in Chiu Chow, while we stayed behind in Hong Kong.

We, finally, found ourselves staying in the same hostel, Eliot Hall at the University of Hong Kong, after the Japanese surrendered to the Allies and peace came to Hong Kong at last. We found satisfaction when we represented Eliot Hall in the 4x100 relay at the University Sports Day. We didn't win any medals but we took part, and that's what counts! A final tidbit about the race was that we did not have any spike shoes to run in, but somehow Ah Mak was able to borrow a pair from a friend and, being life-long buddies, we each put on a single shoe. I think I had the left shoe, but, somehow, it didn't really matter. I seriously doubt that the spikes made any difference because we were not track and field stars, nor did it matter! The best part of it all was that we had fun and we shared what we had. It's our friendship that counts…money and material things do NOT mean a thing.

I went on and graduated from Medical School in 1952 but I regret to say that Ah Mak had to drop out of Engineering School and work in a bank. We still kept our friendship even though I had to leave Hong Kong to travel to the United States for a surgical residency program to fulfill my ambition to become a general surgeon so I could return to Hong Kong and help any who were unfortunate enough to require surgery but were financially disadvantaged.

Eventually, we were forced to return to the United States in 1968 and we lived in Jefferson City, Missouri. We found out that Shiu Liang was now living in Vancouver, British Columbia with his family. We went to visit him and had a wonderful time together. Ah Mak was working as a Customs officer.

One of the interesting remarks he made was when I marveled and inquired about those wonderful dogs they used to detect controlled substances, contraband narcotics, and drugs. He, in his usual nonchalant manner, brushed it off and said, "Those dogs are stupid dogs." When I asked him why he said that, he went on to say, "They howl and fuss like they really find some drugs. But when they quickly open the suitcases they find…dirty clothes!"

I never knew Shiu Liang had a health problem. You remember we ran a race in HKU. But, he told me that he was found to have a heart valve disease and had an operation for it and was taking medication. Anyway, we made plans for him and his family to come and visit us in Jefferson City. Sad to say, it was not to be. A few days before they were due to come see us, his sister Norma called on the phone to say that my dear friend Shiu Liang had a serious problem with his heart and he died. I have nothing more to say, except that one day we will see each other again in Heaven. So, till then, au revoir! 後會有期.

One other rather unbelievable thing that I must relate is that in 1998, I had the great good fortune of answering God's call to serve as Pastor of the Sha Lei Tau Baptist Church in Macau. I shall be relating to you the how, the why, and wherefore that we found ourselves in Macau at my tender age of 70. But, for now, let me just briefly say that in August 1994, I was assigned to be the Medical Missions Administrator of the

Hope Medical Clinic, of the Macau Baptist Mission, under the Foreign Missions Board of the Southern Baptist Convention.

I will have more to say about that later but right now, let me tell you that a conflict arose between the Congregation of Sha Lei Tau Baptist Church and their pastor in the winter of 1996, which eventually led to the dismissal of the pastor. The church, however, was able to carry on its ministry with the help of two interim pastors in the persons of Pastor To Din Lai杜典禮牧師, who was seconded by the Mong Kok Baptist Church of Hong Kong. He also was on the teaching faculty at the Baptist Theological Seminary in Hong Kong. Pastor To was ably assisted by Dr. Lau Tin Yan 劉天恩, a physician in Macau, whom God called into the preaching ministry and thus had a dual ministry.

Two of the deacons of the church, who coincidentally were originally from Swatow, came to see me one day at the Hope Medical Clinic. They were concerned about the future of Sha Lei Tau Baptist Church because of an unavoidable litigation between the church body and the now-terminated pastor, which threatened to be a long, drawn-out, and messy civil suit. By this time the case has become quite notorious. I will have more to say later, but right now, I would like to say that the deacons, Mr. Chan Yiu Tak陳耀德執事 and Mr. Hoi Lok Kun許樂觀執事 came specifically to ask me if I could consider helping at Sha Lei Tau Baptist Church since I am already serving in Macau and may eventually be able to be the pastor-in-residence, since Dr. Lau was planning on emigrating to the United States of America and it was too strenuous on Pastor To to travel from Hong Kong week in, week out. Therefore, toward the latter half of 1997 I began to preach once or twice a week at the church, alternating with Pastor To. After some months of our collaborating in the service of our Lord and enjoying the wonderful musical talents of Mrs. To and their daughter, they came one day with a very pleasant and unexpected surprise. Somehow, Pastor and Mrs. To came and asked if I had ever attended the Kwong Wah Primary School in Kowloon and when I gave them an affirmative answer, they both felt sure that we were in school at the same time and that he was a classmate of my brother, Fred. It was then that I recalled that my mother had mentioned that Mrs. To's parents were Dr. and Mrs. Lo Chi Fai 羅致徽醫生 and that at one time there was a matchmaker who was trying to match her to Fred.

Naturally, I did not tell them about this. The point I want to make is to reiterate once again that our God works in mysterious ways. Imagine that we were schoolmates in primary school and after all these years we found ourselves serving the same Lord in the same church. In any event, it turned out that I was asked by the church to sign a contract to be their Pastor for a period of ten years in August of 1998. At the time, I said I was delighted and willing to sign the contract but I could not promise them that I would fulfill the contract, seeing that I was going to be seventy years old in September. Just to end this story, I did finish the contracted term of service almost three years ago, proving once again that God honors those who honor Him.

XVII

LA SALLE COLLEGE
1937-1941

I graduated from Primary Four of Kwong Wah Primary School and entered La Salle College in Kowloon City in September of 1937. La Salle is a Catholic high school run by The Christian Brothers and is a sister school of St. Joseph's College in Hong Kong. I mention this because my Uncle Henry was an alumnus of St. Joseph's and was quite well known among the Brothers who ran the school. He was very popular, good looking, a good student but best of all he was a very good athlete, especially in track, and was a holder of some records for quite a duration. All this is to say that Uncle Henry was, therefore, instrumental in obtaining a substantial reduction in our school fees.

Patsy and Margaret, my sisters, were also enrolled at St. Mary's Girls' School in Tsim Sha Tsui on Chatham Road. We had moved to a flat in a private house with a garden both in the front and the back on No. 11 Cameron Road. The house was on the northwest corner of the intersection of Cameron and Carnarvon Roads. It was a very nice neighborhood and though the owner of the house was a wealthy Chinese cloth merchant, most of the other houses on Cameron Road were occupied by Westerners.

The house was a squarish two-story house with an enclosed verandah on the east, south, and western sides. The house faced south and was entirely enclosed by a wall, with the front gate situated at the southeastern corner and a gate at the eastern wall allowing access to the garden in the back of the house. There was a back alley behind the northern wall which led to Granville Road and, perhaps by choice, my friend Shiu Liang's flat was on No. 16 directly behind our house.

The garden in the back of the house was, more or less, divided into three sections. The westernmost section was planted full of fruit trees, at least three or four of which were guava trees. The middle section was like a sandlot and that was where I had my friends over to play marbles. The eastern section was a vegetable garden where the owner planted his vegetables. It was appropriate since he was a very devout Buddhist and had converted his living room in his upstairs quarters into an altar and temple big enough for his whole family to worship in. We rented the western half of the ground floor, which had one big room surrounded on the south and west side by the verandah. There was a small bathroom and a small room for dining on the north side with a flight of stairs leading off the dining room down to the the kitchen and the courtyard at the rear of the house. The L-shaped verandah was partitioned so that a master bedroom was made at the end of the southern arm of the angle of the verandah. Between the master bedroom and the front door, we had two beds for Fred and myself. The remaining west wing of the verandah was turned into a workshop in the day time and a corner of it was occupied by a bed for our domestic help. The big central room was partitioned so that there was a smaller area for my grandmother and a cousin to sleep in, while a big double bed was placed in a corner of the "living room" for Patsy and Margaret.

There was a second family that rented the eastern half of the ground floor. On the eastern side of the house, there was a small confectionary store, a cobbler and a Shanghai Laundry.

We probably moved into this house around 1937 because I can remember walking up to Nathan Road to catch a bus to go to school at La Salle in Kowloon City, coming home for lunch, then back to school until 3.30 p.m. Because the buses were often full, catching a bus sometimes became a game of wits and guts. Falls and scrapes were often and inevitable. I had personally witnessed a number of pretty nasty accidents. Little did I think that in later years I would be called upon to patch many a road accident victim, when rotating through the Emergency Room during my internship year at the St. Thomas Hospital in Akron, Ohio, in the USA.

The years between 1937 and 1941 could have been very important formative years for me but I tend to remember them as carefree years. I was acquiring a new language besides being introduced to a lot of new knowledge, though mostly in the three R's, as well as history and geography. The last subject was of particular interest to me and I remember that I did very well the second year I was a student in La Salle, gaining a first place in one of the tests and was awarded with a copy of a World Atlas. Now looking from my vantage as an octogenarian, perhaps this was the seed that sparked my interest and my penchant for world travel. I did manage to travel quite extensively around the world, but for some unknown reason never managed to get to the South American Continent.

One of the peculiarities of the education system in Hong Kong during the thirties when I was studying in La Salle College was that it was named a college and not a middle school or high school. It had caused a few heads to turn when recounting my resume and I had to explain that it was an anomaly, perhaps distinct to Hong Kong, that quite a number of middle or high schools, both for boys and girls, were named colleges. Needless to say, I just want to make it very clear to my readers that I am no "boy wonder" and I did not manage to vault over the process and was able to proceed to a school of higher learning after completing my primary school. On the contrary, I was very much a normal boy and identified with my hero in the series of books written by Richmal Crompton that I loved to read in my early teen years, that of William and his friends. I had to ask Stephen, my son, to tell me who the author was. He has several of those books that I gave him. I just thought that he would have enjoyed William as much as I did when I was learning the English language, learning to grow up a gentleman and learning to be a citizen of the world.

One other peculiarity about the school system that I've never bothered to enquire about was why La Salle, like all the English Language schools in 1937, classified the lowest grade as Class 8 and the highest grade Class 1 and/or the Matriculation Class? As of this writing in 2011, I am sure the system has changed, though I have no idea how many changes it has gone through or what the present system is today! My memories are quite vague about my first days of becoming a La Salle boy. I was quite impressed with the building sitting up on a hill with two massive, curving granite-stone staircases that began inside two massive iron gates that you entered from Boundary Street. I suppose if I were a professional author I would have gone and counted the number of flights of steps and the number of steps in each flight, so I could impress you with it. Suffice it to say that La Salle College was huge compared to Kwong Wah Primary School. And so was the student body!

I should quit belaboring meaningless points and get to the meat of the subject, which is to write about myself and my story. Yet, these are parts of the story about my life, aren't they? And so I was enrolled as a student in La Salle College sometime between August and September of 1937, when I was between eight and nine years of age. I have no recollection of what my first day in La Salle was like, not to mention how I got there. I am sure that I am correct in assuming that my elder brother Fred was given the responsibility to see that I got to school and returned home safe and sound! How else would I be able to write this in the book? Since I do not have a younger brother, I cannot tell you what and how you are supposed to feel to be an elder brother. I have a distaste for psychology and I will not want to attempt to analyze whether my reputation as a "durian" or naughty boy, for the bourgeoisie in all of us, had caused Fred the fear of being "found out" that I was his younger brother. I do remember that when we were about to step into the compound of the school, I was told in no uncertain terms to behave and try not to let anyone know that he was my brother or that I was his brother, whichever is the worse of the two. True! Why should he want to be embarrassed by me?

I do want you to consider the fact that Fred was getting to be a teenager and he had his sensibilities. I bring this up just to tell you another story to illustrate to you that Fred and I are brothers and we love each other very much. However, no matter how you look at it, our age difference probably was a big factor that when he was a teenager, I was still a brat and I imagine he would not want to be caught dead if ever his friends should find out that he had a ruffian for a younger brother. I recall one occasion when he was fourteen and I was eleven and after much pleading and begging on my part he agreed to take me to the movies at the Star Theater not far from where we lived. He just gave me a warning to be ready to leave when it was time for him to go. Naturally, he would not say anything to me after that and it meant that I had to keep my eye on the front door and be ready to run after him when he darted out of the door. Then once we were on the way, he just grunted out a perfunctory remark that I was not to say anything during the movie. Sad to say, I cannot even remember which movie it was, but Fred did take me to the movie.

Let me fast forward to 1947 about ten years later. Fred was "forcefully" removed from Home in 1941 when the Japanese occupied Hong Kong. He was all of sixteen and Mom and Dad thought it wise to let him go to Free (Unoccupied) China with Uncle Henry, Aunt Kitty, Eileen and Gloria since there was quite a sizeable exodus of young people to the "interior" once the hostilities and gunfire had ceased on Christmas, when the British surrendered to the Japanese after eighteen days of glorious and courageous resistance. The three years and eight months of separation had the effect of provoking Fred to voice his regret over his "treatment" of his younger brother—in other words—he missed me and was sorry for the way he was so reserved in his treatment of me. We were later to make up for lost time when we were brought together by chance to be studying medicine at the Medical Faculty of the University of Hong Kong around 1950. I will elaborate on that later.

La Salle College had another distinction in that it had attracted a lot of students of different nationalities and ethnic backgrounds. Perhaps it was because of the nature and cosmopolitan makeup of the city of Hong Kong, though I suspect it is good old common sense to make use of affinity groups to assign students to their classes. I found that when I entered the school for my first year I was assigned to Class 8B and I noticed that all the grades had three classes, that is, from A to C. Upon further observation, I noticed that students assigned to the C classes were all ethnic Chinese. However, students in the B classes tend to be a mix of the youngest and smallest Chinese, all or most of the Eurasians and the occasional other nationals. The students in the A classes were Europeans, Indians and Pakistanis from India, which was a British Colony then plus students of all other non-Chinese nationals. This was a satisfactory arrangement except for intramural sports. Frequently, a soccer match, especially the semi-finals and final championship matches, which would end with only one side a winner. But I suppose it won't surprise you if I were to tell you that the rivalry was often extended into one or a multiple number of boxing matches outside of the school grounds soon after the last bell was rung. It is quite true that we were all indoctrinated with being gentlemen on the playing fields and that we were to exhibit good sportsmanship whenever we were to take part in a friendly match. But, I would be quick to point out that we were also quite familiar with the Marquess of Queensberry rules (1867) of boxing. Our classmates were so used to the proceedings that they would quickly form a boxing ring, the combatants would give their expertise, and after a time they would shake hands and everyone would disperse. There might be some rematches but grudges were few. I've taken part in some of these exercises. This is not recommended in the Sermon on the Mount but it is a process of growing up in a multinational and multicultural environment. You do grow up to be tolerant and understanding of others and I now find it much easier to be a peacemaker, and I don't take it to heart quite so much when I feel I am being persecuted for righteousness's sakes. Obviously, I would never think of challenging you with uttering that well-worn phrase we used in La Salle College, "I'll meet you after school." On the contrary, won't you agree that a better repartee would be, "God loves you and I love you too!"?

My teacher in Class 8 was Mr. Tsang, a man in his thirties, a little on the chubby side with a pleasant smile. I was new to the school and most definitely knew very little English. I was kind of a free-spirited boy and I remember Mr. Tsang throwing some chalk and once or twice even the eraser in my direction, in all probability because I was talking or playing some sort of game with a classmate. As it was a Catholic school, we were required to all line up outside the classroom when the first bell rang; then when it rang again, we marched in to take our seats, but before doing so, we had to say our prayers. We did have a Catechism class and so it did not take too long for me to know quite a lot about the Catholic faith. I considered it fortunate that I was brought up in a Christian home and was quite familiar with the Bible and who God and Jesus are, since I continued to go to Sunday school at the Swatow Christian Church, especially after the chapel was started in Haiphong Road not far from where we lived in Cameron Road.

KENNETH KWONG CHEE SIU

One salient point about a boys' school is the matter of discipline, and considering my early years and the constant reminder from my family and relatives, I imagine that subconsciously I was prepared for a heavy dose of regimentation. Nevertheless, it was still an unknown quality to me and there was nothing to deter my adventurous spirit from testing the waters to ascertain what the limits were. I am sure that Mr. Tsang gave a strong dose of his medicine to me though I cannot say that he meted out anything that stood out in my mind. Though in defense of my "reputation" I would like to plead innocence and furthermore as a new boy I needed to play it safe. After all, a freshman is always a freshman. A new boy is, as my Singapore and Malaysian friends would say, a "Sin Keh" 新客, a new guest or spectator.

Even though we are talking about my junior high school, a first year student was a freshman in every sense of the word. A new boy or girl had to be quiet and learn, especially from the upperclassmen. You speak when you are spoken to and you do not scream or yell when told not to. There were prefects to monitor us, and one of the worst punishments one could get was to be sent to Brother Superior or the Headmaster's Office. I cannot recall that I was meted that punishment in my first year in La Salle, but when I was promoted to Class 7B in the second year, that is a whole new "'nuther story." I was not quite ten years old when school started but would be when September came around. However, though I was getting older I was not getting any taller. In fact, I was teased as a shorty because I could not get taller than 4 feet 8 inches. On the other hand, Fred was quite tall and almost a foot taller than me. As a sophomore year student, I thought I was no longer a new boy, but as is known about sophomores the world over, I was not at all sophisticated enough. Being one of the four youngest boys in the class and also the shortest, we were always put at the head of the line and naturally, we were often picked on by the older and bigger boys in the class. I can still remember the names of my "buddies"; there was Herbert Bush, an Eurasian boy whose father was English and mother was Chinese; then there was Aurelio Cheng, who came to Hong Kong from Panama, where he was born, with his two older brothers Maximo and George, just so they could "learn" Chinese culture and be able to live up to their Chinese heritage—Aurelio would become one of my very good friends; then the fourth boy whose name I have forgotten, except for his nickname, which was "louh syu jai" 老鼠仔, or Little Mouse in English.

Our classrooms were pretty big, certainly roomy enough for the maximum forty students, which was quite common in those days. If I have to give it a guesstimate, it would have to be at least thirty feet squared, if not more. The front wall of the room was fitted with two big chalk boards that extended the whole width of the wall and the height of each board extended from three feet above the platform to the ceiling. There was a platform that extended across the whole width of the front wall and was roughly three feet wide but with a central extension into the center of the room big enough to accommodate the teacher's desk. I mention this just to give you a picture of what the incident I was going to describe would look like to you. I cannot remember the exact reason or what I did, but the teacher of our class, 7B, would have been Mr. Henry Ma. Anyway, I was made to sit on the platform just next to the teacher's desk for my punishment.

The next thing that happened was the teacher asked Herbert Bush to come up to the desk. I told you we were the shortest ones in the class, so Herbert came up and stepped up on the platform so he could see Mr. Ma. I was sitting right there and there were Herbert's feet. I was bored sitting there and so I reached out my right hand and grabbed a hold of Herbert's right foot. Time stood still for a moment. I had not formed any mental image of what was about to happen nor did I have any idea. When Mr. Ma finished telling what he wanted Herbert to do, I heard Herbert say, "Yes Sir." Herbert started to step down. He made the mistake of moving his right foot first, because, in the twinkling of an eye, in that split second, kapoom! There went Herbert! He landed on his butt. His eyes were big and round and his mouth was agape. No one knew what happened! Then Herbert pointed his finger at me. I was Mr. Innocent himself. The class half exclaimed and half laughed. It rook Mr. Ma a few minutes to add two and two together to get four. Siu Kwong Chee was the culprit. Herbert was pointing his finger at me. In a split second, Mr. Ma was on his feet, he came at me, and I had to stand up. He had his ruler in his hand. The command was given, "Put your hand out with the palm facing down." Using the edge of the ruler with the brass strip meant for preventing ink from smudging your paper, he whacked

91

me on the back of my fingers and gave me three whacks. The skin was broken but there was no hemorrhage. Mr. Ma was fortunate he didn't fracture my fingers. But, certainly that was a sadistic move.

The finale was that I was sent outside the room to wait for Bro. Cassian's next round. He was the Headmaster and when he came by and saw me standing in the corridor outside the classroom, his obvious question was, "Why are you standing here?" When I replied that, "Mr. Ma sent me out," his answer, as always, was, "Go to my office." When you got there, you waited until he returned to the office. When he returned, he would ask why you were sent out and after you told him the whole story, he would ask you to bend over on the chair, then, he got his cane out and Whish! Crack! Whish! Crack! Whish! Crack! I guess that meant you were not to do that again. I guess you can console yourself by saying that you always like to try something new once.

The other sophomoric thing I did during my year in Class 7B was that I did not get along very well with my classmate Little Mouse and one way of settling our differences in La Salle was to challenge each other to meet after school. You and your friends and your opponent and his friends would all gather at an empty lot outside of school, your friends would form a ring and you would duke it out. You shook hands. The incident was over. I did have to settle our differences with Little Mouse a couple of times but I didn't hate him nor did I bear a grudge against him.

One other incident that was memorable was that Fred had by now joined the Boy Scouts of Troop 17 in La Salle. He would tell us of the wonderful little things he did or would do at meetings; the picnics, the skills he'd learned; the merit badges and yes the campouts they went on. Early on, some of the stories were fascinating, but some were boring and yet a few would make me envious or jealous. Once or twice, I would broach the subject to my mother, but she would begin by saying I was not old enough, then we couldn't afford it and finally that I was too naughty to join. In other words, if I were a little older, if we were able to afford it, and mostly if I were better behaved, then she would consider letting me join. If you were my age and you were in my shoes, would you not think you might be a little chagrined like I was? I remembered I made a snide remark once to a classmate who was a Boy Scout because of the inner feelings I had and Mr. Ma heard it and he chided me by saying that my brother was a Scout too. Looking back, I realize that Mr. Ma was not quite as mature as he ought to be, given that he and his brothers, Richard and Wally, were all active in Troop 17. I will have more to say about scouting later.

It was time to be promoted to Class 6 and for some unknown reason I was put into 6C under Bro. Wilfred. I was still one of the youngest and smallest in the class but I guess I was reasonably proficient in learning and enjoying it. By now English was not a problem like it had been when I first started in La Salle. I can recall in the first year, I wrote on a piece of paper and feeling quite proud of it—Today is my born day—isn't that something? We had a lot of friends among the Portuguese population or should I say Macanese, now that I know better, in our neighborhood, who were students in La Salle and whose sisters studied at St. Mary's just like Patsy and Margaret. But I suppose we probably sounded strange to an outsider because we had vernacular quite distinct from most: we all spoke a mixture of English, Chinese, Portuguese and patois. Bro. Wilfred, on the other hand, was Italian but he did not have a pronounced accent and he was strict in his way.

Bro. Wilfred would make us buy an extra exercise book and call it our prize book. He would have a column on the side of the chalk board where he would give out the prizes each day. Of course it was not a prize as we know it but rather a punishment. It you were given a prize he would put your name in that column and your prize might vary, like writing "I must not talk in class" fifty or a hundred times on your prize book. He would also remind us that "An idle mind is the devil's workshop" and he would teach us to recite a list of nouns that tell a famous story to keep us from having an idle mind. I often wish I had remembered that list to recite because it is useful not to have an idle mind. I was all of eleven years old but still rather naïve about a lot of things. I was learning but I sensed that my Chinese was not quite up to snuff because we only had one class period for Chinese and that was considered as our second language. Obviously, this is the price you pay for learning English and quite substantially to the detriment of attaining a proficiency in my mother tongue. It was a serious question but there were no easy answers. It was a sad choice that parents had to make—the proverbial horns of the dilemma. We were aware of the invasion of the sovereignty of China by the Japanese army in the Marco Polo Bridge Incident on the 7th of July, 1937 but, given the sad fact that China was caricatured as the sick invalid of Asia and the indifference of the powers that be and the intrigue of international politics, there was not much one could do. However, by 1939, with the rise of Nazi Germany and the dictator Hitler, very quickly we witnessed the fall, one after the other, of the countries in Western Europe. Soon, we witnessed the selling of tiny little tin hats for the Bomber Fund for Great Britain.

Before long, I was promoted to Class 5B and soon it would be 1940 and I would be twelve years old. I was still under 4 feet 8 inches tall but I might have grown and matured somewhat. I was encouraged by my mother that if I did well in school and learned to behave and if I did not incur any bad reports from school, perhaps when I got promoted to Class 4, she would condescend to let me join the Boy Scouts. Of course, at this time, Fred had already been Assistant Patrol Leader and even promoted to be Patrol Leader. He was as tall as 5 feet 8 inches and I think even earned the First Aid merit badge and the Life Saving merit badge in swimming. Actually, the situation in Asia was getting quite tense because there was an embargo on Japan and there was talk of war with Japan. The Scout Masters and some other teachers were mobilized to train with the Hong Kong Volunteer Defence Force. Interestingly, some scouts were asked to volunteer to be ARP's or Air Raid Precaution wardens and some were asked to be dispatchers with the British Garrison at the Kowloon Godowns in Tsim Sha Tsui. Fred was among one of the latter group. We shall come back to this subject later. Right now, let's get back to the story, though I admit, there does not appear to be anything that cries out for me to write about. There is no doubt that I had learned a lot besides English, not the least of which was that subconsciously, I was attaining the standards that my mother had set for me if I was ever serious about joining my brother Fred's ranks of becoming a Boy Scout. Isn't this just typical of us as human beings, the things that we aspire to be or possess, when they seem beyond our reach, the more we like to pretend to be nonchalant and the more we would claim that it is below our dignity to try to stretch ourselves to achieve it? Is this something akin to Pride and Prejudice? Somehow I found myself in that quixotic state of secretly wishing my mother would consent to let me join to become a scout but at the same time trying so hard to show people that I was not the least bit interested and all the time making remarks and hints about how silly Boy Scouts were and how seemingly unsophisticated and undignified were the things they did. So it was that the year went by quite quickly though imperceptibly I gradually won the approval of my mother because she announced that I had won her consent to allow me to sign up when we returned to school again in September of 1941.

That year, 1941, turned out to be a very memorable and significant year in more ways than one. Sometime during the summer holidays, my mother gave me the good news that she was going to let me join the Boy Scouts. I was happy beyond words and was able to cajole Fred into bringing me to one of his scout meetings during the holidays and enroll me in the program. I was close to thirteen years old and would be a teenager by the time school started. I would be entering Class 4, which in effect meant that I would be entering what is commonly known as the Ninth Grade in a senior high school. This was a milestone in my life and in my education, though I must admit I had no idea what I wanted to be when I became an adult. I don't think that had ever entered my mind. Don't get me wrong, I was very much interested in going to school. I enjoyed learning, I enjoyed the new and the old, yet you can't say that I was a bookworm. I was not a dummy either, and I've always considered myself a quick student.

September came. We all went back to school. I joined Troop 17 and became a recruit. I got into a patrol with one of my classmates who had been in the troop a couple of years before. He became my mentor and taught me the Scout Oath, the Scout Law, how to get into formation, how to salute, how to march, and, most importantly, how to tie knots. He taught me all about the uniform and the badges. He showed me the neckerchief which was half red and half purple and how the red should go on the left side, because it represented the left side of the heart where the arterial blood is pumped out. I had to learn all these important things and pass the tests for the tenderfoot rank before I would be sworn in and be invested into the troop. It took all of September, October and November before I finally attained the tenderfoot rank. By then it was time to remind my mother to have my uniform ready so that I would be properly dressed for the investiture.

Finally, by the end of November, I passed all the required tests and the requirements for the tenderfoot badge and arrangements were made for me to be invested on Friday, December 12th in 1941. I was very happy and excited and informed my mother about it. She was pleased that I'd made the grade and she had all the badges sewn on the uniform and had my new uniform all ironed, spic and span, and ready for me to put on for the investiture. I've made it! Maybe I'll be able to live down my reputation as a "durian."

XVIII

WORLD WAR II
1941-1945

As far as I can recall, there was no warning or suspicion of any kind. We had some air raid precaution exercises. To a thirteen year old, life went on as usual. Furthermore, my life seemed quite rosy with the beginning of December. Sunday, December 7th was just like every other Sunday. Swatow Christian Church had had this satellite Evangelistic Chapel 佈道所 in Haiphong Road for a number of years. I usually went there for Sunday school and stayed on for the worship service. That's where I met all my friends like Shiu Liang and Wesley Wu 吳輝鴻. We would all go our separate ways to our respective homes for a simple lunch and I would usually busy myself with trying to find friends in the neighborhood, play some games on the sidewalks, talk and tell stories, but short of that I would be home playing, talking and trying to stay out of trouble.

I've tried at various times to keep a diary but every time that I gave it a try they all turned out to be lost causes. Nevertheless, I somehow had a strong feeling that this particular Sunday—December 7th—had to be different for me. I may not be a quiet person given to reminiscing but I am sure that I am a thinking person with a strong sense of imagination. I am sure that I would have looked with admiration at my new scout uniform—probably many, many times, over and over again, imagining what I would look like in it! I did make fun of the scouts but I am sure you can understand it was a case of sour grapes—and I abhor sour things—ask Betty, my wife and she'll tell you how much I detest anything sour. Even though I did not keep a diary, the happenings and thoughts of that fateful morning have stayed fresh in my memory. I remember thinking to myself: Now my true feelings can be known. I've joined the ranks. I've made the grade. In a few days I will be invested—I will get to learn all the skills, pack my rucksack and sleeping bag—and go on campouts, do outdoor cooking after building a fire—and sleep under the stars!

There's so much to learn and so, so many fun things to do! Yawn! It's getting late. I have to get up early tomorrow morning so I won't be late for school on Monday. Then Tuesday, Wednesday, Thursday and Friday—Scout meeting—Investiture—

Boys of courage! Boys of daring! ...
We are sons of La Salle everyone,
And no matter where we go,
High aloft our heads, we will hold,
And strive that her fame may grow...
Hip, hop, hooray! Troop 17!

It was not yet 8 o'clock on the morning of Monday, December 8th! I was tying my shoelaces and getting ready to get out of the house to catch the bus to school. Whoooo! Whoooo! We could hear a rumbling, boom, boom, boom in the distance. "Was that the air raid siren?" we were asking each other. Fred had already gone to school. My household help came in and said, "The Japanese have attacked Hong Kong! They have bombed Kai Tak Airport and Hong Kong Island!" That was the air raid siren we heard and not a practice.

Not long afterwards Fred came back from school. He was told to hurry home, put on his uniform and report for duty at the Kowloon Godowns. He was given a tin hat and a bicycle. He later on would describe his duty as a dispatcher for the army defending the Kowloon Godowns. We now learned that Japan had joined the Axis of Powers with Hitler's Germany and Mussolini's Italy, and on that same morning of December 8, 1941, Japan also bombed Singapore, Manila, Saigon, Java, and Rangoon, but most significantly, Pearl Harbor in Hawaii.

This was the start of World War II and because of the time differences, the bombing of Pearl Harbor, though taking place simultaneously as the bombing in Hong Kong, was on Sunday, December 7th in Honolulu, Hawaii time. Immediately after the bombing, President Franklin D. Roosevelt of the United States of America declared war on Japan, Germany, and Italy, which officially became the Second World War. President Roosevelt described the day of the bombing of Pearl Harbor as a Day of Infamy. On a much more personal level, it is, in my humble opinion, decidedly a Day of Illumination for me. It may not have looked as clear to me then as when I look back at it now from the vantage of hindsight. But what happened that day seems apparent to me now that it was as if the Lord Jesus had shone His light on me to show me what the forces of evil can do and how your life can be changed in the twinkling of an eye. You can choose to do good, which is definitely the high road, or you can choose to be evil and sink in the process. Whatever it was, my life was changed …decidedly so.

The Japanese took four days and they forced the defense forces to retreat to the Island of Hong Kong. The day before the forces crossed the harbor to Hong Kong the British told Fred and others to discard their uniforms and to go on home. He came on home and gave us the bad news. Bad news? What bad news? You can't be serious! Get rid of my uniform? My new uniform? The uniform that I have earned the right to wear this next Friday? I have to get rid of it? How? No, I can't bury it in the backyard? It's brand spanking new! My mother and father paid good hard-earned money to buy it for me! I earned it! I'll be killed if I were to be found in possession of it? Why would anyone want to kill me for that? What have I done? I'm supposed to do a good deed every day. What's so bad about that? Helping an old lady cross the street is a kind thing to do. Why punish me for that? I promise to do my duty to God and my country! That's an honorable thing to do.

Obviously, there are times when protestations are of no avail. When it was useless to waste any more of our precious time and when it was time to save our energy and awareness to survival…you go ahead and do the inevitable. It was with a heavy heart that I carefully took my brand spanking new well-pressed scout uniform, belt, neckerchief, socks, and everything, went out to the back yard, dug a hole and buried my new scout uniform…never to see it again!

Looking back over the years, that backyard sure held a lot of memories for me, some very good and a very bad one that I just described.

I used to love to play marbles competitively. I had in my possession many different kinds of marbles and we kids would give different names to different marbles depending on their worth. There were marbles of different sizes and though most were made of glass, some would appear to have ceramic objects of different shapes and sizes incorporated inside the marble. I would put my collection in a tin can with a lid and carry it with me every time I went out to play marbles. We would mark out a rectangular shaped area on the sand lot, draw a circle in the rectangle midway between the two shorter sides and a third of the way down the longer side. We would place our marbles for the match in the pool in the circle. We would pitch our "shooting" marble from the circle to the farther end of the rectangle to see who got the closest to the line without being out over the line. The closest one got to shoot first and so forth according to where your marble landed. Your aim was to try to shoot a marble out of the circle, without getting your shooter in the circle, which meant that you would be out of competition. You could also kill your competitor by shooting him twice when you were within two spans of him. It was a fun game for me. I won many marbles in my backyard.

Another memorable thing the backyard held for me was that there were a number of guava trees and in summer when they ripened, I often had a fill of the delicious fruit. There are only two caveats to guavas! The first thing is to be sure that the fruit is ripe before you eat it and try not to eat too much of the seeds in the center of the fruit. Unripe guavas have a sap that is very mucilaginous and together with the seeds will become impacted like rocks in your large intestines, bloat you up and it will be painful when you have to remove them.

The second thing is that typhoons are common in Hong Kong and when severe will require the government to order the closure of schools. It may sound like fun to have no school and you can have a day to play. At least my sister Patsy and I thought so this one typhoon we had one summer, when we were living in Cameron Road. We wound up playing in the wind and rain in the backyard and I was up on the guava tree plucking the ripe ones, throwing them down to Patsy and thoroughly enjoying ourselves to the hilt. We didn't hear a thing when we were out there in the backyard in the typhoon other than our laughter and our chatter and the joy we had in the middle of the wonders of nature. We did not hear any other noise or sound. We did not hear our mother yelling at the top of her lungs for us to come home and wondering where we were. Anyway, when we finally made it home, we were taught a lesson that is still impressed deeply on our minds and our behinds.

I am going to take a break to write a little "appendix" to attach to the end of the book, since this inconsequential organ in my body sidetracked me to spend a good five days in the local hospital in Macau and with the two or three days before and after the illness, altogether put me out of writing for a fortnight. Thanks to the Good Lord, I recovered almost as promptly as any teenager would under the circumstances and I do not feel any worse than coming down with a severe upper respiratory illness. Now all I need to do is to test whether my memory has suffered any from the ordeal. I hope not.

To pick up where I left off, Kowloon was evacuated by the British defenders in four days of a valiant defense of a dire situation due to the hardiness and superiority of the invading enemy. I will not speculate but had information that the enemy's "fifth column" was very active and accurate in the espionage. In any event, the fighting now had turned into a battle of the cannons across the harbor, while the invaders were preparing to make an amphibious assault on the Island of Hong Kong. The night the British retreated to continue their resistance in the Island, the invaders, as is customary in war, would take advantage of a lull in the hostilities and allow their victorious forces, as a sop to their victory, to have a full range of freedom to rape and pillage the conquered territory for the remainder of the night. I remember we were all crowded together on the edge of the double bed that was in the middle of the main living room which we butted against the big double doors that under peaceful conditions would have been used as the main entrance into this section of the house. The door would lead you to the main vestibule which would give you access to the first floor, the east side of the ground floor and, naturally the front entrance.

Sure enough, around nine o'clock in the evening, there was a commotion outside the door. We could hear voices, voices of people, men, speaking a foreign tongue. They had come through the front gate into the front garden and were forcing their way into the vestibule through the front door. We were able to distinguish some gruff and loud voices that were demanding to be heard, and through the commotion, we could distinguish two words that sounded like Chinese to us. We could make out the two words as "Gu neuhng" or (guniang) and we assume they were looking for girls. Soon, we heard the sound as of a shoulder pushing against the door and visibly seeing the bed against the door move ever so slightly. The human voices sounded louder as the crack in the door became larger. I can still see the image of Patsy, Margaret and my mother sitting crouched on the bed clinging to their blankets, with their eyes wide open and staring at each other. Eventually, the door was forced open wide enough for us to see three enemy soldiers holding flashlights in their hands, shining their beams on the girls' faces and making noises. It was at this time that he appeared; he was the owner of the house, Mr. Fong. He came in front of the soldiers and slowly but firmly with his soft-spoken voice, he made some remarks to the soldiers. And, as surely as if by magic, the soldiers left quietly and peacefully. We were never disturbed again after this one incident. We surmised that Mr. Fong, who had retail business selling piece goods and fabric for ladies' dresses and clothing, must have had an extensive business with the rayon producers of Japan, especially during the embargo of the thirties when Japan invaded China and subsequently her ambitions in the Far East. We were thankful that our prayers were answered and we were averted from the danger of the invading soldiers. Meanwhile, the war continued with the new day. One could never be certain of one's life nor one's safety during the vagaries of the war. As luck would have it, the next morning, the dueling of the cannonade continued fast and furious. I began to identify the incoming trio of shells, each burst beginning with a bang, then followed by a sound as if someone is dragging a bunch of bamboo poles across the ground and gradually the sound increasing in a crescendo until it explodes on the object it hits with a loud burst that causes a ringing in your ears, then depending on how close the shell explodes near you, the blast will choke you and you smell the smell of the cordite. If the hit is really close, you may get grit and sand in your nostrils and your ears will be ringing. I'm trying to describe what a thirteen year old remembers of his experience of a war that happened seventy years ago. I cannot say I am scientifically accurate but that one morning, three shells did land on our house, the first one on the first floor on the east side of our house. It burst right in the living room of Mr. Fong, where he housed his Buddhist temple. The roof fell in on him while he was meditating in front of his Buddha. He eventually died from his wounds. The second shell landed on the house next door to ours on the west side and the third one further up the road. Our house was full of smoke and dust and that awful smell of spent gunpowder, quite unmistakable, once you've smelled it. Our parents quickly gathered us together and we went out through the garden in the back to our uncle's house in Granville Road for a temporary refuge until we could find another place to live. That was a close shave! It would be the first of my three close brushes with death during the course of the war!

I must mention this woman who was our household help ever since I could remember. We call her Heung Wong Gu 香黃姑 or Aunt Buddha's Hand, but she was not strictly related to our family, except that her niece was married to Mr. Chan Keih Jaan (Chen Qizan) 陳其讚, whom we call Sahp Suk or Tenth Uncle. From all the family conversations, gossips, information and intelligence that I've been able to gather, which is quite scanty as far as facts are concerned, not to mention the fact that no one in the family would deem it necessary or vital that I should be the recipient of all pertinent information, especially since I was considered quite the brat in the family, I deduce that Mr. Chan's father was probably not a native of Shantou or Chiuh Jau (Chaozhou) 潮洲. Perhaps, like my grandfather, he also came from the Canton area; perhaps, they knew each other and, because of their affinity and their occupation in the governmental circles, became "brothers" so to speak, which is quite common in China. Therefore, by extension, their children were also aligned as brothers and hence Mr. Chan was considered our Tenth Uncle, probably enumerating from my eldest aunt or my father. Anyway, Heung Wong Gu, though not formally educated in the school system then extant, was able to survive and thrive like any modern day go-getter and as it turned out was quite an asset to our family, particularly during the hostilities and the war. This became quite evident with the first close shave we had and the subsequent evacuation and move to a safer place of existence.

103

We noticed that for the past three or four years, life had become quite a struggle for my parents. Working for a father-in-law who has five sons certainly presents quite a challenge. Would you not agree with me that, under these circumstances, there was very little prospect for my father to have a prosperous future and/or any substantial potential for financial growth? Be that as it may, I have learned that my father was a man of honor and a perfect gentleman. I was told that there were factory owners and their sales representatives who made offers of a percentage of their profits to my father, on the side, if he were to direct business their way. Naturally, my father would have none of that and he would stress to them that the company's standing orders would hold true, that the profits would be shared equally among the staff in the export department. My father remained an honorable man to his dying day. He made a decent salary with not much to spare. He did like to go to the races at Happy Valley and he was particularly proud of the fact that he finally became a member of the Royal Hong Kong Jockey Club. We used to say that he diligently took his place each racing day to lay the sod for the ponies to race on. I remember how animated he became when Jeffrey first dated Patsy and then became his son-in-law. They would talk for hours about such and such a pony and so and so jockey. They would always say how narrowly they missed becoming the next rich man by a nose. I do remember once or twice he would take the whole family to the Club for Children's Day, the fourth of April, when they would allow children to go to the races. Strange as it may seem, I was never interested in becoming a punter. Nor do I know why!

I remember for a number of years before the Second World War, when we were living in Cameron Road, that part of the house was turned into a factory. My mother would receive orders from Swatow Drawn Work Company, gather the silk, linen, and georgette material and the hundreds of skeins of silk threads from the famous French thread manufacturer. She would have six to twelve girls who had found their way to Hong Kong from the villages in Chiu Jau, and they would come early in the morning, sit on their little stools and embroider away according to the flowery patterns stenciled in indigo on the cut-out handkerchiefs, blouses, napkins or tablecloths. I have no idea how much my mother made on her labors but I am sure it was not anything to build the Taj Mahal with. I was made aware much later that my parents were often very much in debt and that my mother's health was always so poor that by the time of the Japanese occupation of Hong Kong, her health was so poor that we despaired over her health and wondered if she would survive the war.

I mentioned earlier that we had to vacate our house when a shell landed on the house and killed the owner. We soon moved into a flat on the second floor of No. 41 Nathan Road. It had a verandah, a living room, two bedrooms, a dining area as you entered the front door, a bathroom, two servants' rooms and a kitchen. Also in the interim, Fred left for the interior of Free China with our Uncle Henry, Aunt Kitty, Eileen and Gloria, to continue his studies. He eventually ended up in Gam Jau (Ganzhou) 贛州 in Kiangsi Province, and when the war was over, he entered Lingnan University in Canton.

Hong Kong put up a valiant defense, but was decidedly outnumbered and grossly ill-prepared and less experienced when compared to the invaders.

Rather than writing from memory over something that I had very little personal experience other than the fact that I was a victim of the war, I thought it might throw a clearer light on the subject to include the following extract from Wikipedia.

Battle of Hong Kong

The Battle of Hong Kong took place during the Pacific campaign of World War II. It began on 8 December 1941 and ended on Christmas Day with Hong Kong, then a Crown colony, surrendering to the Empire of Japan.

Background

Britain had first thought of Japan as a threat with the ending of the Anglo-Japanese Alliance in the early 1920s, a threat which increased with the expansion of the Sino-Japanese War. On 21 October, 1938 the Japanese occupied Canton (Guangzhou) and Hong Kong was effectively surrounded.[1]

Various British Defence studies had already concluded that Hong Kong would be extremely hard to defend in the event of a Japanese attack, but in the mid-1930s, work had begun on new defences, including the Gin Drinkers' Line.

By 1940, the British had determined to reduce the Hong Kong Garrison to only a symbolic size. Air Chief Marshal Sir Robert Brooke-Popham, the Commander-in-Chief of the British Far East Command argued that limited reinforcements could allow the garrison to delay a Japanese attack, gaining time elsewhere.[2]

Winston Churchill and his army chiefs designated Hong Kong an outpost, and initially decided against sending more troops to the colony. In September 1941, however, they reversed their decision and argued that additional reinforcements would provide a military deterrent against the Japanese, and reassure Chinese leader Chiang Kai Shek that Britain was genuinely interested in defending the colony.[2]

In Autumn 1941, the British government accepted an offer by the Canadian Government to send two infantry battalions and a brigade headquarters (1,975 personnel) to reinforce the Hong Kong garrison. C Force, as it was known, arrived on 16 November on board the troopship *Awatea* and the armed merchant cruiser *Prince Robert*.[3] It did not have all of its equipment as a ship carrying its vehicles was diverted to Manila at the outbreak of war.

The Canadian battalions were the Royal Rifles of Canada from Quebec and Winnipeg Grenadiers from Manitoba. The Royal Rifles had only served in Newfoundland and Saint John, New Brunswick prior to their duty in Hong Kong, and the Winnipeg Grenadiers had been posted to Jamaica. As a result, many of the Canadian soldiers did not have much field experience before arriving in Hong Kong.

Battle

The Japanese attack began shortly after 08:00 on 8 December 1941 (Hong Kong local time), less than eight hours after the Attack on Pearl Harbor (because of the day shift that occurs on the International Date Line between Hawaii and Asia, the Pearl Harbor event is recorded to have occurred on 7 December). British, Canadian and Indian forces, commanded by Major-General Christopher Maltby supported by the Hong Kong Volunteer Defence Corps resisted the Japanese invasion by the Japanese 21st, 23rd and the 38th Regiment, commanded by Lieutenant General Takashi Sakai, but were outnumbered three to one (Japanese, 52,000; Allied, 14,000) and lacked their opponents' recent combat experience.

The Japanese achieved air supremacy on the first day of battle as two of the three Vickers Vildebeest torpedo-reconnaissance aircraft and the two Supermarine Walrus amphibious aircraft of the RAF Station, which were the only military aircraft at Hong Kong's Kai Tak Airport, were destroyed by 12 Japanese bombers. The attack also destroyed several civil aircraft including all but two of the aircraft used by the Air Unit of the Hong Kong Volunteer Defence Corp. The RAF and Air Unit personnel from then on fought as ground troops. Two of the Royal Navy's three remaining destroyers were ordered to leave Hong Kong for Singapore.

The Commonwealth forces decided against holding the Sham Chun River, which was quickly forded by the Japanese using temporary bridges, and instead established three battalions in the Gin Drinkers' Line across the hills. These defences were rapidly breached at the Shing Mun Redoubt early on 10 December 1941. The evacuation from Kowloon started on 11 December 1941 under aerial bombardment and artillery barrage. As much as possible, military and harbour facilities were demolished before the withdrawal. By 13 December, the Rajputs of the British Indian Army, the last Commonwealth troops on the mainland, had retreated to Hong Kong Island.

Maltby organised the defence of the island, splitting it between an East Brigade and a West Brigade. On 15 December, the Japanese began systematic bombardment of the island's North Shore. Two demands for surrender were made on 13 December and 17 December. When these were rejected, Japanese forces crossed the harbour on the evening of 18 December and landed on the island's North-East. They suffered only light casualties, although no effective command could be maintained until the dawn came. That night, approximately 20 gunners were massacred at the Sai Wan Battery after they had surrendered. There was a further massacre of prisoners, this time of medical staff, in the

Salesian Mission on Chai Wan Road. In both cases, a few men survived to tell the story.

On the morning of 19 December, a Canadian Company Sergeant Major, John Robert Osborn of the Winnipeg Grenadiers, threw himself on top of a grenade, sacrificing himself to save the lives of the men around him; he was later posthumously awarded the Victoria Cross. Fierce fighting continued on Hong Kong Island but the Japanese annihilated the headquarters of West Brigade and could not be forced from the Wong Nai Chung Gap that secured the passage between downtown and the secluded southern parts of the island. From 20 December, the island became split in two with the British Commonwealth forces still holding out around the Stanley peninsula and in the West of the island. At the same time, water supplies started to run short as the Japanese captured the island's reservoirs.

On the morning of 25 December, Japanese soldiers entered the British field hospital at St. Stephen's College, and tortured and killed a large number of injured soldiers, along with the medical staff.[4]

By the afternoon of 25 December 1941, it was clear that further resistance would be futile and British colonial officials headed by the Governor of Hong Kong, Sir Mark Aitchison Young, surrendered in person at the Japanese headquarters on the third floor of the Peninsula Hong Kong hotel. This was the first occasion on which a British Crown Colony has surrendered to an invading force. The garrison had held out for 17 days.

Eighteen days after the battle began, British colonial officials headed by the Governor of Hong Kong, Sir Mark Aitchison Young, surrendered in person on 25 December 1941 at the Japanese headquarters. This day is known in Hong Kong as "Black Christmas".

Isogai Rensuke became the first Japanese governor of Hong Kong. This ushered in the three years and eight months of Imperial Japanese administration. Japanese soldiers also terrorised the local population by murdering many, raping an estimated 10,000 women,[5] and looting.

Prisoners of war were sent to:

- Sham Shui Po POW Camp
- Argyle Street Camp for officers

- North Point Camp primarily for Canadians and Royal Navy
- Ma Tau Chung Camp for Indian soldiers
- Yokohama Camp in Japan
- Fukuoka Camp in Japan
- Osaka Camp in Japan

Although Hong Kong surrendered to the Japanese, the local Chinese waged a small guerilla war in New Territories. As a result of the resistance, some villages were razed as a punishment. The guerillas fought until the end of the Japanese occupation. Western historical books on the subject have not significantly covered their actions. The resistance groups were known as the Gangjiu and Dongjiang forces.

Enemy civilians (meaning Allied nationals) were interned at the Stanley Internment Camp. Initially, there were 2400 internees although this number was reduced following some repatriations during the war. Internees who died, together with prisoners executed by the Japanese, are buried in Stanley Cemetery.

British sovereignty was restored in 1945 following the surrender of the Japanese forces on 15 August, six days after the U.S. dropped the atomic bomb on Nagasaki.

General Takashi Sakai, who led the invasion of Hong Kong and subsequently served as governor for some time, was tried as a war criminal and executed by a firing squad in 1946.

The Allied dead from the campaign, including British, Canadian and Indian soldiers, were eventually interred at the Sai Wan Military Cemetery on the northeastern corner of Hong Kong Island. A total of 1,528 soldiers, mainly Commonwealth, are buried there. There are also graves of other Allied combatants who died in the region during the war, including some Dutch sailors, who were re-interred in Hong Kong post war.

The Cenotaph in Central commemorates the Defence as well as war-dead from World War I.

The shield in the colonial coat of arms of Hong Kong granted in 1959 featured the battlement design to commemorate the Defence of Hong Kong during World War II. The arms was in use until 1997 when it was replaced by the current regional emblem.

Lei Yue Mun Fort has lost its defence significance in the post-war period. After the war, it became a training ground for the British Forces until 1987 when it was finally vacated. In view of its historical significance and unique architectural features, the former Urban Council decided in 1993 to conserve and develop Lei Yue Mun Fort into the Hong Kong Museum of Coastal Defence.

The nearby Sai Wan Battery, with buildings constructed as far back as 1890, housed the Depot and Record Office of the Hong Kong Military Service Corps for nearly four decades after the War. The barracks were handed over to the government in 1985 and were subsequently converted into Lei Yue Mun Park and Holiday Village.

Notes

1 The Japanese losses are unknown. Estimates range from 675 killed and 2,079 wounded to 7,000 killed and 20,000 wounded. On 29 December 1941, the *Hong Kong News* reported 1,996 killed and 6,000 wounded, which Tony Banham called "perhaps the most believable estimate".[7]

References

1. Chi Ming Fung (2005). *Reluctant heroes: rickshaw pullers in Hong Kong and Canton, 1874-1954* (illustrated ed.). Hong Kong University Press. p. 129. ISBN 978-9-6220-9734-6. http://books.google.com/?id=ZTk5HbdCiQ8C
2. [a][b] Harris, John R. (2005). *The Battle for Hong Kong 1941-1945 (HB)*. Hong Kong University Press. p. 55. ISBN 978-9-6220-9779-7. http://books.google.com/?id=8suV69gMia8C
3. "Kay Christie's Story". Hong Kong Veterans Commemorative Association. http://www.hkvca.ca/historical/accounts/christie.htm.
4. Charles G. Roland. "Massacre and Rape in Hong Kong: Two Case Studies Involving Medical Personnel and Patients". http://links.jstor.org/sici?sici=0022-0094(199701)32%3A1%3C43%3AMARIHK%3E2.0.CO%3B2-A.(subscription required)
5. Estimate from Snow 2003 via "The history of Hong Kong". Economist.com. 5 June 2003. http://www.economist.com/cities/displaystory.cfm?story_id=1825845(subscription required)

6. Banham, Tony (2005). *Not the Slightest Chance: The Defence of Hong Kong, 1941*. Hong Kong University Press. p. 317. ISBN 9622097804.
7. [a b] Banham 2005, p. 318

Further reading

Charles G. Roland (2001). <u>Long Night's Journey Into Day: Prisoners of War in Hong Kong and Japan, 1941-1945</u>. Wilfrid Laurier University Press. ISBN 0889203628.

Tony Banham (2009). <u>We Shall Suffer There: Hong Kong's Defenders Imprisoned, 1942-1945</u>. Hong Kong University Press. ISBN 978-962-209-960-9.

No sooner had we settled in our new flat on Nathan Road than, with a heavy heart, we heard of the news of the capitulation of the Hong Kong Defense Forces on Christmas Eve of 1941, after a valiant if oft futile effort to repulse the enemy. It was a few days later, probably no more than two days, that one late morning we heard the sound of marching in the street. I suspect that I was down on the street in front of our flat to watch the British prisoners-of-war being made to march along Nathan Road to the Sham Shui Po Prisoner-of-war camp. It was a ragtag band of soldiers, in all kinds of gear, each trying to carry as much of their personal gear with them as possible. Those who were not physically able would often drop part of their belongings and would hurriedly try to pick them up again, often under the cursing and swearing of the Japanese soldiers who were guarding them and urging them to move on. It was quite a contrasting picture of a victory parade of a conquering army! And so began the tragic occupation of Hong Kong of three years and eight months. I was just fourteen years and three months old when the war started. However, by the time the Japanese surrendered and peace returned in August 15, 1945, I was already a young man, just a month shy of the ripe old age of seventeen. I will have some interesting anecdotes relating to the events and the delay of the resumption of British rule in Hong Kong, some by the forces of events and some by the restraints of circumstances. As the saying goes, "We learn to roll with the punches!"

One of the things that I learned later subsequent to the evening I spent burying my scout uniform in the backyard was that the British forces had retreated across the harbor to Hong Kong Island. As soon as they vacated the Godowns, all those coolies who normally worked under contract through the Five Recognized Coolie Houses 苦力館, located on Canton Road across the street from the Godowns, together with all the people in the neighborhood, began to loot the Godowns. Incidentally, laborers are commonly known as coolie Fu Lihk (Kuli) 苦力 meaning bitter strength. One of the items that our household help was able to purchase and soon became a favorite staple food, especially for Grandfather Choy but very definitely abhorred by Patsy was the little wooden crates of Kraft cheddar cheese. It was good nutritious food. Grandfather Choy would show his enjoyment when savoring a chunk of cheese by taking a bite, closing his eyes and slowly chomping and chewing on the chunk of cheese until it was completely crushed, smashed and melted in his mouth before he swallowed it. He would then open his eyes, search for the chunk of cheese, grab a hold of it, extend it to his mouth, take a bite, push the chunk down, close his eyes and begin to chew and smack his lips at the same time. This would go on until he masticated the whole chunk, when he might go on to take a nap in his recliner chair. I'm going through all this because I want my grandson Austin to read this over and over again so he can revisit how funny it was that Grandfather Choy enjoyed his cheese this way. I cannot remember how old Austin was when I first told him this but ever since then, he has always wanted me to do a "Grandfather Choy" whenever we are eating chunky cheddar cheese. Austin, I hope you get a big kick out of reading this retelling of Grandfather Choy enjoying his cheese.

I came across this devotional reading and immediately thought about Stanley Wong and his parents. Please read on and see of you don't agree with me.

Drawn to Christ

No one can come to Me unless the Father who sent Me draws him; and I will raise him up at the last day. John 6:44

Jesus Christ is the One who introduces men and women to God. Those whom He ushers into the Father's presence all have a loathing of their sin, a desire to be forgiven, and a longing to know God. Those attitudes are the work of God in drawing us to Christ. A response to the gospel message thus begins with a change in attitude toward sin and God.

Beyond that initial change in attitude is the transformation brought about in every believer at the instant of salvation. Christ didn't die just to pay the penalty for sin: He died to transform us.

Deserted by most of His followers, Christ hung in darkness and agony on the cross, crying out, "My God, My God, why have You forsaken Me?" (Matt. 27:46). Those were moments that Jesus felt incredible rejection and hostility. Yet out of those very circumstances Christ triumphed by atoning for sin and providing a way for men and women to be introduced to God and transformed. It was a triumph He Himself would soon proclaim (1 Pet. 3:19–20).[26]

I must admit that I see a lot of truth to this little reading about how futile your efforts at coming close to God could be. Unless you are drawn by God the Father, you will not come to Jesus. Let me see if I can explain it in this following narrative.

I told you earlier that Heung Wong Gu 香黄姑 or Aunt Buddha's Hand, our household help, was quite a go-getter, as demonstrated in her ability to get all kinds of goodies for us like the cheddar cheese we just talked about. One other significant thing she did was when one day she came to my mother with the news that she personally found out from people who knew one of the Heads of a Godown Coolie House苦力館頭 by the surname of Wohng (Wang) 王, that they wanted someone to

---

[26] MacArthur, J. (2001). *Truth for today: A daily touch of God's grace* (128). Nashville, Tenn.: J. Countryman.

"adopt" his ailing grandson. This boy was ill and a fortune teller had told the family that he should be "given" away for adoption, in order to save his life. He was two years old and in all likelihood was suffering from acute glomerulonephritis. When my mother heard about it, she immediately felt it would be wrong to take the child away from the family but instead suggested that we enter into a reciprocity adoption as brothers between the boy and me, even though I was twelve years older than the boy, Ying Gun (Yingguan) 應冠whom we know later as Stanley. It was satisfying to know that his parents agreed and we exchanged gifts of food and maybe clothing, though I am not too clear on the clothing part. My mother would not consider herself a very devout Christian but I am fully convinced that she totally subscribed to the Golden Rule by the way she lived and therefore I see her as a true Christian in every sense of the word. She just had compassion on Stanley and his parents and very much wanted to see him get well. I am sure she probably prayed for him because it seemed that the miraculous had happened. Stanley did not die. On the contrary, he thrived very well and seemed on the road to a good recovery. In fact the miracle did not end with his gaining his health, because he went on to become a Christian and, together with his wife Vicky, are still very active in their church in Vancouver. However, the miracle also did not end with Stanley becoming a Christian, because the amazing conversion was to include his three brothers and two sisters. One of the sisters, Cho Hah (Chuxia) 楚霞 who is married to Pastor Shat, also known as Julia, who majored in vocal music in Taiwan, has made quite a name for herself with her singing and musical evangelism in Hong Kong, Taiwan, and the United States.

One other distinction about Stanley was that he studied Dentistry in Taiwan, practiced in Hong Kong and later came to Calgary, Canada. While in Calgary, he had to have a kidney transplantation, which went well. Not only did he recover and survive but he is now the record holder for being the longest survivor after kidney transplantation. He is now a Real Estate agent in Vancouver and keeps himself busy with being the choir director in his church. That's not all! Because in the 80's, he arranged to have his parents migrate to Canada and he got a flat for them when they settled in Vancouver. His mother had a long history of being affected by glaucoma and was losing her sight very quickly and completely. Stanley's youngest brother, Ying Yuen (Yinyuan) 應元 or Stephen, who was also living in Vancouver then, would often take his parents to church and finally convinced his mother to receive Jesus as her Savior. She was baptized and joined the church. She died in the early 90's and was given a Christian burial. His father became a widower and was quite lonely and despondent. Stephen, being a dutiful son and a Christian, advised his father that since he missed his mother so much, it would be a wonderful opportunity for him to make sure that he would be with her to eternity and all that he needed to do was to become a Christian too. You guessed it! Stanley and Stephen's father did receive Jesus as his Savior and was baptized and joined the church. He eventually passed away and was buried next to his wife—a picture perfect ending—and a wonderful closure to what God can do to those who are open to His Call.

What you've just read is without a doubt one of the most remarkable phenomena and revelations of the miraculous conversions that can only happen through the Grace of God. I am sure that my mother and I, in our wildest dreams and grandest hopes, would never have been able to say the right words or give our most inspiring testimonies to convert Stanley's parents. I'm ashamed to say, I had never tried. But, this is not all that God had done for Stanley, because all through the years that Stanley and his six siblings were growing up, all, except for his eldest sister, one by one, all five of them, an elder brother, two elder sisters and two younger brothers have all become Christians. I guess all I can say is that every Christian should heed what Jesus said in Matthew 9:37 "… 'The harvest is plentiful but the workers are few. Ask the Lord of the harvest, therefore, to send out workers into the harvest field.'"

Now that we have been raised to taste a spiritual high, I am afraid I'm going to have to bring you back down from the mountaintop and into the valley…I almost said…the valley of death, which may be more fact than fiction. I'm talking about the realities we in Hong Kong were then forced to face with the Fall of Hong Kong. We all know now that the Governor of Hong Kong, Sir Mark Young, was forced to announce the surrender of Hong Kong to the Japanese on Christmas Day of 1941. It was a sad and tragic moment, and the beginning of a winter of melancholy that would stretch on for three years and eight months...not a very cheerful way to begin my life as a teenager. How unfair it was to be so abruptly deprived of the best years of my transition from a naïve and sensitive boy into an adult young man! I was too old to have to be cooped up in the house day-in and day-out, but not old enough to go out into the world to find employment. I did ask my father if I could go out with our servant's son and sell/deliver newspapers with him. The idea was quickly quashed by my scholarly father. This brings to mind how different cultures deal with problems such as this. I am sure my friends in the United States of America would chuckle or laugh themselves silly that my father would deem it below my dignity to be a newspaper boy. Just think how many of the rich and famous American entrepreneurs' first independent money-making jobs were to have a newspaper route when he or she was a youngster. Be that as it may, the first few months of the Japanese Occupation were pretty horrible, though I feel reluctant to dwell on it because I am uncertain that we will gain anything by it. As it turned out, when the schools were allowed to be opened, only the Chinese schools were available but learning Japanese was mandatory. With my parents' consent, my option was not to attend school, but instead my father would help me with Chinese literature and eventually we would look for a tutor to give me private lessons so I could continue with learning English, Mathematics, and Science at home.

Not long afterwards, our next door neighbor, who had children about my age, told us that they had found a teacher, who taught in an English School prior to the hostilities but was now unemployed and looking for work. Would you not say that this was once again Divine Providence in answer to our prayers, albeit unspoken? Nevertheless, this happenstance just fit the bill perfectly and so I was able to continue to learn my three R's during those years in question. It was also during the first year of the occupation that I came into possession of a set of books published by the Commercial Press of China, which had a good number of classical English novels, with their accompanying Chinese translations, translated by Lin Yutang 林語堂 and printed side-by-side. This gave me a great opportunity to study both English and Chinese simultaneously, since they were printed side-by-side. I was also able to get many English novels from the Swindon Bookstore close-by and often at a deep discount since they had so few English customers. We had the private tutor perhaps for a couple of years but I can't vouchsafe that my memory is right. One of the reasons was that our next door neighbor's son, who was a twenty-some-year-old young man, was one night taken by the Japanese gendarmes for suspicion of espionage because a few of his friends were suspected of being guilty of helping and abetting the British. The son never did come back home because he died in the gendarmes' hands. In fact, the father was also taken in for interrogation and after his release intimated to us that he was subjected to waterboarding and a number of other forms of torture. Altogether this left an indelible impression in my mind and one that occasionally would leave a very bad taste in my mouth. I am thankful to God that this tutor helped me quite a lot with my English and Mathematics, which put me in good stead in 1945 when the Japanese Emperor surrendered to the Allies and I was able to resume my schooling with only a year's delay. I will have more to say on that later.

I don't think I ever spent any time thinking seriously about what the war meant to me in a philosophical sense, but it was quite obvious to me that the first change I noticed was the loss of my naiveté and whatever sense of freedom I had at that time. I still cannot accept the fact that totalitarian governments could be so intolerant of the freedom of the hoi polloi that it infringes on something as innocuous as a young boy joining the Boy Scouts and/or his Boy Scout uniform! Within days of the Occupation, we were made acutely aware that whenever we walked past any Japanese military sentry we were to face him and bow before we were to proceed further. This fact was clearly demonstrated to us time and again whenever we had the occasion to venture out in the streets to find ourselves given a free demonstration of slaps to the face or a pedestrian being thrown to the ground with a quick Jiu-jitsu throw for not bowing to the sentry of the Japanese Imperial Army. As is often the case with young boys who have a little of the free spirit, I recall the day when I was walking south on Waterloo Road in Kowloon Tong right by the side of Maryknoll Convent School with the intention of turning east on Boundary Street and going to Kowloon City. On the southeast corner of the intersection and across the street from Maryknoll, was the old Gas Company, if my memory is correct. It was a four-story building and had been requisitioned by the Japanese Military and, as was usual, they erected a circular military post for their sentries. As I was approaching the intersection and about to make a turn into Boundary Street, I saw the sentry outside his circular post with his face and body turned to the west looking at St. Teresa's Church. Since the sentry was not looking in my direction and not knowing whether he saw me or not, I did not know whether I should go ahead and bow to the empty post or just go on my way, make the turn and go on down the road. I did not think that I had violated anything but, in a split second, I heard a blood-curdling yell, and there could be no mistake that it came from the sentry. I quickly made a 90 degree turn and with my heart pounding in my throat, with great fear, I could clearly see a rifle pointing straight at me and realized that the sentry had his rifle butt against his shoulder and was aiming the rifle at me, with the intention to shoot me there and then, should I fail to BOW! And, bow I did, not just once but innumerable times. Call me a coward! Whatever! I froze! My mind went blank! I dared not move until I was sure that the sentry lowered his rifle and went on his way. This was my second brush with death. To this day, I still cannot remember what I did right after that close encounter!

Obviously one of the most significant and horrifying realities of any war is the inevitability of death. However, as much as we are aware of this specter, we are never properly prepared to come face to face with it day in and day out and so much in public. Being Chinese, I suppose, starvation and death perhaps may not hold much horror to me as compared to a European. But, this concept certainly has been proven to be untrue now that we have witnessed the Holocaust and even the horrors of the atom bomb. Nevertheless, the first time I saw a corpse on the pavement in the street did give me a fright and a sense of revulsion. This reminds me of the incident my sister Patsy relayed to me when she bicycled with our distant cousin from Tsim Sha Tsui to Kowloon Tong to visit our grandparents. She related to me that as they rode from Nathan Road into Waterloo Road, they came behind a truck, and to their dismay, they came upon a terrifying scene that they were not prepared for. They found that they were behind this van-like truck that belonged to the Sanitary Department, which had its rear door opened and in the truck were thrown willy-nilly, one on top of the other, dead bodies that the workers picked up from the streets that morning. Obviously, these poor souls did not survive the starvation and the cold night, victims of being poor and homeless as a result of the war.

One of the aggravations a war brings is the total exaggeration of facts, falsehoods and half-truths that people love to indulge in, irrespective of their educational level or achievement. The rumor prevalent during the early days of the war was the report that because of the scarcity of food, some had resorted to slicing off the thighs of those who were living in the streets and too weak to defend themselves and left to die, and the meat was sold in the market as pork or beef! Then there were rumors of people eating congee (rice porridge) with meat and spitting out human digital phalanges. However, we must acknowledge that starvation was quite severe during the first few months after the surrender to the Japanese. There is no denying that there was rationing for rice and firewood. I have personally witnessed the less well-to-do running after carts carrying rice and sweeping the grains of rice that fell on the road. But, the most saddening sight was some running after the cavalry and sweeping up the dung that the horses excreted, bringing that home and wash the waste off to collect the wheat or barley that the military fed their animals with.

One could say that I grew up in a hurry, learning the hard truths from the school of hard-knocks. I did have some very positive influences getting myself educated by the many Swatow businessmen who were the leaders of the Swatow Christian Church, which was the church that I grew up with. These men were in the same line of business as my Grandfather's Swatow Drawn Work Company, which is the selling of embroidered blouses, handkerchiefs, pajamas, and tablecloths, mostly imported from manufacturers in Swatow. In fact, when I reached the age of sixteen, we negotiated with our neighbor who owned a store downstairs in Nathan Road called the Ancient Company, selling electrical appliances, to rent me a showcase, which my father arranged with my Uncle to let me sell some of the same merchandise. Needless to say, business was very poor but at least I learnt a little discipline keeping to a somewhat nine-to six routine and how to sell and keep inventory. I had to learn a little Japanese, but a number of times it was scary when a lower-ranked soldier would come in and forcibly walk away with the goods and throw down a few dollars for them. One even threatened to slap me because I tried to resist him. Anyway, this first attempt at retail business did not last too long. This experience coupled with the memory of what it did to my father definitely turned me against this business of buying and selling in favor of my determination to pursue one of the professions. I had read that there were three professions, namely, theology, medicine and law and it sort of planted a seed in my mind as something I should venture for in the future.

One of the songs we learned when I was in La Salle was the song "What is home without a mother?" I've always loved the song and the lyrics. Moreover, it always brings to mind my mother. This past Mother's Day, which was a week ago, I preached on the fact that Jesus showed more compassion than legalism, which reminded me of my mother. You may recall that I was nicknamed Durian by my Uncle Harry and that seemed to have struck a sympathetic chord with pretty much all of my relatives, except, perhaps my mother. She was strict with me but she always showed me her loving and compassionate side. She alone seemed to have the faith and conviction that I would grow out of my naughtiness and change for the better. I can remember numerous times when I misbehaved, she in her desperation would ask me, "When will you grow up?" Finally, I would reassure her that I would grow up and change when I'd reached my fifteenth birthday. You may ask why fifteen? It was the custom in Swatow that a person would have matured by age fifteen from a boy into a man. People would celebrate a boy's fifteenth birthday by letting him eat a whole young rooster by himself; some would have him sit on a flat bamboo basket. This custom was meant to signify that the boy has now grown into manhood and is now no longer a boy but an adult. He is now going to come out of the garden and no longer playing in the garden but instead has to assume an adult role. Anyway, on my fifteenth birthday, my mother did give me a rooster to eat and I assured her that I would leave the garden and enter the adult world. I will leave the judgment as to how well I've succeeded for you to evaluate. I know that for those of you who have experienced your mother's love, you will understand and resound with me my sentiments, exactly!

To be fair, let me state strongly that my father, though a reserved man of few words, besides having my utmost respect, deserves my love as well. He was very definitely strict when I was a boy, though I admit, my siblings and I seldom saw him during the week. We do remember the Sundays when he would take the whole family to a restaurant to have the traditional Yam Char 飲茶. My father, in his way, was concerned that we grow up to be a Christian, a gentleman scholar, a respectable member of society, and a good family man. I may have related this incident before, but it was during the war, and I was not yet 16. I met a girl in the neighborhood, and one evening, we were getting acquainted and we talked at length about different things. By the time I got home, I realized it was past nine o'clock and as I walked into the back door of our flat, who do you think was standing there to meet me? My father! He just sternly told me that if I thought I was old enough, I could go ahead, pack my bag and go. I fully realized that it was the war, I was not old enough and until then, he is my father and I need to obey the rules.

In another sense, I have learned to know by his non-verbal body language, the limitations he has set for me. As the American saying goes, "You shape up or you ship out!" It may have been a couple of years later after this incident or it could have been shortly after the war was over. If you did not know, Chinese New Year is a very happy time, perhaps one of the biggest festivals in the Chinese calendar. It's usually a big holiday and families love to gather together and have fun, food, and festivities. One of the favorite customs for us kids was to receive red packets with lucky money inside whenever we wished an elder a Happy New Year, as long as you are not yet married. This was the time when our parents would give us the freedom to gamble; my favorite thing was to play Blackjack or 21 points. This one New Year, I may have been 17 and a lot of our relatives came to our house to wish us a Happy New Year. We all gathered around a table to play Blackjack. I was winning big and I became the banker. Soon a lot of the cousins dropped out because they lost all the money, except for two uncles. They wanted to win their money back and insisted that I play on. Soon it was dinner time and everybody was getting upset with me for keeping them from the meal. The two uncles forced me to play on and eventually they won their money back. When I got to the dining room, my father was very displeased. He was very silent. Then he spoke to me without raising his voice. He just said, "You don't know how to gamble! You should have stopped when you were ahead." When I heard that, I said to myself, "It wasn't that I did not want to stop. It was the uncles. They were older than me. They should know better. Shouldn't they?" I said to my father in a soft voice, "From now on, I will never gamble…not even for a cent." I have kept my word since then. Call this Providence, if you like, or agree that it was the Holy Spirit who spoke to me to do just the right thing. It has certainly been a blessing to me to be able to subdue one more evil influence on my life.

I am happy to say that by 1944, things were certainly looking up because the tide of the war was definitely turning in the Allies' favor. I had some friends who were of the third country neutrals, some of whom were Eurasians, while others were Portuguese, and some had been able to get news of the war and the good news was that the Allies had landed in Normandy and Hitler's Germany was being driven back. Italy was already almost in the Allies' hands. Though we weren't aware of what the Japanese were doing, we had a pretty good idea that the Allies were gradually getting the upper hand. We could see that by the fact that we began to have air raids by the US Navy's airplanes from the aircraft carriers. I had one frightening experience once when I was crossing the harbor from Hong Kong to my home in Kowloon. We were in mid-harbor when the sirens sounded and soon a series of US carrier planes were dive bombing the Japanese military shipping in the Harbor including the military base in Stonecutter's Island. You can imagine my relief when it was all over and we landed in Kowloon safely. The United States Air Force also got into the act and it was then that I learned about the tactic of carpet bombing. First, we noticed the Flying Fortresses and they would reach their target area and drop tens of bombs like laying a carpet. One of the less fortunate examples was when they did that to the Wanchai district on the island, because it obviously destroyed many tenement flats and killed or maimed many civilians. Then perhaps toward the end of 1944, there were bigger planes, the Super Fortresses and one day in the afternoon, there was a raid and we were all standing in the corridor in our flat on the second floor, third floor for the American way of reckoning, in a four-story row-house. We could hear the droning of the planes and as we waited and prayed, suddenly we could hear the unmistakable noise the descending bombs made and boom! Boom! Boom! Our front door flew open as we felt the house shake, then dust and smoke and the unmistakable smell. Our ears were ringing but as we looked at each other, we were all right. But, it was a close call! How close? I soon found out the next day that three bombs landed on our block, one on the house to the left, the other to the right and the third one a couple of houses to the right. Praise God! It was as close a brush with death as one wants to get. This makes my third close encounter. Fortunately, we were able to stay in the flat and did not have to move.

I must say that I'd had enough of this war and was hoping that it would end soon. We were soon to have our one wish come true though it might be a number of months in the future, but come it did!

IX

Unconditional Surrender
August 15, 1945

It's over! The war is ended! The Emperor finally surrendered!
The date was August 15, 1945. The news that morning was that the
Emperor of Japan was going to make an announcement on the radio
and that the Japanese nationals who could make it were to assemble in
the intersection of Des Voeux Road and Peddar Street and to face the
Gloucester Hotel because loud speakers were to be placed there and they
were to bow to the Emperor while he spoke. What joyous news! What
a glorious victory!

We were told that the Governor of Hong Kong, Sir Mark Young
and all the British personnel who had been interned in Stanley (and
later transferred through various POW camps in China and Japan to
Mukden known today as Shenyang) were released but that there was
insufficient manpower to resume governing the whole of the Colony of
Hong Kong. The arrangement was therefore made that while the British
would resume their sovereignty over the Colony, they would allow the
Japanese to remain in control of the peninsula of Kowloon and the New
Territories until British reinforcements could arrive in Hong Kong.
It was a unique experience and I couldn't help but want to take the
opportunity to have a taste of freedom by taking a little trip across the
harbor on the ferry and get to the Island just to feel the contrast. You'd
be amazed at how such a subtle change in your environment can make
a difference to your psyche! I was quite excited and exhilarated by what
the future held and I was filled with visions of what I could become,

but most of all I wanted to be able to go back to school, to catch up, to learn, and perhaps to go to University. I dreamt of how wonderful it would be if I could get a degree in the three professions and become a clergyman, a physician and a lawyer. Then my thoughts quickly came back down to the nitty-gritty: when would the British Navy be able to sail into Hong Kong through Lyemun Pass 鯉魚門海峽? When would the Japanese be sent back to Japan? When would they open an English school in Kowloon so I could be a student again?

The answers came quite rapidly. We were told that the British Fleet under Admiral Harcourt would arrive on the morning of August 30th. There was word that the Diocesan Girls' School in Jordan Road would be opened late September. Peace was here to stay! The weather was beautiful. Fred would soon return home from China. He had graduated from High School and would be entering Lingnan University 嶺南大學 in Canton to study Agriculture when the new term started in September. What joy! How wonderful to have so many happy events coming one after the other! This certainly was the time to shout aloud with a cheerful voice—God is great! God is good! Let us praise Him together!

I did not tell you this before but, somehow I was able to get hold of a monocular telescope that was shaped like a box camera. It was old but good. On the morning of August 30th, I got up bright and early, took my telescope and went up on the roof. By this time, the owners of the flats that sustained the bomb blasts had repaired their broken roof so it was perfectly safe to go up there. Our house faced east and so I had a ringside seat and a vantage point to focus my sight on Lyemun Pass. It was a bright and clear day with a slight breeze. What a perfect setting for such a glorious event. It is a pity that I was not a poet or I could have composed a fitting sonnet for an occasion such as this so posterity could have a share of my exhilaration.

All of a sudden, I could see through the telescope the shape of a battleship, or cruiser to be exact, with the Union Jack flying on the mast and gradually, one by one, the British Fleet sailed through the Pass into the harbor. After getting over the initial excitement, I quickly went down to our house and then left for the streets. We were living on Nathan Road at the time, which is just a couple of blocks from Salisbury

Road and as I started on my way over there, I could see many young men and boys heading in the same direction. We all were trying to get to Holt's Wharf just to the east of the intersection of Nathan Road and Salisbury Road. The famous Peninsula Hotel is on the right side of the road as you come to Salisbury Road from Nathan Road. Holt's Wharf stood where the Regent Hotel (currently InterContinental Hong Kong) is situated now. There was a building and Godown fronting the road and as we reached the gate we all went in. There was a building on the left side of the gate which the Japanese used as a sentry post and as we entered the wharf, we noticed that the sentries were all sitting very impassively inside the post. They made no attempt to hinder our entry but sat there quite unmoved by all our excited chatter and rush to get in to greet the ship that was attempting to dock at the pier. I was to find out later that the ship was the Canadian Troopship, the HMS Prince Rupert. She was getting close to the pier and truing to dock. We could see the sailors and officers leaning on the side rails, we made our way toward the edge of the pier being careful not to fall into the water below because there were planks missing on the pier, perhaps done purposefully by the Japanese. The sailors on board were trying to secure the ship to the pier but there was no one to secure the hawsers to the pier so we all shouted that we would help. It did not take too long for us to secure the hawsers to the pier and as soon as the ship was securely docked, the ship's officers and sailors were able to lower their gangplank and make their way down to the pier. I saw a Lieutenant leading his landing party as they came down the gangplank, and quickly went over to greet him. I introduced myself and told him about the sentries at the front gate and led them over there to relieve them so as to secure the wharf for the ship. He did that with dispatch and sent the Japanese sentries on their way to Whitfield Barracks on Nathan Road because that was to be the internment area for the Japanese until they were repatriated.

On seeing that everything was now shipshape, the Lieutenant asked me if I would like to have some lunch. I promptly jumped at that suggestion and without hesitation accepted his invitation. I guess my three years and eight months of semi-starvation got the best of me. Very quickly I followed him up the gangplank and we ended up at the Officer's Mess. I can't tell you whether I remembered my table manners or whether my hunger got the best of me. All I can remember is there was white tablecloth on the table; there were beautiful China plates, shiny glass tumblers, salt shakers and pepper mills and shiny silverware, and of course, napkins. There were bread and butter and ice water and all I can remember is we had Canadian salmon for the main course. How I wish I had a camera or a cell phone like you kids have nowadays...I could have taken a few photographs to show you now. I had a most enjoyable meal; one that I will never forget, though, sad to say, with the passing years my memory does grow dim. Finally, the meal was over, the Lieutenant asked if I smoked, I said I didn't but I said, "My father does." Imagine my surprise when he right away went and got a carton of Lucky Strikes and gave it to me. I bid him farewell and came home and gave the cigarettes to my father, which made him very happy, I was sure of that.

As I am about to end this particular chapter, I want to remember that this was very definitely a turning point in my life. Whatever happened in the past was gone and done with. The future was ahead of me with many promises and possibilities. Though I had not heard of the term then, it certainly applied to me then. Carpe Diem! I need to seize the moment. At the same time I need to see that in the end, good conquers evil and as a believer in Jesus, that no matter what happens, no matter how dark the shadow, no matter how deep the valley God is there! I must surrender my all to Him, unconditionally!!!

XX

DIOCESAN GIRLS' SCHOOL
1945-1946

The war ended! The Japanese had surrendered unconditionally. The Emperor's Representative and the Representative of the Japanese Imperial Army were ushered on board the USS Missouri in Tokyo Bay, to sign the document under the eyes of the United States General Douglas MacArthur, the Supreme Commander of the Allied Forces together with all the Representatives of Great Britain, The Republic of China, and France, as well as Australia, Canada, New Zealand, and the Netherlands, and were shown publicly to the World.

It was time now for me to pick up the pieces, begin anew, get educated and build a future. I can't remember how we got the good news, but we were told that Diocesan Girls' School (DGS) in Jordan Road would be opened in late September, but since I did not keep a diary, I am unable to make certain the exact day school started. We were given to understand that because of the shortage of everything, especially expatriate teachers, the authorities could only open Wah Yan School on Hong Kong Island and Diocesan Girls' School in Kowloon for the English curriculum. Needless to say, my sisters, Patsy, Margaret and I made our way enthusiastically, on the morning of registration, toward the school and took our places. Initially, because of the war that lasted three years and eight months, I can imagine with so many kids between the ages of 15 and 20, it would have been difficult to know in which class to put the kids. What the school did was to put the older kids in Class A and the younger half in Class B, with the aim of having us take an exam in October to decide and separate the Class A students into Class 1 and 2, or the Matriculation Class and the School Leaving Class. Similarly the younger group of students in class B was separated into Class 3 and 4 as the case may be, after the exam.

It was a novel idea to have co-education in a school that was a girls' school and it was definitely very different from what it was at La Salle, though I must admit I found no difficulty fitting into the new environment. However, what seemed like a dream come true quickly dissipated and quite unexpectedly my dream world became obscured by a huge dark cloud, reminiscent of the one that rolled over my world when I had to bury my brand new Boy Scout uniform the day Kowloon fell to the Japanese Army. But like all things in life, when everything appears to be dim and dismal, always look for the silver lining and for those of us who believe in Jesus, God will provide. It was three or four days into the new beginning in DGS, I'm not too sure, but the point I want to get across to you is that I was informed by our teacher Mrs. Symons to report to the Headmistress, Miss Gibbons. I am sure you are wondering with me and saying, "What's up? What did I do wrong now?"

This was the first time I met Miss Gibbons. She was extremely nice, however, sad to say, you could tell, even superficially, that the war and internment had taken its toll. I didn't know then that the Diocese had already taken steps to have a replacement soon and Miss Hurrell came perhaps within a month or two but don't quote me on this. Back to the reason for seeing Miss Gibbons—what she said to me struck me like a thunderclap through the brooding dark cloud—I was devastated and completely lost for words. I was crying on the inside but was bravely putting up a stoic front, while desperately trying to compose myself to maintain my equilibrium so as to figure what to do next. Miss Gibbons said that she was sorry that because of the fact that there was a shortage of space and because I was not an old boy from Diocesan Boys' School (DBS), I could not stay and continue my schooling at DGS. Once again I found myself a lowly and helpless little pawn in somebody's chess game. Dejectedly, I made my way home. I brooded. I moaned and groaned around for three days. I was very disappointed and was very upset with the fact that I was not given a chance to prove myself. I was disqualified, not for anything I had or had not done, but just because I was not an old boy from DBS. This was unfair! I was not happy and I showed it. Finally my mother calmly and lovingly came and talked to me on the fourth morning. She said, "If you want to go to school so much, why don't you go and talk to the Headmistress and tell her that you really and earnestly want to go to school and ask her to make a special allowance for you?" I must admit that I was not a very dedicated and regular person then with respect to reading the Bible every morning and spending time in prayer, though I am sure that my mother probably prayed for me in this regard.

Anyway, I went to the school early the next morning and asked to speak to Miss Gibbons. After I was led into her office, I very politely and in my best behavior, gently told her very plainly that I was asked to go home a few days ago because I was not an old boy from DBS, but that I really wanted to have an education and begged her to reconsider my case since there was no other school for me to go to. Imagine my surprise when she got up and led me to the classroom and reinstated me as a student right there and then. I thank God for this great new development and for allowing me to continue my schooling. This is none other than the providence of God, again!

I must admit that I enjoyed being a student again and the new experience of being in the same class with girls and boys. However, it did not take long for me to realize how far behind I was in Mathematics and Science, let alone English Literature. A stark example was in Geometry, because by the time I was given the permission to study at DGS, I found out that the class had already finished the first ten theorems, which caused me to make a mad scramble to learn them myself just to keep up. I knew only a little Algebra, which meant that I had to catch up on Trigonometry, Biology, and Chemistry. Looking back, all I can say is that with hard work, determination, prayer, and a little bit of luck, I passed the special examination in November, and was formally placed in the Matriculation Class. Praise God for His Love and Grace!

I was learning a lot of new things. We were reading Julius Caesar, and for the first time in my life, I was enjoying William Shakespeare, or as he would have said, "Et tu, Kenneth?" Our new headmistress, Miss Hurrell, also taught us Religious Knowledge, and we studied the Old Testament. I'd been to Sunday School all these years but had never studied the Bible systemically and this was quite a welcome change, not to mention that it was an eye-opener to see for the first time how the stories fit together and how it made perfect sense —Sunday School was never like this! I really enjoyed this class and have benefitted from it tremendously. What I am trying to say is that it is uncanny to see how much of what happened over the years since those days at DGS has reminded me of the series of happenstances that I read in the Book of Esther. Let me explain: It is quite remarkable for me to look back from my vantage point on May 24th, 2011, to that day when I sat for the University of Hong Kong Matriculation Examination set in May 1945, then to get the result that I had obtained a Distinction in Religious Knowledge and then to find myself teaching the Old Testament Class as an Adjunct Lecturer at the Mountain View, Missouri Facility of the Southwest Baptist University in Bolivar, Missouri, for the years 2009 and 2010.

Don't get me wrong! My personality would not allow me to become a dull boy because school wasn't all work and no play. We had free time, recesses and lunchtime and besides those we had plenty of other activities like sports and exercises. One activity that we liked very much was a bonus activity because the Padre of the British Army 44th commando unit volunteered to be something like a chaplain to us. He would have some religion classes but the best "class" we had with him was when he came in his army truck and took us out to the New Territories for an outing with food and drink provided. They were real treats!

One of our classmates was Grace Young, whose father was Manager of the Hong Kong and Yaumatei Ferry Company, whose ferries plied between Kowloon, Hong Kong, and the New Territories, which included all the surrounding islands. They also owned a cottage on Silvermine Bay, located in the big neighboring island of Lantau. She would invite us to her home in Silvermine Bay for a picnic, which usually turned out to be a blast because we got to ride the ferry, swim, eat, and hike all in one outing. We were usually quite exhausted on the ferry home, but we had fun!

We also had parties at our respective homes where we danced, ate, drank, and made merry. It didn't take me long to learn how to dance though I wasn't too good at dancing the tango, rumba, or samba, but jitterbug I rather enjoyed, though I must admit, slow and romantic songs were very appealing when you were infatuated with your partner. Anyway, we, like all kids in the world, played all kinds of music and did all kinds of dances, such as boogie woogie, jive, and soon we were drinking rum and Coca Cola, gin, and whiskey, and we even smoked. I did not do drugs of any kind and I do not think any of my classmates did. Personally, I think smoking and drinking are not good for you. But when you are young and foolish, you think that you are so sophisticated to be able to do all that. I will have more to say about that later, so remind me.

One creditable thing I did and I feel rather grateful that I did it even now was that I did take the time and effort to attend the worship services at St. Andrews Anglican Church on Nathan Road midway between DGS and my home. DGS is, after all, the school run by the Anglican Church, hence its name, Diocesan Girls' School. One of the friends that joined me was a classmate of Patsy's named Eileen Peters. We actually were members of the choir and singing in a choir was one of the things I enjoyed doing. There may have been others but I am not sure. Anyway, it was during this venture that for the first time in my life I was asked to sing a solo part once. I have always enjoyed Classical music, especially Bach, particularly the piece, "Jesu, joy of man's desiring." I did take music lessons, I mean the piano, first with Julia Liang, a classmate of my mother's, then with Harry Orr. Maybe I took them because my mother wanted me to take Patsy to the lessons and rather than wasting my time doing nothing, we killed two birds with one stone. I would have continued, except that one day Patsy was given the message by Professor Orr to tell our mother not to waste her money on me because I did not practice like I should. This happened during the war and I really did not feel too concerned about it because I really was too restless and active to discipline myself to spend the time practicing my piano lessons. I'd much rather be outside playing soccer with my friends.

Time marches on! Soon it was time for us to hunker down and prepare for the Matriculation Examination which was to be held sometime in May 1945. We understood then that because of the war and shortage of personnel and the fact that the University of Hong Kong had been pillaged during the war, the reconstruction of the Main building, the Science Building, the lecture rooms, the laboratories, and even the hostels were advancing at a slow pace. The University had to contract with London to set the School Leaving Examination papers for us to do the exam on a one time basis. I am happy to say that when it was all over, I passed with distinctions in Religious Knowledge and Chinese, and qualified to study Science Proceeding to Medicine, Science, or Medicine.

Well done, Kenneth! Now what? You had three choices, which would it be? At one time I had the notion that I would like to do medical research without really understanding what that would involve. I am not like those people who claimed that they knew even before they reached puberty that they wanted to be this and that. Half the time, I wasn't even sure I knew what the world had in store for me. Which reminds me of the story Betty told me about Stephen, our son: We'd always given him Matchbox cars ever since he got his first one from Dr. Ted Paterson's mother when we visited her in Eltham in the UK perhaps in 1961, when we took a trip from Hong Kong to New York. This brought on Stephen's passion for cars and one time Betty took him on a taxi ride when he was still a little boy, and during the ride he was watching the driver with rapt attention, then he announced to his mother that when he grew up he wanted to be a taxi driver. Now, that is ambition. He knew what he wanted to be when he's grown up. Naturally, he never accomplished his ambition to be a taxi driver but he did do motocross in his teens and early twenties and now he sponsors motocross racers. He's also in the signs and decals business and very appropriately many of the racers want to have special logos and designs for their shirts, bikes, helmets and etc. Since I was uncertain about what Stephen is sponsoring, I asked him to give me some specifics, so here it is, right from the man's mouth:

> The term is motocross, without the "r". I sponsor the Missouri State Motocross Series, and I promote the Sho-Me State Pitbike Series, which is a motocross series for people racing modified kids' bikes—ones not originally meant for motocross, but for kids to putt around in fields and woods. They are called pit bikes because, since they are cheap and durable and small, they are popular to have for getting around the pit area of

a race track (which can be miles from end to end). Being racers, the people start modifying them, and naturally the idea for racing follows. We also sponsor individual racers who compete in motocross (which is the outdoor racing), supercross (professional racing in football and baseball stadiums which is done during the winter), and arenacross (amateur and professional racing in hockey and horse arenas, also during the winter.)

But as far as I, myself, am concerned, I didn't have any idea what I should or wanted to be, and so it was that when I got the Matriculation results in my hands and was presented with three choices, I was in a quandary because I had to make a decision and make a choice. I had no one to bounce my ideas with and no one who could really give me any advice. I am grateful that my parents were very supportive and were overjoyed that their faith in me had paid off but they could not begin to help with my choices since they had not had the luxury of having been through higher education themselves and would not have the metrics to help me evaluate the three choices offered me. I must let you, the reader, and the whole world know that they were ideal parents par excellence; they were happy I qualified to enter the University; they were proud but never boastful; they were encouraging, and never for once did they throw cold water on my enthusiasm by mentioning or asking how they were to pay for my University education, but I know that deep in their hearts, they must have worried but they never wanted me to know it. Looking back at what they had sacrificed and done for me, I can't help but wonder if I could ever repay them enough for their love for me!

Anyway, it was time to say goodbye to DGS and after the summer holidays, I went to the University to register. It wasn't long before I found out that I would not be a science student because I would need to take Trigonometry and Calculus and besides I was rather weak in Chemistry. I therefore enrolled in the newly structured course called Science Proceeding to Medicine. However, after a couple of weeks and the poor grade I got on my first paper in English Essay, I decided that this was not my cup of tea either. Hence, by a process of elimination, I found myself enrolled as a medical student, which would require me to spend six years of schooling before I would graduate with a M.B.,B.S. degree; this, plus a year's training as a houseman in a hospital in order to qualify for a license to practice medicine. Then if you wanted to specialize in a particular branch of medicine, it was another six or more years of training, then pass the Fellowship examination to qualify you to be a specialist.

One final thing we were told was that it was compulsory that we lived in the hostel for three years and that we had to provide ourselves with a cot, a mattress, and bedding for the hostel. The University would have a desk, chair, and a wardrobe for us. We would also have to provide for ourselves a folding chair when we attended classes because all the wooden furnishings of the lecture rooms were looted.

As I was writing this, I was bothered by the fact that it sounded like I really was not prepared to make such an important choice in my life and wishing I had a better method. I happened to come across a devotional reading that addresses just such a situation. I am taking the liberty to append it here and hope that this may help you should you be confronted with having to make a hard choice when you have to face such a dilemma.

The test of self-interest

If thou wilt take the left hand, then I will go to the right; or if thou depart to the right hand, then I will go to the left. Genesis 13:9.

As soon as you begin to live the life of faith in God, fascinating and luxurious prospects will open up before you, and these things are yours by right; but if you are living the life of faith you will exercise your right to waive your rights, and let God choose for you. God sometimes allows you to get into a place of testing where your own welfare would be the right and proper thing to consider if you were not living a life of faith; but if you are, you will joyfully waive your right and leave God to choose for you. This is the discipline by means of which the natural is transformed into the spiritual by obedience to the voice of God.

Whenever *right* is made the guidance in the life, it will blunt the spiritual insight. The great enemy of the life of faith in God is not sin, but the good which is not good enough. The good is always the enemy of the best. It would seem the wisest thing in the world for Abraham to choose, it was his right, and the people around would consider him a fool for not choosing. Many of us do not go on spiritually because we prefer to choose what is right instead of relying on God to choose for us. We have to learn to walk according to the standard which has its eye on God. *"Walk before Me."*[27]

---

[27] Chambers, O. (1993). *My utmost for his highest: Selections for the year* (NIV edition.). Westwood, NJ: Barbour and Co.

XXI

University of Hong Kong: Medical Faculty
1946-1952

I can't believe it but I have completely forgotten the exact day we were told we could move into our hostel. I was given a place in Eliot Hall, which was the middle hostel of the three University Hostels or now commonly known as the Old Halls. They were all named after the former governors of Hong Kong; Lugard Hall is the first one you come to as you climb the path leading you there from the Main Building, Eliot Hall is the second one as you climb higher on the sloping hillside and finally the topmost one is May Hall. Each hostel is a three-story rectangular long building. There is a basketball court alongside the outside of the building with a concrete playing surface. The kitchen is at the end of the building as you come up the steps from the path. It adjoins the dining area which occupies the middle section of the ground floor, large enough to accommodate perhaps eight round tables with six stools. At the other end of the dining area there is a common room, and this adjoins the Warden's quarters, which is on the west side of the ground floor. There is a broad concrete staircase leading upstairs at the east end of the dining area that goes all the way to the third level. All the floors are of concrete, and the two upper floors have the same configuration; the bathrooms are at the east end, the doorway is in the middle, which leads you to a small sectioned area that can accommodate four beds, with a French window on each side that leads out to a balcony that runs the whole of the dormitory. As you proceed further in the central corridor towards the west you come to a long open space that can accommodate the beds on each side and with a series of French windows on each side that leads to the balcony. Beyond the stairs there is another small section that is a replica of the one in the east side. It was very Spartan looking and devoid of any ornamentation, particularly because everything wooden was removed during the war and everything was hastily and economically repaired so as to receive the new students who were soon to arrive.

My father had arranged for the coolie who was always called on by my Grandfather's Swatow Drawn Works Company—practically on a daily basis—to move and deliver heavy parcels and crates of merchandise, to come and help me move my bed up to the University hostel. He had to come over to our house in Kowloon with his bamboo pole and ropes and he tied up my metal bed and mattress on one end of the pole and balanced it with my suitcase at the other end. He easily hoisted the pole on his shoulders and off I went with him to catch the ferry to cross the harbor to Hong Kong and then walk to the University. I can't remember whether I had to carry my folding chair and a bag to tote my toiletries and personal belongings or whether he tied up the chair with his load. It was a nice little stroll. I didn't mind the walk because my heart was filled with excitement and because I was going to the University! I felt like an explorer on a journey into the unknown!

If you were to ask Betty about it, she's sure to tell you that I would be the first one to arrive at the hostel and she will be one hundred percent correct, because when we finally made it into the hostel I found out that I was the one and only student to check in at that time and the first one to arrive. It made me feel good because I've always made it a point to be punctual and prompt whenever I have an appointment to keep or a commitment to meet someone. I do believe that it is irresponsible and a sign of disrespect when you never fail to be tardy and are late for a prearranged rendezvous every time. I picked out the area that I would reside, made my bed, unpacked my belongings and tried to make myself feel at home. Yes, this would be my home for the next three years, which is the requirement the University imposed on us and a precondition for graduating. I thought the arrangement was quite appropriate because the last three years of our studies would be the clinical years and we would be required to be at Queen Mary Hospital and at times be at the Outpatient Clinics at Sai Ying Pun, besides having some classes in the University compound.

Before too long, I was joined by a classmate and soon to become one of my best friends in medical school, Kwaan Hau Cheong, who soon picked a spot near mine at the hostel. Then at 6.00 p.m., we both were notified by the dinner bell that dinner was served. We went downstairs and ate our first of many meals at the dining room of Eliot Hall, University of Hong Kong. Presently, the rest of the students residing in Eliot Hall made their separate ways into the hostel and we had students from Hong Kong, Shanghai, Singapore, Malaysia, Goa, Burma and the Seychelles. It was fun getting to know each other and making friends with people from different cultures and nationalities. We all stayed up late but soon had to retire and be awake early next morning for the start of our learning process.

After a false start, I quickly settled down to become a medical student, though with considerable anxiety and apprehension especially when I had no idea what was in store for me. One of the more humorous stories I told Betty, which she thought hilarious, was that on one occasion, before I entered the University, my mother and I were talking about what profession I should take and she advised me not to become a dentist because I would have to deal with the patients' bad breath and dirty teeth. Betty would laugh herself silly and say, "Wouldn't she be surprised if she should find out what smells, odors and dirt you had to deal with as a surgeon?" LOL I'm getting ahead of myself again, but I do have to put down my thoughts into print in the paper as they come to mind or else I might lose them forever. Sorry about that!

As first year medical students, we were required to take three subjects, namely, Physics, Chemistry, and Biology. Fortunately, all of the classes were held in the Northcote Science Building, which was a fairly new building, except for the lack of the wooden flooring, courtesy of the looters. The building is on Pokfulam Road a short distance south of the driveway of the Main Building. I could handle the course on Physics comfortably because I had that in my Matriculation year, but Biology and Chemistry were quite foreign to me and I found them rather taxing in my attempt to master them, and much to my chagrin and shame, I, for the first time in my University studies, had to taste the bitter gall of a failed grade in both of these subjects. After much hard work and determination, I made a passing grade in both subjects in the supplemental examinations. And so it was, I passed the 1st MB exam, the first of three milestones on the way to gaining the M.B., B.S. degree that qualifies me to become a Physician and Surgeon—a medical doctor and a healer! Doesn't that sound impressive? Dr. Siu, I presume?

I guess it is all right to dream now that I have scraped through the first year—and I mean scrape, considering the fact that there were 80 of us when we started at the beginning of the school year but when we appeared the first day of the second year at the Anatomy Building, there were only 66 of us. The ones who failed had to repeat their first year, though perhaps the less determined ones had opted to drop out altogether. Those of us who made it to the second year now could breathe a sigh of relief. Yet we were fully aware that the second MB exam, which was taken at the end of the third year, had the reputation of being the toughest exam and the exam actually only tested us in two subjects, viz. Anatomy and Physiology, both of which were to extend over the two years—the second and third years. We did have to study Biochemistry in our second year but sad to say, I had to take the supplemental exam again, which I passed.

Before too long, third year came and went and it was time to sit for the second most crucial exams of the medical curriculum—the dreaded 2nd MB exam. It seemed like it was only yesterday that we started our second year. The first day in Anatomy Lab was quite a baptism of fire because of the dread of the unknown. I remember we carefully put on our rubber gloves and gingerly touched the cadaver, picked up our scalpels and held our breaths to make the first incision. Every medical student in history has had to confront the excitement mixed with distaste of cadaver dissection. As you get started, each step is fearsome, but as the days and weeks of dissection go by, the work can even become enjoyable and fun. Before I leave the subject, let me say a word or two about our Professor of Anatomy. He was Dr. Banfill, who came over to Hong Kong with the Canadian Regiment just prior to the Japanese invasion in 1941 and unfortunately spent the three years and eight months of the Japanese occupation in the POW camps. Though I didn't get to know him personally, I consider him a hero and worthy of my respect in addition to his being my professor and teacher.

The other personality worthy of mention was our Professor of Physiology and Vice-Chancellor, Dr. the Hon. Sir Lindsay T. Ride. He, without my saying so, was and is still, a very well-known and respected king-sized hero, in a number of ways and among a very sizable if not the whole of Hong Kong. More direct and to the point, it was common knowledge that he was the Commandant of the Hong Kong Volunteer Defense Force and most people in Hong Kong would have read about his escape from the Sham Shui Po Concentration camp quite early on and with the help of the Tung Kong guerillas made his way to Chung King in Free China and while there started the British Army Aid Group (BAAG). BAAG would be responsible for aiding many escapees, especially the Chinese volunteers of the Hong Kong Volunteer Defense Force, to Free China. They also had contacts with the local Chinese who did yeoman work in espionage, though many would wind up being caught by the Japanese and sadly because they were betrayed by traitors. He was a much decorated hero and was to become a very successful Vice-Chancellor for the University. Sir Lindsay and Lady Ride were very much interested in Robert Morrison, the English missionary who was the first person to translate the English Bible into Chinese in 1807, as well as compiling the first English-Chinese Dictionary a few years before that. The Rides were co-authors of two books about the Protestant Cemetery and the Morrison Chapel in Baak Gaap Chauh 白鴿巢 in Macau, which were interesting reads, especially to those who are interested in how Protestantism first got its foothold in China. However, one of the many things that Robert Morrison did had a very bad consequence that is still used by the Peoples' Republic of China to restrict and harass missionaries even today, should they attempt to or apply for an entry visa to enter into and/or travel in Mainland China. The point I want to raise is that I read in one of the biographies of Robert Morrison which mentioned two or three things that he did, which has given fodder to the Communist Government in the PRC to place restrictions on Protestant missionaries when they tried to obtain a visa.

The first faulty move he made was when he was asked to leave Sha Meen (Shamien) 沙面, because he had not met the qualifications to live there, and as a matter of expediency, he moved to Macau. At that time the Chinese government had only allowed the Portuguese to settle there since they first came in the 1550's. Morrison was in the midst of learning Chinese, which incidentally was forbidden to the foreigner, and he was trying to finish his work on the Dictionary and the Chinese Bible, and, therefore did not want to relinquish his golden opportunity. Not long after his stay in Macau, his son died. It was then that he found out that he could not bury his son in the Portuguese Catholic Cemetery and he had to surreptitiously bury him on the Chinese side of the wall that extended from St. Paul Cathedral and the Guia Hill where the lighthouse stood, the wall that separated the Portuguese colony from the Chinese territory. I guess the straw that broke the camel's back was when he no longer had the financial support of his Mission Board. He, therefore, sought or was recruited for employment at the East India Company as a translator. Whether Robert Morrison knew or was ignorant of the fact may be moot, but at that time, the demand for tea, silk, and porcelain back home in England was so great, it drained England of her reserve of silver coins and ingots, particularly when China did not need to purchase anything from England. The Company realized that it was a drain on its treasury to return to China each trip with empty vessels except for the ballasts. Thereupon, they struck on the novel idea of substituting shiploads of contraband opium in lieu of the rocks for ballast. What happened afterwards was history. The tragedy was that it led to the Opium War and the imposition of the Unequal Treaties on China. One unfortunate aspect of all these is that the Chinese Communist authorities seized upon this and lumped everything together and propagandized that the Christians, namely Morrison, used the guise of religion, in other words a missionary, to smuggle into China a contraband, namely opium, to poison the Chinese populace and since then, Christian missionaries would forever be a dirty name because of their association with the smuggling of opium to poison the Chinese people, which led to the Opium War, which led to the imposition of the Unequal Treaties, which led to the humiliation of the Chinese for over the past hundred and fifty odd years. Perhaps it was my naiveté to assume that such a National disgrace and the anger and shame it caused the country, could and would, with time be abated and forgiven; but maybe I was wrong, as I was to find out a few years ago with my personal encounters. It was as if this humiliation on China, though so long ago, would not and/or should not be forgotten but that the insult and disgrace must be repaid or retaliated in one form or another. And who are the culprits on the receiving end? Namely, all Foreign Protestant (Christian) Missionaries would be discouraged if not banned from entering China to engage in evangelism.

Later on in my book, I will be talking about the part I played as a missionary of the Southern Baptist Convention in August of 1994, but at this particular moment, I would like to relate my encounters with the Immigration Authority of the Chinese Government, while I was serving here in Macau between 1994 and 1998, as the Medical Administrator of the Hope Medical Group, which was sponsored by the Macau Baptist Mission of the Southern Baptist Convention. You will soon see what I meant when I mentioned that missionary is a dirty word because China looks upon the missionary Morrison and his ilk as the hypocrites and culprits behind the selling of opium to China, the instigator of the Opium War and the subsequent imposition of the Unequal Treaties.

It all began at a monthly meeting of the Macau Christian Churches Association I attended a few months after we arrived in Macau. While there at the meeting, it was announced that the Association had received an invitation from the Guangdong Provincial Christian Council and the Three Self Patriotic Movement Committee of Guangdong, inviting all pastors to an Exchange visit in Guangzhou in July of 1995. I was quite excited by the prospect and placed my name in the hopper and I was hoping that some of my American coworkers and friends could go too. However, we were soon informed that the invitation would be extended to Chinese members only and all foreigners would be excluded. I couldn't help but feel that this was the first hint of a boycott and a snub to foreigners as a token of retaliation. When we went to Guangzhou for this trip, I was more than a little bit surprised when I found myself seated at the same table with Pastor Fan Sau Yuen (Fan Xiuyuan) 范秀遠牧師, the Vice-Chairman of the Guangdong Provincial Christian Council and Secretary Hung Baak Heung (Xiong Boxiang) 熊伯響書記 of the Three Self Patriotic Movement Committee of Guangdong, during the Feast. Soon the conversation came around to me. The hosts were particularly interested in knowing: Who was I? Where did I come from? Why was I in Macau? What did I do there? What did I do in the past?

After we got through the preliminaries, the Party Secretary and the Pastor told me that there was bad flooding in a town in Northwest Guangdong Province called Lihn Saan (Lianshan) 連山, which is Lianshan Zhuang and Yao Autonomous County連山壯族瑤族自治. Liánshān Zhuàngzú Yáozú Zìzhìxiàn is located in Qingyuan prefecture, Guangdong Province, in southern China. And there was a great need for aid and relief in the hospital in a myriad of ways and they wanted to know if I could assist them in any way? I informed them that I would have to seek my superiors' approval but I saw no reason why bringing volunteer medical teams from the United States to come to Lianshan to assist and relieve the medical needs of victims of floods and natural disasters would pose any kind of problems or disapproval. I will have more to say about this project later. However to hark back to my thesis for this digression regarding the animus of the Chinese Authorities toward foreign missionaries entering China, this is definitely a closed subject, except to say that what I encountered seemed a bit inconsistent on the surface. When the final arrangements were made to bring volunteer medical groups to travel to Lianshan to render supplemental medical services, during my application for a visitor's visa to enter China, the agent at the China Travel Service asked that I produce my Alien Labor Permit ID card together with my passport. When they finally granted my visa, I was told that I had to sign an affidavit that I would not take part in any religious activity because I was listed as a missionary in my Labor permit. This then became a routine formality each time I applied for a visa.

Imagine the feelings that came over me this past weekend of July 1, 2011, when I had the occasion to go to Hong Kong from Macau to help Patsy celebrate her birthday. Incidentally, I have been in Macau since the 6th of January of 2011, to once again pick up where I left off on August 1 of 2008, after serving ten years as Pastor of Sha Lei Tau Baptist Church. Anyway, as we were relaxing in the living room at Patsy's house in the afternoon of a beautiful sunny Sunday, something caught my attention in the Review section of the Sunday Morning Post. The article in question is in page 12 of the magazine and was titled "The war that still rumbles." It has a picture of a smoking opium pipe and the subtitle says, "Author argues the Opium War was elevated from a troublesome skirmish to a national humiliation for political purposes." The author of the review in the newspaper was Bonny Schoonakker and the author of the book "The Opium War" is Julia Lovell, published by Picador. The article began:

> One of the most interesting things about the Opium War (1839-1842), as Julia Lovell argues in her 361-page account, is that it is still being fought. More than 170 years after Britain sent a fleet of warships up the Pearl River to teach imperial (sic) China a lesson in international trade, shots are still being fired.
>
> A recent salvo, as Lovell writes in her preface, comes when Prime Minister David Cameron arrived in Beijing in November last year at the Head of a British trade delegation on a mission. The group was visiting at a time when Britain traditionally commemorated its war dead by wearing an imitation red poppy. This Remembrance Day ritual is "infected by political humbug", as Lovell notes, but no public figure would be seen dead without a red poppy.
>
> However, non-Chinese media reported that Cameron and his delegation had been asked to remove their poppies in Beijing because of the flower's alleged association with the Opium War, when Britain humiliated the Qing army and re-establishing a balance of trade. That controversy was a minor blip during Cameron's visit, if it did in fact happen-reports on it (at least the brief items of wire copy carried by this newspaper) attributed the matter to unnamed British officials in the delegation. Beijing's Foreign Ministry had, wisely, nothing to say on the matter (in marked contrast to the copious newsprint generated by the British Press). Besides, Remembrance

Day's poppies are not the same as the ones from which opium is derived...

From a Chinese perspective, according to Lovell's reading, the Opium War became a war only in the 20th century. Then, the Nationalists (with the help of their in-house spin doctor at the time, Mao Zedong) and the communists needed to find an anti-western cause around which to build a national post-imperial Chinese mythology, elevating that skirmish to the official status of a national humiliation. Lovell may be right that the significance of the Opium War has been exaggerated in China during the past 20 years as a deflection from the crackdown on the demonstration in Tiananmen Square.

But it was another cruel, shameful period in the history of the British Empire. At one point Lovell describes how the inhabitants of Canton, after the city fell to the foreign troops, were murdered in cold blood while "inland, women were divided for rape between the invaders (the prettiest reserved for the white British, the rest for Indians)". You don't have to be Chinese to find that outrageous even 150 years later. thereview@ scmp.com

Well, that was not what you would call a minor diversion, would you? I hope it made for interesting reading, since what I have to tell you about my medical schooling would certainly be very dull and boring to read. I have racked my brain to recollect and find something interesting to tell but it has been quite futile, I'm sorry to say. We all knew that one of the two most difficult examinations we had to pass was the Second MB at the end of the third year and I might have told you that already. We all worked hard all through these two years and spent long hours trying to remember all the mnemonics to help you recall the order and arrangement of the nerves, arteries, and veins in different parts of the body. I get a chuckle when I think of those ingenious students in bygone days in different parts of the world figuring out all those clever ways to recite the correct answer to the examiners questions in a viva exam. One of the cuter ones that I remember well was "Tall dames are never hot", but I am not sure that I remember what they stand for correctly. Anyway, it is the mnemonic to help you remember the structures that are behind the medial malleolus, the ankle bone on the inside, so you can quickly recall which tendon, artery and nerve that is there and the relations they have with each other. Anyway, Anatomy and Physiology are tough subjects to make a good grade but very important to understand why we get sick and how to get well. I didn't mean to get all philosophical but the point I want to get across is that it was with a deep sigh of relief, at the end of the third year, when the results were in, that I found out I had passed the second MB exam.

It was altogether a wonderful feeling of joy and a beautiful sense of hope and anticipation for the future. However, one of the relatively more pressing things to do was to arrange for my reliable coolie to help me move my belongings back to our home on Nathan Road. I had stayed my required three years in a University hostel and now I was free to live wherever I pleased, but more to the point, it was a sensible and economical move to live at home and commute each day by ferry and bus to the University and/or Queen Mary Hospital, a further distance on the bus that goes further to the south beyond the University campus.

And so it was, the transition of my station from a pre-clinical to a clinical period of studies where we actually were physically in the hospital, making clinical rounds with the Professors and his professorial staff, accompanied by the matron or assistant matron and her nursing staff, all-in-all a very impressive retinue. Naturally, I need to admit that we, the medical students were the least important of the whole entourage and, needless to say, the butt of all the jokes and disparaging remarks, depending on the mood of the Professor of the day in question. Some of my classmates, especially the eager ones, would appear with white coats, medical bags, stethoscopes, and all the available paraphernalia. Some of us, who came from families where we pinched our pennies with a press, could only after considerable deliberation procure the bare necessities at the last moment. All told, it was a heady period for us, and it was quite an excitement to attend our first lecture in the lecture room on the Medical Floor at Queen Mary Hospital.

All kidding aside, I realized the seriousness of my studies, much more than I could have imagined. In my first year, I was giddy with the awareness that I had made it to a prestigious university and it was quite an awesome feeling. But all at once reality struck, and I realized it was not child's play but rather it meant serious study and maturity in time management and training to remember important things and avoiding cluttering the mind with nonsense and trivia. Now, having succeeded in entering the clinical years and having to deal with matters of life and death, I gather, on a daily basis, one finds one's mental and emotional state change quite perceptably with respect to the truism of the "reverence for life," as taught in the Judeo-Christian religions and culture. Simply put, I began to study seriously because there was so much at stake, and certainly uppermost in my mind was the love and sacrifice of my parents, and particularly, my mother, who had been so ill since the war years and had suffered so much. It is to them that I owed a great debt of gratitude!

Nevertheless, teachers are human, with some showing more of their human frailties than others. I have already given an example of one teacher in La Salle, whom I hope had not allowed his aggressiveness to really harm a student. In my fourth year of medical studies, we had to study Pathology. When we were nearing our new term, we had heard that the Professor was Professor Hou Pao Chang who had come down from China. During the course of the year, he began to have tutorial classes with us once a week in the afternoon. He would have us ask him questions, whereupon he would give the answers. I was, at that time in my life, still quite reserved and nervous about speaking up in public, since I was rather introspective and timid and self-conscious. Therefore I did not ask any questions for quite an extensive period. Anyway, one afternoon, he stopped in front of me and said that I had not asked any questions and he wanted me to do so. After a few minutes, when I still did not ask him a question, he went to his desk, picked up his can of Lucky Strike cigarettes, brought it over to me, offered me one and said for me to have a smoke and he would return and he would expect a question from me. A few moments later, he came back and said, "Siu, do you have a question?" I was not a heavy smoker, so after I took a drag, I asked him, "Does cigarette smoking cause lung cancer?" (Remember, this was 1949. He was taken aback, a little. I can't remember his answer. What I remember, very clearly, was the finals of the Pathology exam. It was my turn for the orals. When I entered the room and closed the door behind me, there he was seated in his chair, with a look on his face that reminded me of the movie of Clint Eastwood, when he said that famous statement, "Go ahead, make my day!" The man never said a word. On the lab bench was a microscope and beside the scope sat a slide. It was quite obvious, he was really savoring and enjoying himself to see me suffer or squirm and pay for my "insolence" during the tutorial a while back. I was able to understand that he wanted me to tell him what I saw in the slide. I knew I couldn't tell him enough to get a passing grade. As I left the room, I could detect a twisted grin on his lips. I knew that I had to take a supplemental exam for it a few months later. I was not going to let him defeat me because I passed the supplemental exam. Teachers should never be vindictive. Not that it's any consolation, but cigarettes now have warning labels on them that state in no uncertain terms, "Smoking can cause lung cancer." I've also stopped smoking a long time ago...but that's another story.

As I'm mulling over what to write next, I chance to take a peek at the calendar and as of this moment it is now the 29th day of July, 2011. Summing it all up, I really ought to be ending my story...before some uncontrollable event...at least something quite beyond my control, should put an end to the story; and who but little ole me would be able to end it the way I wanted it to end?

There is no doubt that going through medical school is extremely interesting and exciting, at least to the medical student. But, to an outsider, it is decidedly boring and dull as ditch water. I would not want to bore you with all the detail of making rounds, checking your orders, re-ordering your medicines, talking to the patients, checking them and a thousand and one things.

One of the more novel things that we had to rotate through was the outpatient department at Sai Ying Pun, and one of more "exotic" specialties we had to go through was the V.D. (Venereal Diseases) department. It was there that we got to see all the different kinds of sexually transmitted diseases. (Please do note that this was before the first case of a new sexually transmitted disease, namely, AIDS, was discovered.) The other thing we were encouraged to do was to give the patients their intravenous injections of their medicine for their syphilis. The only drawback and revolting thing to me was that some of my classmates were eager to try their hand at venipuncture, but if they were not proficient and the medicine was inadvertently injected into the soft tissues, it would cause a necrosis that might take a lot of bother to get it to heal. Anyway, I had an aversion to VD and the associated "oldest profession" that brought that on. I recall during the Japanese occupation perhaps in 1943, I was helping a distant cousin of my mother's in his store in the Yau Ma Tei area on Nathan Road just north of the intersection with Jordan Road. I would go on my roller skates in the morning and return home in the late afternoon. He had a store that sold tablecloths, blouses and the usual embroidered stuff from Swatow. I enjoyed the work except for the fact that on the first floor above the store, there was a brothel! Normally, it would not bother me except when their business was slow, the girls would sometimes come down and congregate around the door of the store to eat their snacks and gossip. It was altogether quite revolting, especially when they would occasionally have sores on their face and limbs and that's when I wished they'd go somewhere else. Anyway, as things turned out, one afternoon, on my way home, as I was trying to coast down the sloping road on one skate, my skate slipped forward and while trying to break the fall with my hands, I dislocated my left elbow. I got home without too much trouble and mother sent our servant to get a Chinese traditional bone-setter. He came and had me sit on the edge of my bed while he sat opposite me. He got a hold of my left arm, put his dirty, and smelly foot on my chest and proceeded to straighten my left elbow. I know he did not feel any pain, nor did he ask me if it hurt. He put a poultice of herbal medicine around my elbow, wrapped it with cellophane and placed a cloth sling to support my arm. He changed the poultice every few days and I noticed that the skin was all blistered from the herbs and wine. He took everything off after about two or three weeks. Perhaps, subconsciously, it was then that I decided it might be a good idea I go into medicine and do it right! My dislocated elbow, however, succeeded in dislocating me from my job downstairs from the brothel.

One of the rotations we had to go through was in Obstetrics and Gynecology. I did rather well in these two specialties, but one of the requirements that turned me off the specialty was that we had to deliver a minimum of fifty babies, either through natural birth or otherwise. We all had to spend a month at the Tsan Yuk Hospital in West point. Altogether, it was a hectic, busy, and sleepless month, and it really did not take us long to accomplish assisting at the fifty deliveries, even though there were five of us medical students with two of the midwifery students taking part in the mix of the rotation. I was more than satisfied when I reached my quota and since so many of my classmates were so eager to do more, it was quite easy for me to let them take over the excess deliveries. In case any of you are interested, the name of the hospital is made up of two words; the first is Tsan Jaan (Zan) meaning to praise 贊 and the second word is Yuk Yuhk (Yu) meaning to give birth 育. Maybe a good name, but could it have been a tad of a misnomer, considering the size of Hong Kong and the population. Hong Kong really does not need any encouragement or praise for its birthrate, does it?

There was a lot to learn, old things, historical facts, and truisms. It would be boring to just list them and talk about them. In the end, the important thing for any of us students to keep foremost in our minds was to pass the exams and graduate, which is the thing that really matters when all is said and done. It was an ordeal, having to sit through the written examinations for the three subjects and then wait our turns to do the orals. To make the long story short, there were 55 of us sitting for the final examinations, and when the results were posted, twenty two of us attained the passing grade, with the rest being informed that they could repeat the examinations within six months. I thank God that I passed in the first round. We were informed that there would be a formal banquet for the graduates with a black tie affair. I had to scramble to have my white tuxedo tailored so I could take part in the banquet. My parents were elated and so were my sisters but, sad to say, my mother was unable to attend my graduation. My father and both my sisters did come to the ceremony as well as my Uncle Geoffrey, my mother's brother. I should be able to dig up some photographs to grace this book for the occasion. So ends another chapter in my life! A rather important and auspicious milestone in my life's journey!

XXII

THE APPRENTICE SURGEON
1952-1959

I graduated with the degree of M.B., B.S. (HK), that is Bachelor of Medicine and Bachelor of Surgery at the University of Hong Kong Medical Faculty, May 1952 after completing the grueling six years of study and hard work. Upon graduation, we were required to work as a Houseman at a Government hospital or as a Clinical Assistant in one of the three Clinical Faculties of the University of Hong Kong at the Queen Mary Hospital in Hong Kong before we would be registered with the General Medical Council, which would allow us a license to practice as a Physician and Surgeon or a Gynecologist and Obstetrician anywhere in the United Kingdom. Each of these clerkships would be of six months' duration and we had to do two in order to qualify and be registered as a licensed Physician and Surgeon with the General Medical Council. Initially, after the examination results were posted, there was a mad scramble by the more eager and ambitious classmates to see who could land their most favored posts. I was never quite able to get myself to that level of intensity and eventually I was able to obtain a position as a Houseman in the Surgical Department at the Queen Mary Hospital, mainly under Dr. Morgan Lu, a Thoracic Surgeon, but also working under the General Surgeon, Dr. Kong Hoi Kit and the Ophthalmologist Dr. Chan Yik Ping. It turned out to be just the right post for me and I soon found out that I had quite a knack for surgery, a specialty that I finally settled upon as my career, which has allowed me the privilege of introducing myself as the Great Cutup.

Dr. Kong was a Fellow of the Royal College of Surgeons and was the Surgeon in charge of one of the surgical units at Queen Mary Hospital, which is part of the Medical Services of the Hong Kong Government. He was a very nice and soft-spoken gentleman and very early on in my training, he asked me to come to his office, gave me a writing pad and a pencil and asked me to draw straight lines in the pad. He asked me to take the pencil and pad with me to my quarters at the hospital and told me to practice drawing those straight lines every day. He then gave me a couple of shoelaces and taught me how to tie knots, especially square knots; with both hands and with the right and left hands. He said to me to tie one end of the lace to a bed frame and practice tying whenever I had time on my hands. It didn't take me long to master the techniques of making a straight incision and to be able to tie knots on the catgut or silk or whatever material the sutures were made of. I am really thankful for teachers and masters such as Dr. Kong, who can generously pass on gems such as these to their apprentice surgeons.

Dr. Lu, on the other hand, was a good teacher in another sense of the word. He's a man of few words. He did a sizeable number of thoracoplasties for patients with fairly advanced stages of pulmonary tuberculosis, who had had numerous artificially induced pneumothoraces but the disease was not controlled and the belief at the time was that a surgical procedure be done whereby a number of ribs were resected which would allow the muscular chest wall to collapse on the useless lung with the hope that it may arrest the further advancement of the tuberculous process. I guess I should have warned those of you who are leery of these bloody details to skip this part. Anyway, the die is cast. Sorry! Back to my story! Because these procedures sometimes could incur a loss of a good deal of blood, Dr. Lu would like to have the assurance that enough blood be typed and matched and be available for the surgical procedure. Therefore, part of my job as the Houseman was to make sure that some preoperative lab work be done and the patient had enough blood typed and cross-matched so that it would be available for his operation. Furthermore, in order for the transfusion to be carried out expeditiously, I had to perform a cutdown on the patient preoperatively; i.e., we used a local anesthetic and made a small incision on the inner side of the ankle, in front of the ankle bone. There, we would locate the very prominent vein called the Long Saphenous vein and when we had secured it, we would control it with sutures, cut into it and insert a metal cannula (this was later replaced by ones made of plastic, which are disposable, as soon as they were available). I need not belabor the point, but, while Dr. Lu gained a lot of experience and notoriety performing these thoracoplasties, I, at the same time, gained a lot of expertise and proficiency doing cutdowns; experience for which I am very grateful, because in my later years of residencies and private practice, I was able to put to good use my facility in performing cutdowns in all kinds of emergencies, such as when pediatricians and nurses had difficulty infusing intravenous fluids and nutrients to their dehydrated and malnourished babies. I was quite prepared to provide the assistance they needed...many of these cutdowns definitely cut down on the morbidity and mortality rates of the patients...!

Our duties as Housemen, also required us to rotate through the coverage of the Emergency Room, but because the nursing staff at Queen Mary Hospital was quite well staffed with well-experienced nurses, our work load at the Emergency Room was relatively light. I do remember one night, perhaps a couple of months after we first reported for duty at Queen Marry Hospital in June, 1952, I was asked to see a young man in the ER. After examining him, I determined that he had acute appendicitis. I could call on my senior Medical Officer but if I felt capable, I could go ahead and take care of things myself. I talked to the Anesthetist on call and he encouraged me to go ahead and do the appendectomy myself and if I needed to, he would be happy to assist. He had qualified a couple of years ahead of me in China. Anyway, I did it, my very first surgical case, my first solo appendectomy. The man left the hospital after a week and he made a complete recovery. My classmate, Alice (Hwang) Low, wrote me a month or so ago and said that we all got together and agreed that we ought to help each other out when we had emergencies or problems. She also reminded me that I was proud that I did the operation and told everyone that I did the operation through an incision only two inches long. That's quite a big buttonhole! It tickles me to think back to the time when I was the Chief Surgeon and Head of the Department of Surgery at the Alice Ho Miu Ling Nethersole Hospital in 1959, when Pauline, Choy Wing Ping, had to have her appendix out and I did it through a real button hole incision. She later on went to the UK for her higher studies and when she had her preliminary physical examination, the examining physician was questioning her medical form whether she had made a mistake in listing that she had an appendectomy because he could not find a scar?!

One of the many outstanding character traits of Dr. Lu was his ability to remain calm and unflappable in the face of what to outsiders could be a sense of impending doom and danger. To be able to remain cool, calm and collected is most assuredly an advantageous asset to possess when you are suddenly confronted with an unexpected danger and possible catastrophe. To remain as cool as a cucumber is a delicacy and a delight in the surgical theatre; it is as welcome as an accompaniment to your hamburger in your favorite luncheon venue.

It was a lovely fall day and the autumn leaves were falling. We admitted this teenager for surgery who had a history of pericarditis and now the pericardium had enough fibrosis to restrict his cardiac functions. Anyway, the symptoms were quite marked as to cause him to suffer from heart failure. Dr. Lu intended to strip and remove portions of the pericardium to allow his heart to function at its normal capacity. This would be a very interesting case to see and assist in.

As the surgery progressed, everything was orderly and under control and the procedure was advancing at a normal and timely pace. As the fibrous pericardium was stripped away, we could see clearly the heart muscle pumping away, as if it was so pleased with the sense of being released from the constricting scar of the diseased pericardium… the proverbial bird being let out of the cage, if you want to be poetical about it. Dr. Lu had been working from the base of the heart towards the apex. He was about to stop, because he knew that the myocardium is thinnest at the apex, partly from the disease process and partly because it is naturally thinnest at the point. He had his left index finger at the apex of the heart and his scissors were in his right hand. He said, "I think I'll take one more …cut." Before he could finish saying it, there was a sudden hemorrhage under great pressure…and Dr. Lu barked out a series of orders, "Suck!" "Sponge!" "Suture!" I could see the Senior Medical Officer, Dr. Chan Shui Luen, was moving frantically to help. As a second assistant, I knew better than to get in the way. I just hung on to the retractor to make sure that the exposure was adequate and nothing got in Dr. Lu's way. He very quickly had the situation under control by placing his index finger over the cut, thereby stopping the hemorrhage with his pressure. He was suctioning the blood out and very effectively the field was cleared and when the nurse handed Dr. Lu a suture, he deftly placed a cross stitch with one hand without lifting his finger from the cut in the heart. He allowed Dr. Chan to tie the suture and very soon everything was under control. One could say that the hemorrhage would ironically tell us that the stripping of the pericardium was more than adequate to release the myocardium from the restricting pericardium and, in a sense, the mission was accomplished with success.

It's as I've always said about our kind of work, "In surgery, we deal with millimeters and milliseconds. To be a good surgeon, means that you must know your anatomy well and have the knack to stay out of danger. Know what and where you are cutting! (Always bring your color-coded anatomy textbook into the theater with you and have the nurse sterilize it for you. I'm just being facetious.)"

The die is cast! My roommate, Lim Ping Thiam was telling me he planned on applying to do a medical residency at the Jersey City Medical Center and my classmate, Kwaan Hau Ming was going to apply to do his surgical residency in the same hospital. I found out that Aunt Lillian's husband, Chau Sek Hong, was a resident in surgery at St. Thomas Hospital in Akron, Ohio, so I wrote them and asked them to send me an application. I sent in my application, finished my surgical Houseman's rotation of six months, then went on to do my six month's rotation as Clinical Assistant under Dr. Stephen Chang of the Medical Department of the University of Hong Kong.

My application was for a position as a Rotating Intern, i.e. I would be required to spend three months of internship in each of the following specialties: Internal Medicine (includes Pediatrics), Obstetrics and Gynecology, Surgery, and Pathology. The hospital sent me their acceptance of my application, which placed me on an Exchange Visitor status, thus allowing the Department of Immigration and Naturalization Services to grant me a visa to enter the country. This, in turn, allowed me to apply to the Consulate of the United States of America in Garden Road in Hong Kong to process my application, make an appointment for an interview and then a physical examination. I suppose I should have reminded you that I had to apply for a British Passport before getting the visa. It may surprise you, but the one thing that caused anyone any alarm or concern was the day I put my appearance at the doctor's office at the Consulate. I was 5'8" tall, but when I stepped on the scales, the needle stopped at 104 lbs. The doctor was flabbergasted and perhaps surprised that I was up and about and talking to him. Anyway, he really gave me a thorough check up and after ordering some lab work and chest X-ray, I was eventually given the green light and my visa.

During this time, Patsy was working at Dodwell's, a British firm that also dealt with shipping lines. She booked me on a freighter, the SS Bronxville, which carried twelve passengers, pretty much on a First Class basis. The trip took altogether 21 days; two days from Hong Kong to Kobe. Some friends met me and took me to Kyoto. We saw some beautiful places and saw the old Capitol and Palace. A couple of days later I took the train to Tokyo and was met by other friends. Eventually, I went to Yokohama to meet up with the Bronxville for the trip to San Francisco. I was met by an Episcopal priest who took me to the YMCA in Chinatown. The next morning I went out and found a diner and had my first American breakfast, a java and a sinker, which I had learned from comic books, and it consisted of a cup of coffee and a doughnut. Naturally, I really cannot say that I had arrived in America, the Land of the free and the home of the brave, because I was really still in China since I was deposited there and I wouldn't get into the good ol' US of A until I got on the train tonight and let the train take me to Akron, Ohio. I did have to have a haircut so I found a barber shop nearby and had my hair cut. I did have two bits but since I don't get very hirsute, I did not ask for a shave. I also didn't want a shampoo because I thought to myself that since I would be taking the train and whenever I watched a movie, the trains looked very well equipped and I thought, now knowing what I know...quite erroneously, that I would be able to shampoo my hair before I settled down to sleep. Well, I'm sure you've heard the old cliché, "I'm afraid you're barking up the wrong tree." or "Don't count your chicken before they're hatched." Whatever it is, I was sadly mistaken. How was a poor boy from Hong Kong, like me, going to know that at that stage in my life and at that particular moment, there was and always will be, a great divide between what I could afford and what Hollywood portrayed to us on the silver screen, how the other half of the world, the so called upper crust or what is better known as "the rich and famous" lived and traveled in their Pullman coaches! And as luck would have it, the Episcopal priest who met me at the pier also purchased the train ticket for me and it was a third class economy, coach ticket. To my dismay and to add insult to injury, when I got to my seat, it was at the end of the car and the back of the seat was up against the back of the cabin which prevented it from reclining, which meant that I had to sit bolt upright. We left San Francisco at 7.00 P.M., and coupled with the fact that I had all the snippets of hair on my shirt collar and down my back, it was sheer torture! I was not able to sleep. All night long, I heard the engineer or conductor announce the stops we reached and the stops ahead. There I was, feeling down in the dumps, defeated, dejected and a little desperate; tired, hungry and a tad angry; wanting to sleep but unable to. What could I do?

As the train sped eastward at a good speed, the different towns we went through, most I'd not heard of but a few sounded familiar. In the small hours of the morning, with nothing to keep my mind busy, I tried to listen to the announcer giving the names of the towns we were approaching. Suddenly, my ears perked up! I thought I heard a familiar name. I listened carefully and sure enough, he did announce that we would be in Cedar Rapids, Iowa sometime in the morning. I knew that Aunt Leona and the boys were in Cedar Rapids, though Uncle Ted was not. I decided that it would be a nice break for me to get off and pay them a visit before going on to Akron Ohio, even if it would mean one more day's delay. In fact, because I took the freighter instead of flying, I had already obtained permission from the hospital to grant me the excuse for my late arrival. My mind was made up without too much debate as I looked for the conductor to help me unload my trunk and two suitcases as I was determined to disembark from the train at Cedar Rapids, have a day's rest before completing my trip to Akron. At the Union Station, I found a pay phone and called my Aunt Leona. She might have heard that I was planning on going to Akron to do an internship but I had not planned on visiting relatives or friends on my way there, especially since I was already short on time and would be late in arriving by three to four weeks. I knew she was not prepared for an unannounced visitor but the way I was feeling that morning and the harried condition I was in, I was not too concerned about committing any social blunders. No matter how embarrassed I was, but with the condition I was in and the discomfort I was experiencing, I was quite ready to throw all caution to the wind, just as long as I could get a shampoo and a bath and jump into some clean clothes! And, perhaps to sleep…and dream!

I was sure that I surprised Aunt Leona with my surprise visit, definitely unannounced. I am sure that what I did must have infringed on a very delicate rule of order, and was certainly not to be done among the socially elite and those who are socially and politically correct. I know that I can't apologize enough for this breach of social etiquette, but to an uncouth young man…it was the worst of times and it was the best of times. You have no idea how good it felt when I heard her voice on the phone and that she would be right over to pick me up.

It was the first time I met Mrs. Spryncl and she very matter-of-factly told me to put my things in the room, go take a bath and lunch/dinner would be served as soon as I was ready. That was the best bit of good news that I'd heard since they announced on the S.S. Bronxville to come to the dining Room for the Captain's Dinner. I had almost forgotten how good a hot bath and shampoo felt. I lost my sense of time until I heard a knock on the bathroom door and a voice asking if I had drowned in the bathtub. (Joke!) It felt so good! I thought I had never had such a good feeling until we got to the dining room. It smelled so good! This would be my very first American home-cooked meal. We had fried chicken, mashed potatoes, corn on the cob and ice tea. Have you ever seen the size of the corn? I found out what Iowa corn is like. Then, to top it all off, we had Bing cherries for dessert! I had never known that there were fruits called Bing cherries. First time in my life! I love Bing cherries. Thank you Mrs. Spryncl and thank God for the wonderful and tasty meal. It truly was an end to a perfect day!

It was time to push on, definitely imperative if I were serious about pursuing my ambition to become a bona fide, well-trained and competent surgeon. Surprise! Mrs. Spryncl handed me a brown paper sack in which she had packed a piece of fried chicken and some Bing cherries and told me that the train would be stopping in Chicago and

I would have time to enjoy my sack lunch, before getting on the train again that would take me to Akron. That was another first for me. I finally arrived in Akron a little after eight in the evening and was met by my tenth Aunt and tenth Uncle-in-law and Yvonne. St. Thomas Hospital here we come, but first I'd spend the first night at Aunt Lillian's apartment and then report for duty the next day. It was close to August now and this meant that I was late reporting for duty by about a month. Naturally I wouldn't be taking any vacation during the year to make up for the lost time. Come to think of it, the whole process took a whole year from the time I thought about it to the time I finally assumed duty as an intern at the hospital. I must admit that as I reminisced on that very meaningful day in September of 1945, when after I was sent home because I was not an old boy and the lack of any vacancy in the Diocesan Girls' School; and when three days later, my mother encouraged me to go and ask Miss Gibbons to allow me to study there; and now seven years almost to the day, I found myself at the beginning of a process that would take me another eight or nine years to finally qualify as a Board Certified General Surgeon of the American Board of Surgeons in 1962. I knew it was going to be a tough row to hoe, but at the same time, I knew I would have an enjoyable time in the process...and, needless to say...I would be, obviously, learning a lot of new and wonderful things, many of which might even qualify to be presented in Ripley's Believe It or Not? Anyway, I was quite determined that I must strive hard to complete my residency training, even if it meant competing for excellence so as to be awarded the Chief Resident in Surgery post after three years of a graded residency program. This would then qualify you to take the Board Exams, the written and the oral.

As I began my internship year, I was very thankful that I had a year of experience to fall back on and so I did not regret too much that I had to do an extra year of internship. One thing that was helpful to me was that I was not a complete novice in many of the situations I encountered, particularly in the Accident Room in St. Thomas Hospital which was on the North side of Akron, right on Route 18, if my memory serves me right. I have always said that when you are on-call in the ER, you will have your hands full, taking care of all the auto accidents. I got to know the Sheriff and his deputies very well and of course, the ambulance drivers too. I also became good friends with the Head nurse in the Accident Room, Miss Mary DiDonato. You could say that we had a mutual admiration situation going; she was an intelligent and efficient nurse who knew her profession well and she was impressed with my proficiency and abilities. I remember a very humbling experience, when she paged for me and asked me to proceed to the ER right away. When I arrived, she very quickly told me that another intern was in the ER attempting to do an emergency tracheostomy, which is to place a tube into a patient's windpipe to allow him to breathe because of an obstructed airway. He did not get very far when he cut into a transverse cervical vein inadvertently, which obscured his field of vision and in a word, he was in trouble. I thank God that I was able to control the bleeding vessel and very quickly relieved the patient of his breathing difficulty. I was thankful that Miss DiDonato had so much confidence to call me instead of some senior resident or an Attending Surgeon and happy that her confidence in me was not misguided or misdirected. On the other hand, this event certainly helped to boost my confidence and determination to push ahead and finish my training to become a well-trained surgeon, which would go a long way toward my unstated goal of returning to Hong Kong and helping those who may be less well off to have the luxury of up-to-date surgical care.

One other boost to my morale that Miss Didonato did was when she put in a good word for me to the premier Orthopedic Surgeon on the staff of St. Thomas Hospital, Dr. Fowler B. Roberts. He was a rather distinguished looking gentleman who carried himself graciously besides being an excellent Orthopod and I remembered well one thing he told me when he came to the ER to treat a patient with a Colles' fracture (a fracture of the wrist). He taught me how to reduce the fracture with an injection of a local anesthetic into the hematoma of the fracture site, reducing the fracture with the thumbs and index fingers, and then applying a cast. His aphorism about putting a cast was that, "It takes just as much time and effort to put on a neat cast as a sloppy cast; so always put on a neat cast." He allowed me to finish the cast and later on he told Mary DiDonato that I was a "quick student." Mary said that it was a good compliment coming from him. If you say so, Mary, I am not going to quibble with you.

It could have been late September or early October that Uncle Ted came to Akron for a visit. It could have been that he'd known some of the folks before, but in any event he brought me to the Swedish Covenant Church in Akron and introduced me to some of the finest people I'd ever met. I think he spoke to the church but the people there were very nice to me and they made it a point to come and pick me up every Sunday for the duration. Then when it was close to Thanksgiving, a young couple invited me to their house for dinner. He was a Scotsman and I think she was Swedish. They did not have children then. It was my first Thanksgiving Dinner and my first taste of turkey and all the trimmings. We had so much to eat that we just had no room for the dessert, which was going to be pumpkin pie and perhaps ice cream. The host suggested we go outside in the yard and throw the football around a bit. It had snowed some and so the ground was covered with a layer of snow. Akron does get snowed on a lot and so I had my first taste of snow too. I need not tell you that it was not the kind of football that I had known and played with during my childhood. I must admit, I just did not get the hang of it. Anyway, we had our pie and then it was time to get back to the hospital. It was a thoroughly enjoyable DAY! It was also a very appropriate name for this very special day. Yes, indeed! We must always give thanks to our God for so many reasons. The Swedish friends were very good hosts and they had so many interesting foods to eat, especially around Christmas. I remember being invited to a church smorgasbord and got introduced to a number of "new" foods, like Swedish meatballs.

On a lighter note, I was asked by the nuns at the hospital to join their chapel choir and was honored by their asking me to sing a solo at one of the masses around Christmas.

One rather somber detail was when I rotated through Pediatrics as part of the Internal Medicine rotation and had a young boy who suffered from Idiopathic Thrombocytopenic Purpura. Perhaps you could classify it as one of the blood dyscrasias or bleeding disease due to the failure of the cells that produce clots. It was the first time I'd taken care of such a patient and I was thankful that I was able to get the much needed blood transfusions to him when he needed them with my facility in doing cutdowns when needed.

While my experience at St. Thomas Hospital was not gained completely through the eyes and ears of a complete novice, there is no doubt that I have gained from the added experience, which will never be taken away from me. I had made many friends but there was one undeniable fact, which was that the hospital had not yet gained the approval of the American Board of Surgery to qualify as a hospital which provided a fully approved program for the required four years of training for the Boards. The program as it stood at the time was that the training would have to be supplemented by a year's study at the University of Michigan at Ann Arbor, Michigan. Rightly or wrongly, I somehow had a strong negative feeling toward this arrangement and, therefore, I began to make inquiries about other programs quite early on. I remembered that when I was doing my Clinical clerkship at the University of Hong Kong under Dr. Stephen Chang, we had treated a missionary from China. He was Bishop Ralph Ward of the Methodist Church and I remembered that he told me his brother was a Clinical Professor of Surgery at the Johns Hopkins University Hospitals in Baltimore Maryland, Dr. Grant Ward, a Head and Neck Cancer Specialist. I wrote Dr. Chang and apprised him of the situation and my desire to locate a hospital where they had a four-year approved program. I thank God my prayer was answered when I received a letter from Professor Warfield Firor at Johns Hopkins, informing me that, in his position as Head of the Department of Surgery at the Maryland General Hospital in Baltimore, he was offering me a position as a First Year Resident in Surgery there and to report for duty July 1, 1954. An application to that position was enclosed with the letter, which I duly completed and dispatched to the Hospital Administrator, Mr. Stewart B. Crawford.

A number of human interest stories that happened to me while in Akron were that it was known as the rubber Capitol of the world in more ways than one and that there is a road that is paved with a mixture of rubber and other things as an experiment and is supposed to be the first of its kind.

It was in Akron that I experienced my first cold winter and first snowfall, so I had to buy myself a topcoat, a hat and a pair of rubber outer shoes. The first time I went to the department store for the coat, the man told me they didn't have my size and he suggested that I go down to the boys department because they would have the sizes that fit me. I was quite surprised then but not anymore! A few other inconsequential things I learned about Ohio was that it is a dry state, which meant that restaurants do not serve alcoholic beverages and you can only purchase alcoholic beverages in licensed package stores. However, you can go to the State Parks and get 3% beer at the food concessions. I learned a new term when we were there with the interns, residents, and nurses at one of our evening outings on a weekend. We could order pitchers of beer, fill our glasses, and drink chug-a-lug, which means bottoms up,

One of the more sedate things I encountered was when the Social Page Editor of the Akron newspaper made an appointment with me for an interview. She was a very nice and mature lady and I was pleased to find out that she later on went on to Hong Kong and visited my parents and my siblings. They even went out and had a Chinese feast and when she returned to Akron, she wrote an article together with the picture taken at the dinner. I know that I have the newspaper clipping somewhere in my files and I should dig it out and include it with this write-up.

The other worthy and memorable thing I did was that when I first worked at Queen Mary Hospital, I saved a good percentage of my salary and gave it to my mother. However, when I was about to leave Hong Kong for the US of A, she handed me an envelope and told me to open it after I got on board my ship when she sailed out of the harbor. Well, she surprised me once again and once more showed me how much she loved me...which greatly exceeds my most extravagant expectations. What she did was she saved up all the money I gave her as a token of my love for her, and she had the Hong Kong money exchanged into US dollars and gave it all back to me. Not wanting to be outdone by her, I saved all that money and early in the Spring of 1954, I went downtown to the store that sells silverware and fancy stuff like that and I picked out a set of sterling silver for twelve in a lovely pattern called Classic Rose and had that mailed to my mother and father for their Thirtieth Wedding Anniversary in May. I rejoice over that because I finally found a way to show my love and appreciation for their love and sacrifices for me over all those years. Perhaps the only regret I have is that I was ten years too late…you will remember that I told my mother I would behave better when I reached my fifteenth birthday, the day when I was to leave the garden and be a grownup man.

I completed my year of internship on the thirtieth day of June. The next day, I bid my farewell to all my friends, got to the train station and headed for Baltimore, Maryland. I arrived in Baltimore around nine in the evening, took my bags (I got rid of my trunk), got out of the station, hailed a cab, and asked the driver to take me to Maryland General Hospital. The Main Building looked like it was built in the 1800s, with red brick walls, a flight of stairs made with ten granite steps shaped in an arc with two brass rails on each side and the steps narrowing at the top to a set of wooden doors. The meter showed my fare was $5.00. I didn't know then, but a few days later when I had some free time to walk around the neighborhood, I found out that the train station was no more than four blocks away from the hospital. I guess I was taken for a ride! That's not a very nice way to welcome a stranger!

I was soon taken across the street to the doctors' quarters and shown my room. I quickly unpacked and soon went to sleep. I was sure that the next day would be a busy day!

It didn't take too long for things to fall into place and a routine to set in. As residents, our lives and duties were quickly set out for us. The on-call list was soon posted all over the hospital and we were all given as many copies as we need to remind us of our daily duties, working hours, and the days we could get off. It may sound complicated but it is actually very simple because, in a practical sense, it was a very logical arrangement to divide the entire house staff into two teams. Each team would take turns being on call and as an example, while everyone would be on duty five days a week from Monday to Friday, 8.00 a.m. to 5.00 p.m., Team "A" would go on call at 5.00 p.m. on Monday, but would be off on Tuesday at 5.00 p.m. The team would be on duty again on Wednesday at 5.00 p.m., then off duty on Thursday and Friday nights. However, Team "A" would be on duty both Saturday and Sunday. This rotation would go on *ad infinitum*.

I might mention that the "surgical house staff", as we were commonly known, was made up of the Chief Resident, a third year resident, two second year residents, three first year residents and two interns.

With this arrangement, it is quite obvious that there was a process of elimination each year and only the fittest person would survive to be the Senior Resident by the time the four year rotation was completed. In fact when I was the third year resident, there were two others that had survived the cut and I was glad that I won out in the end and became the Chief Resident and the other two had to delay their turn for a year. I was also glad that the program at Maryland General Hospital gained the full four years approval for surgical training the year I became the Chief Resident, which took a big load off my mind and gave me the crowning glory to my six years of hard work following my graduation from Medical School. I was glad that I could finally heave a sigh of relief and give my thanks to God for His Providence once again.

When I first joined the residency program at Maryland General Hospital, the program had just recently attained the American Board of Surgery's approval as a hospital that could train residents that would be qualified to be Board certified. In fact, the hospital still had an arrangement with the University of Maryland in Baltimore to allow the resident to attend the Surgical Anatomy course that would be equivalent to a year of residency. It was a good feeling to know that I would not have to do that, though the course in surgical Anatomy was so good that I went ahead and attended the classes because it was something extra that would be beneficial to my armamentarium and a bonus that will not be taken away from me.

As I was nearing the end of my surgical training, I was given an opportunity to work at the City Morgue under Dr. Russell S Fisher, who also became one of the first medical doctors to assume the position of the Medical Examiner of Baltimore. I soon was able to become the Pathology Resident at the Women's Hospital in Baltimore under Dr. William Lovett, who was an Assistant Medical Examiner of Baltimore. I do believe that next to anatomy, pathology is the other subject that is of great importance to a surgeon and I have never regretted completing the eighteen months I spent in Pathology. In any event, during the interim, I passed the written exam for the American Board of Surgery. Eventually, after a few twists and turns, I was all geared to take my beautiful wife, Betty nee Mary Elizabeth Faber, our pretty, cute and intelligent daughter, Ravenna Kay, plus our ready to be born son, Stephen Marcus, and head for Hong Kong to assume the duties of the Acting Head of the Department of Surgery at the Alice Ho Miu Ling Nethersole Hospital on Bonham Road on the Island of Hong Kong, in November 1959. But that's another story...and I will continue that in the next chapter.

XXIII

METAMORPHOSIS: TOTAL TRANSFORMATION

Cling to what is good.
Romans 12:9

As a servant of Jesus Christ, God wants you to bind yourself to everything good, to whatever is inherently right and worthy. That task requires the use of discernment. With the help of God and His Word, you must carefully evaluate everything and thoughtfully decide what to reject and what to cling to (1 Thess. 5:21–22).

As you separate yourself from worldly things and saturate yourself with Scripture that which is good will increasingly replace that which is evil. Then, you will fulfill Paul's message to the Romans: "Do not be conformed to this world, but be transformed by the renewing of your mind, that you may prove what is that good and acceptable and perfect will of God" (12:2). [28]

Before I continue with my story, I would like to, if I may, digress a moment to relate something that is quite significant as far as my life was concerned. I was just about to begin to write about some of the big decisions and some equally momentous actions and events that would have made some profound changes in my life; some of which were decidedly deliberate and well thought out; but some were very definitely not those in which I could claim, as some do, that I had wanted to do or to be ever since I was a little "wizard" who had just been "potty-trained" but had always wanted to grow up to be some sort of a famous

---

[28] MacArthur, J. (2001). *Truth for today: A daily touch of God's grace* (211). Nashville, Tenn.: J. Countryman.

personality; and then there were those that magically happened to everyone…like falling in love with a beautiful girl! But I was reminded by something so meaningful that happened to us these last two days that I am compelled to digress and tell you about what happened.

Anyway, just for your information, what I am writing about in these next few paragraphs is that today is Monday, August 22, 2011. It is now around 9.00 p.m. so I have plenty of time to tell you about this very beautiful event, which took place yesterday, Sunday evening, the 21st of August, 2011. This was the eve of our Jade Anniversary, i.e., our 55th Wedding Anniversary, the 22nd of August. About three dozen of the folks at Sha Lei Tau Baptist Church, including the lovely and smart, two years and six months old Constance Hong Ching Lam, 林康晴, threw a wonderful party for us at the Fian Style Café on NAPE in Macau in the evening. They sang praise songs accompanied by Song's許爽爽guitar, and they sounded angelic and beautiful. After their singing, Mr. Hoi Lok Kun, 許樂觀, the Deacon prayed and then we were served a lovely buffet dinner, which ended with dessert, a decorated Happy Anniversary cake and a Home-made cheese cake expertly decorated by Cathy Chan陳可君. If you have Facebook, do go in and look at some of the pretty pictures that Wilson Lam林耀權took. We all had a lovely time and Betty and I really appreciated this wonderful and loving gesture from our church family and friends at the Church.

Then, today, Miss Tam Wai Chun譚惠诊, Mrs. Ip Wai Chun葉慧珍, Mr. and Mrs. Hoi Lok Kun took us to a Cantonese lunch at the Tou Tou Gui Restaurant 陶陶居 to celebrate our anniversary one more time, this time on the exact date and we had delicious Cantonese food, which we all thoroughly enjoyed. I must admit it was a very praiseworthy, lovely, and fitting ending to our fifty five years of wedded bliss. God had been and continues to be "very good" to us and He has been so ever since He first uttered those very same words, when He pronounced the results of His Creation as "very good" back in the days of the Genesis!

Now, let me get back to my story. When I left you, I had just finished telling you about my training at the Maryland General Hospital and transferring my training to Pathology at the Women's Hospital in Baltimore. However, there are a number of things that happened to me while I was doing my stint at Maryland General that I would not want to leave out. So if you don't mind, please bear with me and listen to what I have to say. One of the most important tidbits of information that the Maryland General Hospital gave me soon after I reported there for duty was that the hospital is affiliated with the Methodist Church and a couple of years after I got there, the Methodist Church became united with the United Brethren Church to become the United Methodist Church. The Mount Vernon Place United Methodist Church that is affiliated with the Hospital is in Mount Vernon Place and is the second oldest Methodist Church in Baltimore. It is located on the Northeast corner of the famous Mount Vernon Place at the intersection of Madison and St. Paul Streets and across the street from the well-known Peabody Music Conservatory. At the center of Mount Vernon Place stands the first monument built for George Washington. The Nursing School at Maryland General Hospital is closely affiliated with the church and holds its graduation ceremonies there. The church is about four blocks from the hospital and is within an easy walk from the hospital. Dr. Grant Ward that I mentioned in the last chapter is a member of the church, and his brother was Bishop Ralph Ward, a missionary to China whom we took care of at the Queen Mary Hospital in Hong Kong when he was ill. Another doctor that is a very active member of the Church was Dr. Harold C. Dix, an Ophthalmologist, who together with his wife, were very hospitable to me, when I became a member of the church.

Whatever it was that moved me, I must admit that I do not recall anything that remotely resembled a momentous decision on my part, but perhaps my guilty conscience was trying to goad me though not sufficient enough or it could have been the Holy Spirit who decided to let me know that it was time for me to take a different track and make an alteration to the erratic direction I was sailing in my voyage through my course in life. In simple common sense terms, I was not doing myself or my parents any favor. I was living a selfish and childish life rather than the "childlike" and "innocent" Christian life I was meant to be living. No matter how it happened, it was quite imperceptible at first. I was not even aware that ever since I entered the Medical School my spiritual life had taken a decided laissez faire attitude. On the other hand, I became much too interested in dating. Fortunately, one big dampening effect was that I was often out of pocket money and so that was a blessing in disguise. Besides, medical studies were definitely not for the less-than-absolutely-serious student, and the threat of flunking out was always threatening at every corner.

And so it was…at first, more a curiosity…but, surprise! Let me tell you, one should never underestimate the importance of a dedicated and good usher. The two I remember well at Mount Vernon Place United Methodist Church were George Taylor and Bill. I never used his last name so I only know him as Bill. They were so good at ushering that I even asked to work with them as an usher for a spell. They are the kind that never forgets a face and a name besides remembering where your favorite pew is. They made sure that you would want to go back the next Sunday!

The church had a good organist and a good choir. I joined the choir. I found out that the church paid a small stipend to the organist and the four principals; bass, tenor, alto and soprano members, who were students at the Peabody Music Conservatory. This is such a great arrangement and the church would always get to enjoy good music during the worship services. What a joyful symbiosis! But, most of all, the reason that this downtown church was so well-liked and her membership was so high was, I think, due to Dr. Albert E. Day, the Pastor. I thoroughly got involved with his sermons that I anticipated each Sunday when I could find the time to go. Then as I got to know him better he gave me a copy of the book he wrote titled, "None of these diseases." I think he was very much into prayer and healing and his parishioners just were enamored with him. It didn't take me too long to join the church as a member and I soon found out that the people of the church were also very friendly. I will have more to say about being a member of this church family when eventually Betty and I were married there and all five of our children were baptized there.

The way Betty tells it, it always makes me come out like a cad! I looked up the meaning of the word in the dictionary and it says that a cad is a man who behaves dishonorably, which means I am not a gentleman. That is so far from the truth. The truth is that the first time I saw her was when she worked as a pinkie in the hospital. She was then a senior in Patterson Park High School in Baltimore and the hospital had a program for high school students who were interested in a career in nursing. They could come and work as a pinkie, or a Nurses' aide, after their school hours and get some training; they were given a pink uniform to wear and worked at the direction of the Head Nurse on duty. Anyway, there she was and I saw her...I was quite awe-struck with her beauty...blonde hair, blue eyes, beautiful smile...I was busy in a patient's room, changing his blood-soiled dressing and making sure everything was under control...the room was a mess with soiled gauze and bandages all over! Then this apparition...she walked in and asked if there was anything she could do to help. What do you think I said? She thought I was being fresh and said something that she thought I was flirting with her. She really didn't care about me then. Actually I was quite overcome by her looks and really wanted to know her better. Anyway, it's her words against mine. But, I was disappointed I did not make a good impression on her. She later on told me that from that day on, every time that she came to work and I happened to be on the floor, that I would follow her everywhere she went...even into the utility room...now why would I do that? But, she would tell the story that there was an elderly patient who was very observant and told Betty that she was sure that this Oriental doctor, meaning me, must have a crush on her and she wondered if Betty knew because the doctor was always following her every move every time she came on the floor.

Quite mysteriously, in spite of my diligent observation and search, all of a sudden, she was nowhere to be seen. Where could she be? I did find out that her name was Mary Elizabeth Faber but not much more. Sad to say, it certainly looked as if I had missed my opportunity to make any kind of a favorable impression on this gorgeous damsel and now she had disappeared. Gone, vanished into thin air. I had missed the boat and now it was too late to do anything about it. Oh where, oh where has my pretty girl gone?

Naturally I was disappointed not to have done a better job of being more assertive and, perhaps, introducing myself when I first saw her and knowing more about her. However, I did not get myself too despondent and, to console myself, I insisted on looking at the bright side of things. Lo and behold, by the time February 1956 rolled around, which was at the most about a couple of months after her disappearance, the buzz heard in the cafeteria at the hospital were that there would soon be a bunch of new nursing students coming to the Nursing School. Betty was entering the Maryland General Hospital Program in February. Betty just confirmed to me that one day, though I was not aware of it, I was having lunch with another doctor and she and her classmates all came into the cafeteria for lunch...all decked out in their new uniforms... which made them doubly attractive. Yes, you guessed it, my fellow doctor and I were ogling the new arrivals and sizing them up; and my cohort said, "I'll take that one" as he was pointing to one of the girls in the group; however, as I am sure you've guessed it by now; I right away saw the girl of my dreams, the girl that I thought I had lost. Anyway, I pointed to Betty and I said, "I WILL take that one," as I fixed my gaze on her and pointed to Betty. I suppose it was a good meal but I can't tell you what it was I ate. When I came back down to earth, I very quickly realized that we had yet to be formally introduced and I had yet to get to know her. Still, it was a consolation to know that she would be around for a while...all I needed was an opening and an opportunity. Meanwhile, I had a job to do and a profession to learn and master.

It was not all that easy to get to know a girl even though you were both working in the same hospital and what's more is that there is a saying that goes like this: "Patience is a virtue, sometimes found in women but seldom found in men!" Is there any truth to that?

Strange as it may seem, there's a girl in Betty's class named Isenhour, but I've forgotten her first name. She was quite friendly to both of us and she surprised me one day when she called me on the phone and told me that if I wanted a date with Betty to quickly call her at home. She found out that Betty's date that evening was ill and would not be able to take her out. So I did just that and sure enough I was successful and took her out on our first date. We ended the evening by parking our car at the Loch Raven Dam in Baltimore and talked. It was hot and so we had to keep the windows rolled down and consequently we were both pretty much eaten alive by the mosquitoes...yes! I know! Mosquitoes don't eat humans, but we were stung pretty badly. Eventually, in memory of that wonderful itching and romantic witching hour, we thought it would be nice to name our first daughter Ravenna, in memory of Loch Raven Dam and the town in Ohio near Akron called Ravenna. Finally, the reason we chose to name our daughter Kay was because nearly everyone in the hospital had trouble pronouncing my last name Siu properly and no one was able to pronounce it so you could tell whether they were calling me or Dr. Su! They wound up by calling Dr. Su, Dr. C Su, and calling me Dr. K Siu. So, Betty and I decided to name our daughter Kay. I imagine Kay would rather we chose another name but that is the prerogative of parents and the bane of children to have to suffer the consequences of an odd name that parents dream up for whatever reason. Anyway, after that first date, Betty and I got along very well and I had very strong indications that more dates would be forthcoming. I want to make a note here that we did not have any language difficulties, which reminded me of what Betty told me about a conversation she had with Dr. Mervin Trail one day when they were having a meal together at the cafeteria. Mervin was a second year medical student at the University of Maryland in Baltimore and was working at the hospital as an extern, or someone who helps in the Pathology and Clinical laboratory. They were discussing how disgusted they were with the resident doctors in the hospital that were from Korea, Argentina, Mexico and Japan. While they were deeply engrossed in their mutual disbelief and dismay at the standard of the fluency and intelligibility of their spoken English among the non-English-speaking foreigner doctors, I happened to walk by their table and I just stopped long enough to say a few words to them by way of a greeting. I'd sort of had Mervin under my wings because of his likeability and mental capacity. I would teach him various things, such as sewing up lacerations, putting on casts, and such odds and ends that would be valuable to him when he became a doctor. I had never had a chance to make her acquaintance since she came to the hospital as a nursing student up till then. Later, Betty was to tell me that she remarked to Mervin about how good my English was, how I had no accent except perhaps a little of the Queen's English. In a nutshell, Mervin said to Betty, "Of course Ken's English is good! He's from Hong Kong."

I am thrilled to say that we dated with greater frequency as time went on and we enjoyed finding out different things about ourselves and the kinds of family lives we led. We very quickly fell in love with each other and we found later that we were thinking of each other all the time. One day, when you have the chance, you should ask Betty about the nick name she gave me when she first met me and also when she was doodling, who the subject of her doodling was.

Meanwhile, just in case you should be wondering, let me tell you that I was making very good headway in my training program, perhaps because of the stiff competition inherent in the type of residency program prevalent in the United States at the time. If you were found wanting, you were politely invited to find your way out; no one was allowed to continue in the program or advance to the next level if you were not doing up to par. We were also told from the beginning of our entrance into the residency that depending upon our performance, we might be scheduled to assist certain Attending Surgeons and sometimes we would be advised early on to diplomatically, efficiently, and judiciously appropriate the scalpel before the Attending Surgeon and accomplish the procedure to avoid harming the patient. This is especially important when the Attending Surgeon is elderly and perhaps even senile. Later on in my own situation, I suppose this could have been one of a number of factors that encouraged me to take early retirement, and I've never regretted taking that plunge.

One of the slightly unkind monikers that were given to some forbidding but efficient Nursing Supervisors was the "Battleaxe." I used to tease the one OR Supervisor at Maryland General Hospital because she was always putting on this fierce appearance, especially if you happened to be a less-than-smart nurse or a resident who was verging on being incompetent. One late afternoon, during my tenure as a second year resident, I heard my name being paged on the PA system. It was a page from the OR Supervisor asking me to go up to the Operating Room right away. When I arrived, she gave me a rundown on the reason for the page. She said that the reason she called me was she wanted me to scrub up right away and get into the operating room and help Dr. Rafful. He was a third year resident and was doing an appendectomy but was having a hard time finding the appendix, which according to the Supervisor was about five hours prior to her paging me. I did scrub in and happy to say that I got the appendix out within fifteen minutes. I thank God that sometimes under certain circumstances when you call on Him, He will provide you with a cool head and a pair of supple hands for occasions such as these.

One of the better known, and perhaps busiest, General Surgeons in private practice was Dr. Lester Chance. I was happy to gain his confidence and therefore, by the time I was a third year resident, I was often given the chance to help Dr. Chance (pun intended). He was from North Carolina and people would tease him about how in North Carolina people don't wear shoes and that is why someone from North Carolina is known as a tar heel. He also liked to tell me about a philosophy of life he learned when he was growing up as a kid in North Carolina: "Don't run, when you can walk, don't walk, when you can stand. Don't stand, when you can sit. Don't sit, when you can lie down." Needless to say, I gained a lot of experience and practical skills from working with Dr. Chance the last two years I was at Maryland General Hospital.

One of the benefits of knowing Dr. Firor a little bit was having the privilege of assisting him in surgery. He had a particular talent about him and a skill that I had not seen in any one else. He was a missionary doctor in Lahore, Pakistan when he was younger and now was Clinical Professor at Johns Hopkins University Hospitals. It was a delight to assist him when he did an abdomino-perineal resection of the rectum for cancer. I was amazed the first time I assisted him when he completed what we call the pelvic sweep with under half a dozen movements of his hand. I was glad when subsequently I was able to accomplish a similar maneuver. Finally, it was a blessing to have him endorse my advancement to be the Chief Resident of the training program and then to the completion of my surgical training in July of 1958.

Now it's time to turn my attention to something very meaningful and even monumental figuratively speaking that was about to happen to me, but first let me quote a few well-known verses of Scripture to set it in motion, namely the words from the Teacher/Preacher in Ecclesiastes 3:1-8:

> **1** For everything there is a season, and [29][l]a
> time for every matter under heaven:
> **2** a time to be born, and a time to [30][m]die;

---

[29] [l]ver. 17; ch. 8:6

[30] [m]Heb. 9:27

a time to plant, and a time to pluck up what is planted;
[3] a time to kill, and a time to heal;
a time to break down, and a time to build up;
[4] a time to [31n]weep, and a time to laugh;
a time to mourn, and a time to [32o]dance;
[5] a time to [33p]cast away stones, and a time to [34q]gather stones together;
a time to embrace, and a time to [35r]refrain from embracing;
[6] a time to seek, and a time to [36s]lose;
a time to keep, and a time to [37t]cast away;
[7] a time to [38u]tear, and a time to sew;
a time to [39v]keep silence, and a time to speak;
[8] a time to love, and a time to [40w]hate;
a time for war, and a time for peace. [41]

At this moment I want particularly to highlight verse 8 and specifically to the word love. I understand that there were and will be skeptics who would say that, "Beauty is but skin deep," or that, "Love is but a fleeting feeling." However, when we are talking about love that is in the heart and the permanence of love that is exhibited by God toward men and women who reciprocated His love and have abiding faith in the Creator God, we're talking about something quite different...and that is what I am talking about...love that abides 天長地久 or the sky that stretches endlessly and the earth that exists for ages and ages. (My translation).

By the time June 1956 came around, I was assured of being promoted

---

[31] [n] [Rom. 12:15]
[32] [o] [2 Sam. 6:14]; See Ex. 15:20
[33] [p] [2 Kgs. 3:25]
[34] [q] [Isa. 5:2]
[35] [r] [Joel 2:16]
[36] [s] [Matt. 10:39]
[37] [t] [Prov. 11:24]
[38] [u] See Gen. 37:29
[39] [v] Amos 5:13
[40] [w] [Luke 14:26]
[41] *The Holy Bible: English standard version.* 2001 (Ec 3:8). Wheaton: Standard Bible Society.

to be the third year resident and there was good indication that, barring unforeseen circumstances, there was nothing to stand in my way of being promoted to be Chief Resident in the following year. I just needed to keep my nose clean, mind my own business, study hard, keep abreast of new advances, be a good manager, keep the residents ready and give keen discipline where discipline is needed, and praises where praises are due. I must adjust to being a leader and teacher and settle down. Coincidentally, I'm getting to the age where I should settle down in more ways than one. Mervin was getting to be a pretty good friend and we became mutually buddies in a sense. I had used up my vacation time due me in June 1956 and I needed to check the calendar and with Dr. Charlie Su the Chief Resident if I needed to take time off in the summer and autumn of 1956. I had strong indications that Betty would not mind being married to a Chinese doctor and I suspected Hong Kong might have tempted her some. Mervin said he would be honored to be my Best Man, especially if the wedding would be held before school started. One final thing that I had to check was to see how many dollars I had in the Bank, and to my dismay, a quick glance in the stubs showed that I did not have any kind of a balance that would allow me to get married and have a honeymoon!

Yes, you guessed it! I had not yet gotten to the point of popping the question, no idea where to get some money, had not yet purchased a ring, arranged for vacation, or asked the Pastor and the church for availability. One very bright point was that Betty had attended worship services with me at Mount Vernon Methodist Church periodically and seemed to favor Dr. Day, his sermons, and the church just as much as I did. I also had the situation figured out and soon took the appropriate actions so we could get married around August of 1956.

Naturally, I could not expect to marry Betty if I did not propose to her. At that time, though some of my friends told me that I had a slight resemblance to Gregory Peck, I never managed to befriend a movie director or script writer, so I had to resort to my own initiative. Furthermore, since I had neither made the acquaintance of De Beers, nor did I have a rich uncle, therefore all I could offer Betty was my undying love when I made my proposal, which she accepted! To put it in simple English, I just asked in my usual refined manner and in an even and well modulated tone, "Betty, will you marry me?" And, she replied, "Yes!" We kissed and we were happily engaged. We briefly discussed the few facts that needed to be decided on; we agreed that we would have a small wedding, at the chapel in Mount Vernon Place United Methodist Church. We would ask if we could have it on August 22, 1956, either at ten or eleven in the morning. We would most likely have Mr. Elmer Lambert the Associate Pastor to officiate. I would ask Mervin Trail to be my Best Man and Betty would ask one of her classmates Shirley Kane to be her Bridesmaid. Betty's mother Mrs. Fannie Mae Cuppett and her stepfather Mr. Russell Cuppett would give Betty away and I would try to contact Uncle Ted Choy and Aunt Leona to come and witness the wedding. Among a small number of friends we had invited to attend would be Mrs. Sherri Hurka, the Radiographic Technician from Maryland General Hospital and a few of Betty's high school classmates. Meanwhile Mervin helped me in getting our marriage license from City Hall while I went to Carl Schoen's to get a wedding band.

One important thing I did was to send a telegram to my parents and make a request to them to remit to me immediately $200.00 and saying a letter was to follow. Then I wrote Aunt Lillian to lend me $200.00, as a sort of contingency fund for our wedding and honeymoon (I was able to repay Aunt Lillian before too long, though she did remind me of it.). Lastly, I also wrote a letter to my parents in which I said that by the time they were reading the letter I would have been married and that I would eventually send them some pictures. I tried to give Uncle Ted a call but found out that they were on a camping trip somewhere in Pennsylvania. I was finally able to contact the campsite and spoke to the ranger who told me that he would not disturb any camper unless it were an emergency and so I explained to him that it was an emergency to me even though it may not be so to him. He was amused and became very nice after I explained to him the reason for my call and went and got Uncle Ted. Uncle Ted took everything in his stride, took the whole incident nicely and in the morning they made their way back to Washington, D.C., then came to our wedding. The most important thing as far as we were concerned was that we made our vows to God even though it was a small wedding ceremony and we took the vows seriously. We returned to Betty's home for a small reception, cut our cake, took our bite and soon left on my/our Mercury Hardtop convertible for the big Apple—New York. We got to the Hotel McAlpine somewhere near Times Square and had a room in the back with a view of the brick wall of the back of the building next door. It really was not something that bothered us because we only had eyes for each other...so who cares about a view anyway?! We made our way to Chinatown, found an authentic Chinese Restaurant in the basement of a building and had a good Chinese meal. Betty loved mustard and I made sure she had the baptism of fire when she had her first taste of the real thing. You should ask her to tell you about her experience. (Let me give you a hint—she thought it was like French's mustard but I did not tell her but just sat across from her in the booth and quietly watched her reaction.)

The next day we went to the Empire State Building and wrote in the Guest Book on the Observatory Floor, "Hong Kong or bust!" We also had our lunch at the Automat—not very good but it was something new. After three or four days we left for Front Royal in Virginia to see the Blue Ridge Mountains and drive on the Skyline Drive. We went to a café for breakfast and I was glad I had an interpreter with me; otherwise, I might have starved because the waitresses were speaking a foreign language. Lucky for me Betty understood their language. The Skyline Drive is really beautiful. Soon, too soon, our honeymoon had to come to an end...and so it was...the newly married couple, Dr. and Mrs. Kenneth Siu had to make their way back to Freedom Way in Baltimore, Maryland. I went back to work and was as busy as ever. Betty had to leave the School of Nursing because nursing students were not permitted to get married unless they were in their last six months of training...quite an archaic rule, but what was most distasteful was the fact that Betty had to return the $100.00 scholarship she was awarded when she began her schooling because she did not finish her training so she had to forfeit the award. She later got a job at Hinson, Westcott, and Dunning, a Pharmaceutical company where she worked in the lab as a technician. This went well for a few months but when she figured that her pay was not going to be sufficient to cover her expenses on her cosmetics, she decided to resign from her job.

Meanwhile, Betty had joined Mount Vernon Place Methodist Church too and she became involved with teaching the kindergarten or first grade Sunday school, while I became involved with the Sixth grade class, which was quite a challenge. I was able to attend the worship service at least every other Sunday, which was pretty much pre-determined by my on-call schedule at the hospital. We had also moved to a furnished apartment in a building which is across the street from the hospital and right next door to the doctors' quarters, which made it very convenient whenever I was on call. In 1957 I was elected to chair the Missions Committee at the church because I was quite interested in Foreign Missions. My training in surgery had been going very well and I fully expected to, if possible, return to Hong Kong to help the indigent and the poor, especially when surgery is involved. You could say that God was urging me along those lines and making me realize how much time and opportunities I had wasted in my younger years, particularly all through my medical school days. In sober retrospection, I had really drifted since the war ended in 1945 and now in 1957, I was scrambling and hoping that it was not too late to wake up and pray that God would give me a new start. The Mission Committee chose to study the life of John Wesley, which turned out to be truly a blessing for me. Just as John Wesley had his heart-warming experience, I also benefitted from a change of heart. Just as the following quotation had said about the result on John Wesley, I was happy and joyous to be able to pray God to receive Jesus into my heart and to know that it is by God's grace through faith that I can gain forgiveness of my sins and Eternal Life because Jesus died for my sins on the Cross and was resurrected on the third day. He ascended into Heaven and will return one day to judge the living and the dead.

Quotable

"John Wesley, founder of Methodism, received this witness at a meeting on Aldersgate Street, London, as he listened to one reading Luther's Preface to the Book of Romans: 'About a quarter before nine, while he was describing the change which God works in the heart, through faith in Christ, I felt my heart strangely warmed. I felt I did trust Christ, Christ alone, for salvation: and an assurance was given to me that He had taken away my sins, even mine, and saved me from the law of sin and death' (Wesley's Journal, May 24, 1738)."

"For some this confidence dawns gradually. For others, it is a sudden discovery at the moment of faith. EACH OF US CAN BE ASSURED OF OUR ACCEPTANCE WITH GOD!"—"Four Great Emphases of United Methodism"[42]

I may have mentioned it in another place that we went to New York once to apply to the Foreign Mission Board of the United Methodist Church to send us to Hong Kong as missionaries, but we were told that they did not send missionaries back to their country of birth. Anyway, Betty and I were convinced we wanted to give our lives to Jesus, one way or another and, therefore, we prayed one night together and pledged to give our lives for the Lord. In any event, we were both committed to follow Jesus wherever He leads us. I find this following quote very appropriate and certainly applicable to me:

Yet he saved them for his name's sake.

—Psalm 106:8

What is imported in this "Yet," in God's saving *notwithstanding?*[437]The text is speaking of impediments on the sinner's part. God saved Israel here, notwithstanding dreadful sins. God can save you with an everlasting salvation, notwithstanding the most grievous provocations that you have been guilty of and the greatest impediments that you have laid in the way.

He can save for his name's sake, notwithstanding *grievous guilt and heinous transgressions.* Thus his name is declared to be a God forgiving wickedness, rebellion, and sin. You see mercy courting you, notwithstanding this very objection.

He can save for his name's sake, notwithstanding *long continuance in sin.* Mercy follows you with many a "how long, how long": "How long

---

[42] Richards, L. (1990). *The 365 day devotional commentary.* Includes index. (774). Wheaton, Ill.: Victor Books.
[43] [7] Ibid.

will these people treat me with contempt? How long will they refuse to believe in me?" (Num. 14:11).

He can save for his name's sake, notwithstanding *many apostasies and backslidings.* "Let the wicked forsake his way and the evil man his thoughts. Let him turn to the LORD, and he will have mercy on him, and to our God, for he will freely pardon" (Isa. 55:7).

He can save for his name's sake, notwithstanding *enormous neglect and contempt of God* until now. See Isaiah 43:25, "I, even I, am he who blots out your transgressions, for my own sake, and remembers your sins no more."

He can save for his name's sake, notwithstanding *grievous, rebellious hardness and contrariness.* "He kept on in his willful ways. I have seen his ways, but I will heal him; I will guide him and restore comfort to him" (Isa. 57:17–18).

He can save for his name's sake, notwithstanding *outward afflictions and poor circumstances* in the world. Though you are an outcast and nobody cares for you, he may save you for his name's sake, for he "gathers the exiles of Israel" (Isa. 56:8).

He can save for his name's sake, notwithstanding *degradation, unworthiness, and pollution,* for there is a fountain opened. "On that day a fountain will be opened to the house of David and to the inhabitants of Jerusalem, to cleanse them from sin and impurity" (Zech. 13:1).

—Ralph Erskine[44]

We used to teach our kids a short simple prayer that goes something like this: "God is great, God is good, let us thank Him for our food. By His hands we all are fed, Give us Lord our daily bread." This is nothing short of saying God is our Provider. We were soon to expect another of God's provisions for us. I was securely situated in my Chief Resident position and soon Betty was to tell me the good news that we would become parents in February of 1958. We welcomed the good news and made preparations accordingly. It would be convenient, at the very least, since we were living just across the street from the hospital. Betty consulted Dr. Mansfield, who was the Chief of OB/GYN at the hospital

[44] Wallis, D. (2001). *Take Heart: Daily devotions with the church's great preachers* (202). Grand Rapids, MI: Kregel Publications.

and she had excellent prenatal care. As 1958 came along, we were pretty much stuck in the hospital and the apartment. On the morning of the 18th of February, we were all digging out of a snow storm that hit us the night before. Dr. Mansfield was stuck in the hospital because of his deliveries and I was busy with emergencies all night. Around six in the morning, I saw Dr. Mansfield in the cafeteria and as we were talking, I kind of mentioned that Betty was due or maybe overdue and asked if he had anything to do that morning and whether he was scheduled to do anything special. He answered that he had nothing planned or pending. So I asked if it would be all right if we went ahead and bring Betty over to the hospital and see if we couldn't expedite the delivery. He agreed and so I gave Betty a call and asked her to get ready and I would be over to get her and bring her over for the delivery. Fortunately the snow had stopped and the road was cleared up nicely. I got Betty to the hospital without any slips or slides and Dr. Mansfield saw her and got the nurses busy and very quickly she was in the Labor Room and soon delivered a healthy and pretty girl, whom we named Ravenna Kay Siu. Betty said that as soon as she got back to her room she was inundated with well-wishers and friends that she had no time to rest.

Time really waits for no one. Betty brought Kay home and we had the joy of seeing her grow. Betty would remind me that I often would return to the apartment late at night and she would be in bed and often I would bring Kay over to the bed and play with her. One incident that happened that brought salutary effects was that we used to smoke and one night I came in late as usual and tried to reach my bedside table for a cigarette but found an empty package. I was more than a little put out and asked if Betty knew she smoked the last cigarette. She admitted she knew which prompt me to lose my temper and berate her for not going to the store to get a fresh pack or two since she had the time during the day. Later, when I cooled off and thought about the state I got myself into, I began to evaluate the situation. It was not worth losing my temper because of a cigarette, especially against someone I love and the mother of someone I love. I apologized to Betty and decided there and then to stop smoking. It was not worth losing my character and personality over something so useless and harmful, not only to my health but to the well-being of my family. I have not smoked another cigarette since that night.

I thank God that it was so easy and simple. Just like the way I stopped my fondness for gambling and my weakness for alcohol. Yes, God is good!

I completed my surgical residency at the end of June, assumed my position as resident in Pathology at the Women's Hospital and finalized my requirements to take the written exam of the American Board of Surgery. I took and passed the written exam and attempted the Oral exam but did not wait for the results because I had applied and was accepted as the Acting Senior Surgeon and acting Head of the Department of Surgery at the Alice Ho Miu Ling Nethersole Hospital in Hong Kong and returned to Hong Kong with Betty and Kay in November 1959 to a very heart-warming welcome of my family and friends.

XXIV

ALICE HO MIU LING NETHERSOLE HOSPITAL
1959-1962–1964-1968

The New Nature

Having been born again, not of corruptible seed but incorruptible,
through the word of God which lives and abides forever.
1 Peter 1:23

When we become Christians we are not remodeled, nor are we added to—we are transformed. Christians don't have two different natures; we have one new nature, the new nature in Christ. The old self dies and the new self lives; they do not coexist. Jesus Christ is righteous, holy, and sanctified, and we have that divine principle in us—what Peter called the "incorruptible" seed (1 Pet. 1:23). Thus our new nature is righteous, holy, and sanctified because Christ lives in us (Col. 1:27).

Ephesians 4:24 tells us to "put on the new man," a new behavior that's appropriate to our new nature. But to do so we have to eliminate the patterns and practices of our old life. That's why Paul tells us to "put to death your members which are on the earth: fornication, uncleanness, passion, evil desire, and covetousness" (Col. 3:5).[45]

Wow! What a welcome! We landed in Kai Tak Airport and made our way out of the plane, and after clearing immigration and customs we exited into the arrival hall. Then it struck us. It looked as if the whole

---

[45] MacArthur, J. (2001). *Truth for today: A daily touch of God's grace* (171). Nashville, Tenn.: J. Countryman.

arrival hall in Kai Tak Airport was filled with my friends and relatives and when they saw us enter the hall, they all gave a loud roar to welcome us. It was a beautiful sight! It was a heart-warming experience.

It was almost six and a half years since I left for Akron, Ohio to do my internship and subsequently my surgical residency training. I left Hong Kong in August of 1953 and by the time I left Baltimore, Maryland, to come home, it was November of 1959. I had finally completed my training, taken the examination of the American Board of Surgery and best of all, returned to Hong Kong with a few changes that reminded me superficially of the changes God made on Jacob, the son of Isaac and the grandson of Abraham. The one striking similarity was that God changed Jacob's name from Jacob the deceiver to Israel, the one who struggled with God and won; God did not change my name but did change me from a nominal Christian to one who is dedicated to serve God in whatever capacity the Lord deemed best.

Every faculty you have is to be used for God's glory.

In Romans 12:1 Paul pleads with believers to present their bodies to God as "a living and holy sacrifice," which is an appropriate and acceptable act of worship. But as someone has rightly said, the problem with living sacrifices is that they tend to crawl off the altar. That's because sacrificial living demands spiritual discipline and constant dependence on the Holy Spirit. We as Christians aren't always willing to do that.

According to Paul, the motivation and ability for self-sacrifice are found in the mercies we've already experienced in Christ. In Romans 1–11 he mentions several of these, including love, grace, peace, faith, comfort, power, hope, patience, kindness, glory, honor, righteousness, forgiveness, reconciliation, justification, security, eternal life, freedom, resurrection, sonship, intercession, and the Holy Spirit. Because you've received all that, you should gladly surrender every faculty you have for holy purposes.

"Body" in Romans 12:1 also includes your mind, for verse 2 says, "Do not be conformed to this world, but be transformed by the renewing of your mind, that you may prove what the will of God is, that which is good and acceptable and perfect." A transformed mind is the key to transformed behavior.

Prior to your salvation, you had neither the desire nor the ability to make such a sacrifice. But because you are a new creation in Christ, you are not to "go on presenting the members of your body to sin as instruments of unrighteousness; but ... as instruments of righteousness to God" (Rom. 6:13). One practical implication of this is to abstain from sexual immorality. "Know how to possess [your] own body in sanctification and honor" (1 Thess. 4:3–4).

You are a holy priest, and your priestly work begins with presenting yourself as a living and holy sacrifice. Is that your desire? Are you a faithful priest?[46]

After we got over the noisy reception and the excitement of the family and friends in their first encounter with Betty and Kay, we finally made our way to 53 Nathan Road, where my parents, Margaret, Fred and Helen and their baby daughter, Leslie lived. Patsy and Jeffrey Sun were there too. We were joined by Uncle Henry, Aunt Kitty, Eileen, Connie and John, and also Mr. and Mrs. Wong Sek Fai 王錫輝, the parents of Dr. Stanley Wong 王應冠. But, where is Gloria?

An interesting story to tell about this trip was that we found out that Betty was going to have another baby, a boy who was due in December of 1959. Because I reckoned that I would have taken my Board exams by then, I was thankful that I was able to apply for and was successful in becoming the Assistant/Acting Chief Surgeon at the Alice Ho Miu Ling Nethersole Hospital in Hong Kong. We also found out that because Betty was Rh neg while I was Rh pos, there was a possibility our new baby would have complications from that incompatibility. We, therefore, arranged beforehand with British Airways about securing our seating on our flight to Hong Kong. Lo and behold, when it got close to flight time in November, British Airways did an about-face and said they would not fly us to Hong Kong.

[46] MacArthur, J. (1993). *Drawing near*. Includes indexes. (July 9). Wheaton, Ill.: Crossway Books.

Was it a case of Murphy's Law or somebody's incompetence in British Airways?

Fortunately, Helen, my sister-in-law, was working at Pan Am at the time and was able in short notice to get us seats on one of the first Boeing 707 flights from the US to Hong Kong, with stopovers in Hawaii or some other island in the Pacific, then Tokyo for a change of planes, before we went on to Hong Kong.

We spent the night at one of the hotels nearby, then came over to the house for breakfast. Dad was having his usual breakfast of toast, butter and coffee. We sat down with him and Betty liked the toast so much, she ate all of it. Fortunately Dad already had his quota of a slice of toast and as usual, he again dutifully left the last bite of his toast in his plate.

I wonder what a superstitious Chinese family would think of a new daughter-in-law in the family who has such a voracious appetite for food. Personally, Betty is just a healthy person who enjoys her food. Yvette, our youngest daughter would say in later years, "Mom how is it that every time I see you eat, you seem to enjoy every bit of it so much, but when I try, I never find it so appetizing? Also, you are like a vacuum cleaner when you are eating because every bit of food just disappears in no time, while I am still struggling with my first bite!"

After breakfast, we made our way to Nethersole Hospital, where we were met by Dr. Ashton, the Superintendent of the hospital, who took us across the street to our flat on No.1 Bonham Road, 1st floor.

Following is an abstract about the hospital for your reference:

"The Alice Ho Miu Ling Nethersole Charity Foundation ("Foundation") has been established with a history of over 120 years since 1887. In 1887, Sir Ho Kai generously made a donation for the building of the Alice Memorial Hospital in memory of his beloved wife who died in 1884. It was the first hospital in Hong Kong that served the local poor Chinese with western medicine. The Hospital, under the management of the former London Missionary Society (now known as the Council for World Mission), aimed to serve patients and the community with the love, tenderness and care of Christ. Two other hospitals, Nethersole Hospital and Ho Miu Ling Hospital, were commissioned in 1893 and 1906 respectively. The three hospitals were then incorporated by Ordinance under the corporate name of The

Executive Committee of The Alice Ho Miu Ling Nethersole Hospital ("EC, AHNH") in 1954. The Hospital was relocated from the Hong Kong Island to Tai Po, the northern part of the New Territories, in 1997. It is now a district acute general hospital and a member hospital of the New Territories East Cluster of the Hospital Authority.'

Figure 13. Arrival in Hong Kong at 53, Nathan Road.

I was soon able to fit into the routine of the hospital. The day started at 8.00 a.m., and if surgery was scheduled, we hoped that the first incision would be made promptly at the stroke of the clock, which means that anesthesia would start earlier in time for that to happen. However, before the blade met the skin, one of the nurses would be asked to lead in prayer so that everyone would be in the proper spiritual preparedness. Quite often, there were two or three operations going simultaneously depending on the patient load and the operations would go on until the last scheduled case was completed, which might be sometime in the late afternoon. To be more precise, general surgery was scheduled for Mondays and Thursdays, while gynecology and obstetrics were scheduled for Tuesdays and Fridays. Every Wednesday, we would have Grand Rounds where all specialties met in the morning during which we would report to the medical team the results of our findings in the operating room and for any further dispositions of the referrals. The medical team would then refer all their new cases to the group, where we would discuss what surgical procedures need be taken. This was a very profitable session and really pointed out the benefits of the aphorism that "many heads are better than one."

One of the duties that I enjoyed doing was teaching and lecturing to the nursing students. I love teaching except for the fact that it had to be done in Chinese. This turned out to be much more difficult than I first thought. The fact was that at the University, everything was done in English, all my books were in English and all the training I had was in English. In the end, according to my rough calculation, it took me four hours to translate and figure out a one-hour lecture. I was happy to be able to do it and gladly accepted the challenge. Indeed, technical jargon can be very difficult to master and translate, but once you've learned it then it's like second nature.

It wasn't too long after my initial acclimatization when it was time for Dr. Edward (Ted) H. Paterson to take his furlough, which then allowed me to assume my position as Chief Surgeon and Head of the Department. It was nice to know that the Halstead model of intern and resident training was alive and well at Nethersole Hospital too, and I did have a resident under me and an intern that rotated into the surgical department every six months, under an agreement with the University of Hong Kong and the Hong Kong Hospital Authority. The School of Nursing at the hospital was also approved by the Nursing Board and her graduates were eligible for licensure as RNs in Hong Kong.

In case you thought I had forgotten, not long after we were moved in to begin my job at Nethersole, I contacted my classmate, Dr. Hu Shih Chang 胡世昌 who was the Pediatric Specialist of the University of Hong Kong at Queen Mary Hospital and we consulted him about our soon to be born baby regarding the Rh incompatibility situation, He checked the medical history and ordered a number of blood tests. Coincidentally, Nethersole Hospital was host to a missionary Lab technician from New Zealand, who upon learning of our concern for our expectant baby's hematologic problem, reassured Betty that in her experience and understanding, she thought that chances of our baby having any problems with the blood type incompatibility was very slim because Betty's blood type was "O" and mine was "B". Finally when Stephen Marcus was born at Queen Mary Hospital, the birth and the placenta were all within normal limits. There was a bit of an icteric tinge in his sclera and there was a slight yellowish tinge to his facial skin, but all these cleared up within days with the use of the ultraviolet light. Blood tests were also within normal limits. We praised God for this good news and we thank God for the wonderful doctors, nurses and technicians for their expertise and loving care.

Meanwhile, Kay was showing an extraordinary keen sense of her desire to learn and would often ask us while pointing to a new letter in a book or newspaper, "What's this?" We would tell her what the letter was and she would be looking for another letter to ask us. Sometimes we would play a game with her by writing a letter on a blank page in a writing pad and ask her if she knew the letter and she would give the right answer, then we would write another and so forth. Anyway, by the time she was twenty months old, she knew all the letters of the alphabet and some simple words. Sometimes, I would take her over to the hospital and soon one of the senior nurses in the Obstetrics and Gynecology Department by the name of Sister Tam Wai Ling譚慧玲 would take her to the nurses' quarters and introduce her to all the nurses there. Kay soon was able to learn all their names and she also learned some Cantonese language.

Betty also took some Chinese (Cantonese) lessons and soon they were both able to understand some very basic colloquial Cantonese, though we all know how difficult it really was for a foreigner to master the nuances of pronouncing the nine tones of spoken Cantonese. I am sure we have all heard of the funny faux pas foreigners made when they first attempt to venture into their initial rites of passage with the language. One afternoon, Kay came home after spending some fun time with Sister Eva Tam and as usual they had to pass by the hospital kitchen when she smelled a very strong odor from the kitchen. They asked Mrs. Sun, the Supervisor of the kitchen, who was the mother of Mr. Jeffrey Sun Hon Kuen, our brother-in-law. Mrs. Sun told Kay that they were brewing some Leuhng char (涼茶) [cold tea in Chinese medicine, a concoction drink of many herbal ingredients to drive off the 'heat' in human body.] It has a very distinctive smell and it must have left an indelible impression on her mind, because when she got home she told Betty, "Mom, they were cooking this "two tea" and it was very stinky." They came and asked me what it was. At first I couldn't make head or tail of what they were talking about until I finally realized that Kay must have had the tone wrong. She had mistaken the word 兩 (leung) for 涼 Leuhng), though they were both given the same phonetic intonation of Leuhng. The word 兩 means two and the tea is not two tea 兩茶 but 涼茶. Let the speaker beware!

Imagine the congregation's surprise when their new missionary pastor was preaching his first sermon after he graduated from language school, and the first words that came out of his mouth was:

"Ngoh hou jung yi tong yahn." 我好中意劏人 which means 'I love to kill people very much. Of course, what he meant to say was:

"Ngoh hou jung yih tohng yan" 我好中意唐人 which means 'I love the Chinese people (唐人), the people of the Tang dynasty or commonly known as Tohng Yan very much.' Anyway, I got a good laugh when Dr. Ashton first told me about the perils missionaries face out in the mission fields. But then again, I fail to see the wisdom in the position Mission Boards take about not sending nationals as missionaries to their countries of birth! Imagine the amount of resources the Boards could save were they to send nationals and foreigners to wherever missions are done! I am talking about the resources, frustrations and time expended in acquiring the necessary language and cultural skills and customs each foreign missionary had to incur could be put to better use if the Boards would consider doing away with the restriction of not sending candidates to their countries of birth. Let me say here categorically that as long as it's God's call I'm responding to, I will do everything possible to fulfill what God has prepared and purposed for me to do, with or without a Board! I know that as long as God wants me to serve Him, He will provide for me to do His Will. I will wait for His call and while I am waiting, I will spend my time and effort to prepare and be ready to "Go!" when I get the "Call."

Yes indeed! Trust and Obey. There is no other way to be happy in Jesus but to trust and obey. Simple truths; simple enough to do, provided you get your ego out of the way; but once you submit to it—even miracles can happen. Yes I've found this to be true numerous times—too numerous to count—and besides, I don't have enough fingers to count them.

There was also a little song that I learned when I was studying in La Salle years ago which I've found to be very true and I am sure has helped me through many times in my life, such as when learning new skills and new categories in school and in coping with life's intricate problems in general. The song goes something like this: "Once or twice, you should fail, try, try again. If at first you don't succeed, try, try again." Sometimes I would hum this tune over and over until I got over the blues of my failure and just try harder.

Let's just say that, on the whole, we were enjoying our lives very much and Stephen was growing and thriving like a normal kid. We had made a friend who lived just to the West of us and he would drive by and pick us up on Sunday mornings and take us to the English Methodist Church. His name was John Chambers and he worked in the Hong Kong government as an Administrative Officer and he sang in the choir. I was getting along really well in my job and especially when the Head Nurse, Frances Wu was a classmate of Aunt Janet, one of my mother's younger sisters, who also was from Swatow originally. I must admit she was quite partial towards me, though in my defense, I never gave her any reason to entertain any negative feelings towards me. I think I have always endeavored to earn other peoples' respect by a strong sense of doing the right thing at the right time, treating people fairly and honestly and avoiding idle gossip at all times. I've always treated my junior doctors fair and square and I've always treated the novice nursing students gently and I feel that they were never afraid of being scrubbed in with me even if it was their first case. I have never liked those surgeons who yell and scream at everybody and throw instruments on the floor if the nurse should hand them the wrong instrument.

Now, I can't move on without making sure that you have not been given a wrong impression. There is no way that I can get away with leaving you with a totally false mental picture of Kenneth Siu, that he has now, by his own cunning, turned himself into the masterful surgeon that he is by the sheer dint of his mental superiority and manual dexterity. On the contrary, I have feet of clay just like anybody else, as well as the statute in King Nebuchadnezzar's dream, and just as susceptible to be smashed by the rolling stone cut out not by human hands! (cf. Daniel 2:31-34) What I was trying to convey was that whatever accomplishments I had came in large measure from determination, hard work, observation, and study. However, successes more often came because of prayer, a pure motive and most certainly through the Grace of God. That said, I must be careful to reiterate that the blame for any and/or all of my failures should, of necessity, be laid at my feet. Anyway, just when everything appeared rosy and I was basking in the glories of running a surgical department, the dreaded bad news came to me in the form a letter from the American Board of Surgery that I had failed the oral exam and that I could apply for a re-exam after showing proof of further studies and an interval of six months since the first exam. In any event, I had to continue working at Nethersole Hospital until Dr. Paterson returned from his furlough. I made sure that I was registered for the exam in 1962 and eventually made plans to return to Baltimore in time to take the exam. You may say that I am prejudiced, but after all these years and the numerous exams I've taken, I'm of the opinion that oral exams and interviews have no place in society or the workplace, solely because human beings have this inborn predilection for prejudice over anything...often unrelated to whether you are qualified for the job or not. Worst of all, you have no control over any particular examiner's prejudice, whether it is justified or not…and it could be triggered just at the second the examiner lay his or her eyes on you, quite apart from what you may have or have not done! Another puzzling factor that I cannot fathom is why it is that your mind can play tricks on you just at the moment you are forming your answer and the words that come out of your mouth are not quite the words that your mind is searching to use, but by then, your fate is doomed! (Sort of like a slip of the tongue, which often gets worse as you try to correct it—like a comedy of errors, except it's not funny.) Trust me, I'm speaking from some of my painful experiences. I know what I'm talking about because I've taken more than my quota of exams!

Anyhow, it was my own cross to bear and there was no reason that Betty or Kay and Stephen should have to put up with my misery, and so, I asked Patsy to help make us an itinerary that we could enjoy and have fun and remember for the rest of our lives. We left Hong Kong in July of 1961 on the Asia of Lloyd Triestino, in a cabin all to ourselves and arrived in Singapore for a three-day layover. We went ashore and toured Singapore and were accompanied by my friend, Lee Wee Soon who was my classmate in the Medical Faculty at the University of Hong Kong prior to his leaving for Singapore. I think Kay and Stephen enjoyed visiting the zoo as much as anything else. We left Singapore and soon arrived in our next port of call, which is Madras on the eastern shore of India. Since the ship we were on was a passenger ship, it had a large cargo capacity. Therefore, at every port they would stop to off-load and load on new cargo depending upon their business volume. At the same time, we were told that they would also replenish the ship's supply of soft drinks, candy, and naturally, ice by the block. Madras was a short stop and we were soon off to Colombo, Ceylon or more appropriately Sri Lanka.

Again after a short delay we were on to Bombay or what is now known as Mumbai.

I'm not sure if it was a famous personality who said that 'Life is like a comedy of errors', but I do want to give credit to whoever it was due. We were treated to just such an incident that I feel I would be amiss if I do not repeat it one more time and, therefore, I apologize to those who have heard it before. I do not intend to make fun out of someone's misfortune, but I do feel that life is already too severe, if we do not make an attempt to find an escape, if only to lift our spirits somewhat.

The amusing episode I'm about to relate happened one evening just at the end of our dinner. This young Indian gentleman boarded the ship in Madras and we were between Madras and Mumbai. He was travelling alone and was seated at the table just next to us. We had just finished our dessert and as is the custom, we would be served cheese and biscuits from the cheeseboard and a choice of beverage. At that point, I quietly intimated to Betty and the kids to pay attention to our fellow-traveler when his order of cheese and biscuits would be served him. We didn't have to wait long and as the man leaned forward to taste his order of Gorgonzola cheese, he bolted back on his chair from his stooping posture and threw his head back, as if to say, "Good heavens! What have I got here? However can you call this food?" He quickly got up from his chair AND STORMED OUT OF THE DINING ROOM!

As we approached land in Mumbai, we immediately were made aware of an interesting phenomenon. Suddenly, we felt the boat took a sharp list to the right and we heard and saw the coffee mug that was sitting on the table was very briskly caused to slide across the table, prevented from crashing to the floor only because of the wooden rails on the sides of the table. Simultaneously, we also heard a loud scraping sound as the suitcase under our bunk slid along the floor. The kids were wide-eyed with apprehension, not knowing what was taking place and I had to explain that this phenomenon happens because of the wide continental shelf and the tides that begin its ebb and flow in the evening as a result of the rising of the moon. This was the best I could do and I apologize to the weatherman and scientists for my amateurish attempt to educate my kids.

As we docked in Mumbai, I noticed a large number of vultures in the sky and noticed the building where they gathered and realized that Mumbai had a rather large population of Zoroastrians who believed in placing their dead on the rooftop to allow the birds of prey to consume their carcasses and would later collect their bones for burial.

As we admired the city from the deck, I noticed that Mumbai probably has the largest automatic Laundromat in the whole world. I'm only speaking in jest because as a matter of fact they have the largest automaton laundry vats in the world. What I'm saying is that they have these large squarish wells all over their compound and a large number of workers doing the laundry by hand and then hanging the wash out to dry. The workers looked and acted like they were robots. It was quite a sight!

I imagine they took on board a large quantity of block ice per usual and our kids would have free access to drinks when they played in the nursery during the day, at the dining room and in our cabin. Betty noticed that Stephen was burning with fever as we departed from Mumbai but fortunately he soon recovered once we were on our way. We soon reached Aden and in short order we entered the Suez Canal. I noticed that the boat had to reduce her speed while in the Canal because traffic was quite heavy. It gave us a chance to see the Pyramids at a distance. Soon, we were in the Mediterranean Sea and on our way to Naples. The

Captain was very accommodating and knew how to please his customers because he took the ship around the Island of Capri and played the tune "'Twas on the Isle of Capri that I found her, beneath the shade of an old walnut tree..." on the PA system, just so we could have a look at the famous island, especially for those who are the romantic types. The next morning in Naples we took a walking tour around our hotel and we each had an ice cream cone for the occasion. The next day we went on a tour of Pompeii and we had to carry Stephen when we were walking around the site where the volcanic eruptions had caused the most damage. It is surreal... especially the charred victims and domestic dogs and cats that were solidified in mid-motion. We ended our voyage at the last port of call in Genoa. It was altogether a memorable journey for us, though I suppose Kay and Stephen would have a better recollection of every point of interest were they a few years older.

A couple of days later, we took the train and went on to Caux sur Montreau in Switzerland and took part in a conference sponsored by an organization called Moral Rearmament, which was the eventual body that was begun in Oxford University called the Oxford Movement. The tenets of the group stress Christian principles, particularly with regards to the morals of the individual. I must admit that Caux is a lovely place and the surroundings were ideal for anyone who aspires to the spiritual and moral betterment no matter your religious orientation. But basically, if one really sticks faithfully to the teachings of Jesus, is always mindful of being obedient to every word Jesus taught, exercises due diligence to live each day the way a believer ought to live, prayerfully seeks the guidance of the Holy Spirit each day to help you resist the devil's temptations and to be mindful to abide in Jesus, there is no need for anyone to go through extremes to achieve what God has freely given you!

> *"How can a young man keep his way pure?*
> *By keeping it according to Thy word.*
> *... Thy word I have treasured in my heart,*
> *that I may not sin against Thee"*
> *(Ps. 119:9, 11).*[47]

A few days later, we bid farewell to newly made friends at the conference, took the train and headed for Calais, France to catch the cross-channel ferry to Southampton, the UK. On the way there, we had a stopover in Paris in the morning and we were given hard rolls and cold cuts for breakfast, which left poor Kay and Stephen out...and we could not get any ice cold milk...what a tragedy! Then to top it all off, it appeared that we were in a train depot and the train was in a complete stop. It was impossible to find any train personnel to inquire where and why we were where we were—nowhere. I did find a man but when I asked him if he could tell me what was going on and when the train would be leaving for the United Kingdom in English, he just shook his head, turned around and just went on his way without saying a word. This was the second time that I have encountered the rudeness and boorish behavior of the French, and it really puzzles me. While trying to figure out what I ought to do and thinking that we might have to find another train that would take us to our destination, I thought we ought to get off the train to investigate and find out. I took this course of action because it appeared that we were the only passengers in the carriage we were in.

---

[47] MacArthur, J. (1993). *Drawing near.* Includes indexes. (October 8). Wheaton, Ill.: Crossway Books.

It was difficult traveling with three suitcases, a mother and two kids. I managed to get the bags down to the platform while Betty and the kids were looking at busy old me through the window. I was about to get back on the train to help Betty and kids alight from the carriage, after placing the suitcases neatly side by side on the platform, when suddenly the train started to go forward. I ran back to get two of the suitcases and attempted to catch up with the train. To my dismay, as I headed toward the train, the train did a reverse on me and went back the way we came. I was completely puzzled and befuddled and thinking to myself, how would I be able to find them again? Just as suddenly as it started, the train came to a halt. I managed to get the suitcases on the train and finally, the conductor did come by and all was well. I finally gathered my confused and stray thoughts and surmised that all the maneuvering was because they had to change the locomotive and the back and forth movements were done because of the uncoupling and coupling of the aforesaid locomotives. Nevertheless, I still think the French are very rude and lack the virtue of hospitality.

The ferry ride to Southampton was calm and enjoyable except for one thing. We went to the dining room for lunch, and we were all eager for some food and drink, I think, but the drink that was readily available was hot English tea and not anything else. I'm sure that Kay, Stephen and Betty would enjoy a cuppa, but at that particular moment, we would happily take a second choice. You could say that living in America and Hong Kong for that matter, we get pretty spoiled. Complain, complain, complain...that's all I seem to be doing! But, there is more. When we reached our destination, we had to clear customs and immigration. Betty holds a U.S. passport as well as the kids, while I carry a British document...so we had to go on separate lines to queue up. Betty had to struggle with the kids, the diaper bag and her purse, while I had my hands free behind my queue, but I couldn't do anything about it. We did get to our hotel in London. While there, we had an opportunity to ride down to Eltham to visit the elderly Mrs. Paterson, Ted Paterson's mother. We later went on the train at Waterloo station to go down to Southampton to catch the Queen Mary to sail to New York. We were greatly and pleasantly surprised while we were sitting on the train to see Mrs. Paterson walking down the platform looking for us. We went down and greeted her when she surprised Stephen with a gift—a Matchbox car! This was the first time in his life he'd ever set eyes on a Matchbox car. I kinda chuckled when one day not long ago, when he said he wished his mom had helped him to safe-keep it. The Atlantic crossing was smooth and the kids had a great time as usual in the nursery with parties, party hats, tooting horns and the whole lot.

When we reached New York, everybody got on the deck to see the welcome by the fireboats shooting their water cannons to welcome us. Then we all saw it… the old lady herself that had welcomed so many of the hundreds and thousands of new arrivals and visitors to the shores of the great Land of the Free! It was quite a sight and it did bring goosebumps—even to the most hardened individuals—I'm sure! Betty's mother and younger sister Yvonne were there on the pier to welcome us as we docked in our berth. It was a nice Welcome Home, indeed!

It was time to settle down somewhat and appraise the situation carefully so we could strategize what kind of a future we would end up with, although I fully understand that whatever plans I visualize, they would not be realized unless they fit in with God's plan for me. Nevertheless, we knew we needed a place to stay, a car to get us around and a decent job to help us have food on the table so the kids could grow up and thrive. I praise God I was able to get my old part-time job at the hospital in the Bethlehem Steel Plant at Sparrows Point near Baltimore. I was able to get a Rambler wagon and I was able to rent a home at 4611 White Avenue in Harford County just northeast of Baltimore City. It was a quiet neighborhood and the house adjoined a Mobil Gas Station. There was also a neighborhood store with a butcher and that was the first store that Kay went to purchase something on her own because it was just down the street from our house and she did not have to cross any streets to get there. Kay also went to a neighborhood kindergarten on their school bus and Betty just cried her heart out the first day she went to school. We have pictures of Kay and Stephen playing in the pile of maple leaves in the front yard that Betty raked up that autumn. Stephen enjoyed riding his pedal car full speed up the path and then bang it into the front gate. It was an idyllic place. Finally, the most memorable sight and sound was to hear our next door neighbor yelling at his dog to, "Git in here!"...every day!

I can never forget Stanley C. Bociek M.D., the Chief Plant Physician and Surgeon—how kind and compassionate he was! He had somehow found out that I was hoping to be able to go to Chicago for a Post-graduate Review course for the American Board of Surgery exam, but was having difficulty raising up enough money to do it. He asked me pointblank how much I needed and wrote me a check for the 400 dollars needed for the registration fee as a loan to me. The course was very helpful and I was able to pass my Board exam. I thanked Dr. Bociek profusely and assured him that as soon as I saved enough money I would pay off my indebtedness to him immediately. Not long after that, he summoned me to his office and when I walked in he handed me a small slip of paper on which he wrote the following: "I O U $400.00. Paid in full. Signed, Stanley C. Bociek." What a generous man!

Eventually, I joined the Central Medical Center in Downtown Baltimore as their surgeon, doing mostly Industrial Medicine. This was definitely a stop-gap job, while I applied to the Immigration Service as a Permanent Resident so that I could get a Green Card in preparation to becoming a US citizen. I had also made preparation to return to Nethersole Hospital and assume the position of Chief of Surgery. Meanwhile, I also took and passed the examination for the Board of Healing Arts of Maryland to obtain my license to practice medicine in Maryland.

There was plenty of good news on the home front because Debbie was born in Maryland General Hospital on January 30, 1962 and Becky was born July 4th in 1963 at Bon Secour Hospital. Betty decided that she needed to go to a hospital where she was not as well known as at Maryland General because she could not get any rest when Debbie was born. We ultimately made it back to Hong Kong sometime in the early part of 1964. I picked up where I had left off; Kay, Stephen and Debbie all enrolled at Glenealy Junior School, together with Dr. Gilbert Chapman's daughter and son. Gilbert was the missionary in Internal Medicine from Adelaide Australia. The kids used to tell me that when he drove them to school in his Holden wagon, he would give them a thrill and make the wagon jump like a kangaroo. Gilbert was soon to tell me that I would not be Chief Surgeon because I did not have a higher degree from the UK. In another part of this book I related that the hospital sent me to the UK in January1966 where I obtained the FRCS Edin. in May.

XXV

JEFFERSON CITY, MISSOURI, U.S.A.

It was not an easy decision to make and yet at the same time the situation was such that to stay was to put my family of six dependents—my American wife, our son and our four daughters—the youngest of whom was yet to be born in October of 1967—at a risk which seemed, after much prayer and consideration, to favor our evacuation. I remember an incident I encountered when I took Kay down to the Rediffusion TV studio for a performance by her class at the Glenealy Junior School. I was parked by the pavement in front of the studio and as I was approaching the car, I noticed a gallon can under the front of the car and naturally I thought the worst of the situation—a bomb—someone must have planted a bomb under my car—but why??? It didn't help me one bit at the time, when I was reading and hearing from the newspapers and television about the heroic sacrifice of almost all of the bomb disposal personnel of the British Army and Police Force in Hong Kong from trying to defuse all the bombs placed by the communist terrorists. It was also around this time in 1967 that as I was reading my copy of the Journal of the Christian Medical Society, I came across an ad by a Christian doctor in the United States who was advertising for a physician partner who was interested in medical missions to join his practice. I answered the ad and soon received a reply from the doctor, who said that by coincidence he was planning a trip to Hong Kong. He came and witnessed my performance as the Head of the Department of Surgery at Nethersole Hospital. I informed him at the time that Missouri's medical practice ordinance was still back in the dark ages because to practice medicine in Missouri one had to be a citizen of the United States, which meant that regardless of my being licensed in Maryland and being certified by the American Board of Surgery as a Specialist in General Surgery, I would not be qualified to be licensed in Missouri. I should add that I had chosen not to apply to become a naturalized citizen of the United States when I decided to return to Hong Kong to work at Nethersole Hospital and was, therefore, not a "Green Card holder" simply because I did not anticipate having the luxury of returning to USA once a year to keep the status current. I informed Dr. Stuart Exon, the surgeon who had placed the ad that he should look into this matter and deal with it before I could join him. He assured me that he would and subsequently asked me to prepare to join him in May or June of 1968. Perhaps, if the situation in Hong Kong had not got so desperate, I would have made sure my licensure was properly dealt with before taking the whole family on the journey. Alas, sometimes desperate situations result in desperate measures and hindsight is always the proverbial 20/20 but I will not belabor the point.

Having gone past the point of no return, what remained was to make the best of a bad situation. I became a State employee and the surgeon and physician of the Missouri State Penitentiary in Jefferson City, and was remunerated on an hourly basis, which, for beginners, was arranged prior to my arrival by Dr. Exon at four hours a day, five days a week. The arrangement he had made also allowed me to assist him in surgery with the proviso that I would be paid US$20.00 an hour. As it turned out the assistant's fees were satisfactory because he was rather slow and would spend twice to three times the amount of time it would take me to finish the operation. However, this became quite intolerable when he embarked on what the nurses derisively termed an "Exonthon", with apologies to the marathon runners, which meant that the operation might last sometimes ten to twelve hours. But more often than not it might be days on end before he got a major operation that would require my assistance. Consequently, I petitioned the Warden of the Penitentiary to extend my hours of employment just so I would be able to provide sufficiently for the family. We were renting one of Dr. Exon's houses on Belair Road and the Belair Elementary School is just at the other end of the street, which made it very convenient for the kids and for Betty, who soon became a bus driver. It was a lovely neighborhood and in the summer, the kids joined the swim team and were practicing in the park which is just a few blocks away from the house.

Just when life seemed to settle into a new routine, then something like a recurrent nightmare once again appeared in the horizon and turned our world topsy turvy all over again. I have no idea what Dr. Exon did or did not do, but someone had reported to the Board of Healing Arts in Jefferson City accusing Dr. Exon of aiding and abetting an unlicensed person to practice medicine, namely me; and I was accused of practicing medicine without a license. As far as I knew, I was permitted to assume the post of "Medical Officer" and to practice medical and surgical care at the Missouri State Penitentiary. As to my assisting Dr. Exon in surgery, the extent of what I did was no more than a nurse or surgical technician would do, which would not constitute practicing medicine, no matter how you look at it. I did not have any contact with the patients either before or after the surgery and they were complete strangers to me. I was paid the assistant's fee by Dr. Exon according to the hours I spent helping him in surgery and I never personally charged the patients or contacted them for payment. I did not work or enter Dr. Exon's office during this time and therefore I had no knowledge or awareness of his charging procedure. When we appeared before the Board, Dr. Exon had Mr. Tom Graham and Mr. David Brydon to represent us (I am surmising that they represented me because I never received any summonses nor was I ever interviewed by anyone.) We were told that we were guilty and we were to cease and desist from any further activity on my part as a surgical assistant at once and I was to restrict my medical practice to the State Penitentiary only. The only conclusion I can come to at this time, after all these years, was that Dr. Exon could have, without letting me know and without getting my consent, been charging the insurance companies and/or Medicare with respect to my assistant's fees according to a physician's scale rather than a technician's scale, but, turning around and paying me according to the latter scale. (This was because friends of ours had told us during the course of time that I had been referred to as Dr. Exon's money tree!)

It was obvious that something ought to be done to change the law existing in Missouri at the time regarding the licensing of physicians who were not citizens of the United States. Fortunately during the year of 1969, Mr. John Danforth was campaigning to run for the position of Attorney General of Missouri and the Women's Auxiliary of the Missouri State Medical Association headquartered in Jefferson City, of which Betty had become an active member, was helping in his campaign. Mr. Danforth had used the slogan "I dare you" in his campaign and had ads in the newspapers and flyers all over the state. Betty, therefore cut one of these ads from the newspaper and mailed it to him together with a cover letter "daring" him to repeal the licensing law the moment he became the Attorney General. Many doctors, including some in Jefferson City, also petitioned him to change the law. It was very exciting and emotional when Mr. Attorney General Danforth immediately declared the law restricting licensing of non-citizens unconstitutional the moment he was elected. I was able to go down to the office of the Board of Healing Arts the next day and immediately obtained my license to practice medicine in Missouri, after paying a fee of US$10.00. Praise the Lord that in January of 1970, I began my practice with Dr. Exon. It was an interesting aside that the Board ran out of application forms for licensure, because there were so many physicians throughout the State who were in the same situation I was in.

I soon found out that being in partnership with Dr. Exon was going to be a very difficult affair. Looking back, I felt that he was not at all fair with the way he remunerated me, which reflected in the less than generous way he approached life. It was evident that he wanted all the benefits to go his way and everything that he did he wanted to be to his advantage. Money tree indeed! One of the two incidents that convinced me to make my move to terminate our partnership became very clear to me was the occasion when I asked and got his permission to attend a medical meeting in New Orleans towards the end of my first year with him as a partner. I'd also told him that it would mean much to Betty and me personally because our Best Man Dr. Mervin Lee Trail was now a "Big-man-on-campus" at LSU Medical School as well as a VIP in the sports world and city politics. He agreed that I could go to the meeting and so I made all the necessary arrangements and reservations. Imagine my surprise and his temerity when a few days before we were scheduled to leave for New Orleans, he told me that Anne, Mrs. Exon, wanted him to take her to the Big Easy—New Orleans because it was some sort of anniversary day for them! I had to put my foot down and told him we were going to New Orleans, regardless. We had a GREAT time! But, the incident did not help our relationship with Dr. Exon one iota, especially with respect to our partnership. I couldn't help but notice that he had taken at least two mission trips but had yet to advise me on how I should go about taking part in one of these mission trips because I was quite a novice in these ventures. By the time I began my second year with the partnership, he just gave me a 50% raise on my lowly monthly salary, but did not initiate any conversation about when and how I would or could enter into being a bona fide partner with him. By this time I was fully convinced that I was being taken advantage of, and since we had not had any written agreement signed, I began to plan my move to sever our relationship.

Over the last couple of years I came to know Monsignor Kaiser of the Roman Catholic Diocese of Jefferson City quite well. We were introduced through our mutual friend Mrs. Winnie Hall, who was in charge of working with the physicians who were employed to do the medical evaluations for the applicants to the Social Welfare Department for their medical disabilities. I was able to obtain a position as a medical consultant, which allowed me to supplement my income at the time when life seemed so desperate. I, therefore, made an appointment to visit Mgsr. Kaiser so that I would be able to discuss with him the ethical and moral issues involved with terminating my partnership relation with Dr. Exon and the establishment of my solo practice in Jefferson City. The first favorable thing that we agreed on was that everything Dr. Exon and I did was concluded verbally and we did not commit anything we agreed on by putting it in ink on paper. Everything was tentative especially prior to my licensure. After I was duly licensed, I could not say that he was the least bit inclined toward being generous with my remuneration. When my licensure was achieved he made no indication or effort to offer me the terms of partnership. On the contrary, I was made to feel I was still an indentured hireling. We didn't need a prolonged conversation to conclude that both ethically and morally, I was in the clear to proceed and establish my own practice. It was consoling to know that I did not answer the ad and join this venture under false pretenses. Even though

I could not claim that I took part in being a medical missionary, my consolation was that I had determined that I will be a Christian Surgeon and do everything completely ethical and moral but most of all above board.

We moved into our first home at 1009 Fairmount Blvd., on the west side of Jefferson City the day before Thanksgiving in 1971 during a slight snowfall. The house was built in the twenties, a Victorian style two-storied house with a basement, a detached two-car garage and a storage shack in the back. It was a nice house in a street that is off the main street, on level ground and a nice neighborhood. There were four bedrooms and a nice den in the basement that was my study-cum-guest room, plus a nice family TV room in the other part of the basement. After we got all our boxes and boxes of things in the house and scattered over the living room, Becky came in the living room, looked around, sat down on one of the boxes and with a loud voice, asked in an incredulous tone of voice, "Mom, are we *rich*?" Bless her heart! Of course we are rich—not in a worldly sense, Becky—if you know what I mean!

I also interviewed Bev Cearlock sitting on our boxes and hired her on the spot. We would be getting my office ready for patients by January 3, 1972, when the office furniture and equipment got moved into the office at 915 Leslie Boulevard. Dad, Fred and Helen would be coming for the dedication by Rev. Gene Rooney, Pastor of First United Methodist Church the day before. I thank God that my practice got off with a good start and it continued to be a lot better than I had anticipated. I am grateful that God has gifted me with a good mind, perfect vision, a pair of dexterous hands and a good constitution. Of course, it was helpful that He has also blessed me with a friendly disposition which allowed me to treat my colleagues in a courteous and friendly manner while at the same time, receiving their goodwill and much welcomed referrals. I thank God that He has given me the good fortune to have the gentle touch which allowed the surgical wounds to heal well and with very minimal scarring. It was most gratifying at the height of my practice to hear from Mrs. Spencer, a retired nurse who started a business making brassieres and fabric implants for post-radical mastectomy patients to volunteer the information that she was always able to tell her clients that they were patients of mine without their volunteering that information.

Her clients would ask her how she knew they were my patients and she would say that she could always tell because of their beautiful scars. That was quite a testimonial!

Eventually, because my practice was getting to be too busy and because of the demands from the referring doctors, and while I hesitated because of my sad experience with my previous partnership, I was reluctantly forced to seek a partner for the sake of the patients and the referring doctors. Still smarting from the shabby treatment I received from someone who was so miserly when it concerned money, I therefore sought to make the conditions as equitable as possible without giving him everything and the keys to the kingdom as well. By this time, we had transferred ourselves and joined the First Baptist Church in Jefferson City, because, the Pastor of the First United Methodist Church where we were members before, was deep into being a practitioner of Neuro-Linguistic Programming, a rather bizarre mixture of psychology, visualization and linguistics and a somewhat obscure quasi-religion. The young surgeon concerned was being discharged from the military where he obtained his surgical qualification. I offered to have him work for a year on a trial basis at an adequate monthly salary and if everything was satisfactory, I would let him be an equal partner with pension and all benefits on a profit-sharing plan. I was sure I was more than generous and fair with my offer and my intentions, but, alas, in spite of my good and honorable intentions, things did not turn out the way I had envisioned. In the end greed reared its ugly head once too often. He just seemed intent on grabbing all the business and referrals and hinted that having half a loaf was not quite enough and hinted at entering into a productivity arrangement. His ingratitude just made me so disappointed, I was completely devastated. I evaluated my situation carefully; Betty had managed the Alpha & Omega Christian Bookstore for almost fifteen years, Kay graduated from Central Methodist College, went on to University of Missouri in Columbia and finished her Master's course in Journalism but did not want to write the thesis for her Master degree and married Stephen Dinolfo and was working as Director of Communications at Missouri State Medical Association; Stephen graduated from Washington University, then went on to University of Missouri Medical School, obtained his M.D. and was a resident in

Pediatrics at University Hospitals in Columbia; Debbie graduated from Kansas State University and got her R.D. (Registered Dietitian) degree at University of Missouri; Becky also graduated from Kansas State University then obtained her Master's in Special Education at University of Missouri, and last but not least, Yvette graduated from Northwestern University and went on to the Dental School at University of Missouri in Kansas City. I am hoping I have not jumbled any of the facts but this was around 1990 and I was going to be 63 years old in September, so I talked it over with Betty and told her that during my residency days, I had decided that I would not work until I am too old to make straight incisions or when my hands become weak and shaky. Our children had all grown and finished their college education and all had gone on to post-graduate schools and careers except for Yvette who was still on her way. I, therefore, thought it was time to retire from surgery and try to find a position where I could serve God in a more concrete and substantial way.

And so it was! I decided to retire from Surgical Specialists Inc. on June 30, 1990 and go in search of an opportunity to serve the Lord, wherever it may be. It was very appropriate and poignant that one of the proficient, propitious, and productive surgical triumphs that had befallen me was the series of slick, swift and successful parathyroid adenoma exploration and excisions I did over the course of the last five years. How fitting it was that my last operation on June 30, 1990 was the last in this wonderful series of parathyroid adenoma excisions. As I took my gloves off that day, it was to bid a fond farewell to a career well spent and well blessed by God for the benefit of mankind. No regrets! Just a grateful heart!

XXVI

From Healing the Body to Healing the Soul

*"Therefore, my brothers, be all the more eager to make
your calling and election sure.
For if you do these things, you will never fall,
and you will receive a rich welcome into
the eternal kingdom of our Lord and Savior Jesus Christ.*
Peter 1:10-11 NIV[48]

I had never met Dr. Osborn before.

I recall it was a day in January in 1994, but I can't remember the date nor the time of day, though it could have been sometime in the afternoon. When you get to be my age, it is a tad hard to remember every detail.

Betty and I had arranged with D.L. to visit the Administrator, J.D., at Hope Medical Clinic in Macau. D.L. and I had studied in Midwestern Baptist Theological Seminary the year before. He had gone to Hong Kong on assignment and we made the arrangement to take the trip, when we visited Hong Kong. We left Hong Kong on the jetfoil and in 55 minutes arrived at the new jetfoil ferry terminal in Macau. It was quite a difference compared to the slow steamers in 1951.

After clearing immigration, seeing that it was lunchtime, we made our way to one of the ubiquitous noodle cum coffee shops in a storefront in the International Building close by the pier. As I looked at the area

---

48   *The NIV Study Bible.* Zondervan. Grand Rapids, MI. USA.1985

around the pier, seeing all the new construction — modern ferry pier, a second bridge, tall buildings, wide roads, flyovers and the jetfoils — I couldn't help but wonder; how things have changed!

Figure 14. Macau Ferry Terminal's interior 1994.

I'd only been to Macau once before and that was perhaps in 1951. I was still in medical school in Hong Kong and went to Macau on an overnight trip with the youth group of the Swatow Christian Church in Tsim Sha Tsui. The ferry ride took nearly four hours! I don't remember having to travel with a passport or other types of travel documents. I'm not even sure if we had to go through Immigration then.

Macau then was a far cry from the one in 1994. What a difference forty years made! Macau in the early fifties was more like a nineteenth century town than a twentieth century city. There may have been a few quaint single houses left in Macau in 1994, but one would have to travel to Coloane to see one. The bungalows and two-storied houses with their own gardens were long gone.

Figure 15. Pedicab in Macau circa 1951, still in use 2009

Figure 16. Pedicab and low buildings

Figure 17. Pre WWII house

Figure 18. Another view

But, I digress!

We ate our lunch of chicken noodles in broth and finished the meal with a cup of hot Ceylon tea with milk and sugar that the British colonials in Hong Kong used to enjoy during the halcyon days of the British Empire. The drink became a favorite of many, and I must admit that the "chefs" in these ubiquitous Chinese coffee shops have the art of brewing tea honed down to a T (no pun intended). We had a good lunch and besides it was — I won't say cheap— very economical.

It was time to head to the Hope Clinic for our appointment. We hailed a taxi — and to this day it is still a mystery to me why the driver did not know how to get us to the clinic but left us outside the Polytechnic University. We had to ask for directions and found out we were about two blocks away from the clinic — not a difficult walk and one that might have helped our digestion a bit — but still we felt slighted. We headed north on the street named Sidonio Pais and passed by Ye Long Hau Park, which has a little zoo and an aviary situated at the foot of Guia Hill. The hill is the site of one of the world's last remaining lighthouses with revolving mirrors. Macau's people are eager to make sure the lighthouse remains visible all around and to make certain, there is an ordinance limiting the height of surrounding buildings.

XXVII

HISTORIC MACAU

Figure 19. Guia Lighthouse viewed from the west

Figure 20. Guia Lighthouse and Chapel

Incidentally, this lighthouse has now been designated as a National Monument by the World Heritage and Antiquities Society. [49]

The name of this area of town, Ye Long Hau二龍喉, means twin faucets or "two dragon throats" if directly translated from the Chinese name. At the right side of the entrance gate are two water faucets made in the shape of two dragon heads with water flowing out of their throats, thus the name.

Because Macau has been a Portuguese colony for over four hundred years, the city has a number of surprising and quaint Chinese and

---

[49]   Guia Lighthouse is the oldest lighthouse on the coast of China. Construction of the lighthouse began in 1864 and was completed in 1865.

Originally, the light beam was lit by paraffin, operated through a wooden wheel and a rope to make the lantern rotate. The original designer, Carlos Vicente da Rocha, was a Macao-born Portuguese. In 1874, the lighthouse was damaged by a typhoon and stopped operating for over 30 years. After long repair works including the installation of mirror reflectors, the lighthouse went into operation again on 29th June 1910 and it has been in smooth operation ever since. *Macau Heritage net.* Home page.

Portuguese street names that result from some less-than-erudite translations and transliterations over the years. The city's name Macau is derived from the name of a Fujian goddess A-Ma, whom fishermen credited with having saved their lives from a storm that wrecked their ship. They originally named the rock overlooking the beach where they washed up "A-Ma" Gau or Bay of Ma.

Macau was very different in many ways from "British" Hong Kong. It was "settled" by Portuguese traders and adventurers in the 1550s with the tacit agreement of the Chinese government. These first newcomers were lone Portuguese men, though, perhaps, some may have brought along women with whom they had co-habited in other ports such as Malacca, Goa and Timor.

As time went on, some local Chinese women, through their employment or various marketplace contacts, became common-law "wives" of these Portuguese men, which over the years resulted in a Eurasian population now known as the Macanese. This distinct biracial group, while able to speak and understand both Portuguese and the local Chinese dialect known as Cantonese, also spoke their own special language know as "Patua."

Patua was descended from the late medieval Portuguese of the navigators, along with lexical and syntactical characteristics derived from local languages. [50]

---

[50] Brookshaw, David. *Visions of China Stories from Macau*. Gavea-Brown Publications, Hong Kong University press. Hong Kong. 2003. p.12..

XXVIII

HOPE MEDICAL CLINIC

We finally reached the clinic after a quarter of an hour walk and found that it occupied the first and second floors of a twelve story building.

Figure 21. Hope Medical Clinic

Perhaps because of Macau's proximity to Hong Kong or perhaps because Portugal is like the rest of Europe and the United Kingdom, the first floor in Macau would be called the second floor of a building in the United States.

I will not attempt to describe in detail what the interior of the clinic or the layout of the clinic was like, except to say that it was spacious and well-equipped.

As you entered the first floor, you came into a large waiting room with about twenty chairs, surrounding the medical records office. The clinic also housed a pharmacy, a clinical laboratory, a radiology unit and a physical therapy department besides a surgical theater and three examination rooms.

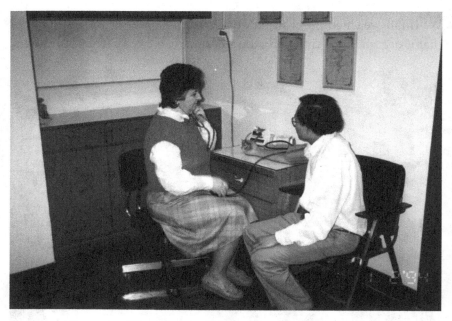

Figure 22. The administrator checking our friend's BP

On the upper floor, there was an accounting department along with classrooms and a conference room.

We met the Administrator and our friend introduced us and told her that I had applied to the Foreign Mission Board as a volunteer with the hope of filling the position left by her retirement.

I expressed my appreciation of this distinct privilege of meeting her and to have the advantage of seeing firsthand how the clinic should be managed. We had a very cordial and constructive interview, and I was happy to find out what the job entailed, and how the place functioned.

I wanted to ascertain whether I was qualified to assume the duties of the Administrator.

Figure 23. The administrator

We were taken on a tour of the facility and were introduced to all the members of the staff. I was surprised to learn that there were twenty two members of the ancillary staff. There was even a lone gentleman who served as the evangelist cum interpreter, both verbal and written, among the group.

He was also the preacher at one of the four Chinese Southern Baptist churches in Macau. Although all career missionaries learned to read, write, and speak Cantonese, volunteers who came to be short-term missionaries at the clinic would need the help of Mr. Lam Im Wah, the preacher/interpreter.

I was introduced to Dr. Osborn at the end of the tour. Dr. Darryl Osborn was a quiet, sedate man with a kind disposition.

He and his wife had served as a medical missionary and missionary worker in Africa for over twenty years, and were about to retire to Canada. Dr. Osborn had postponed his retirement for two years and volunteered to help at Hope Clinic, while Dr. Keith Morgan, the Medical Director and the lone medical doctor at the time, prepared to go on a scheduled year-long furlough.

When we were introduced, he said to me,

"You used to treat peoples' bodies. Now you are going to treat their souls."

Wow!

I had never thought that what I was about to embark on as my career could be summarized or phrased in quite such dramatic words, but they seemed to strike a responsive chord in my heart.

You see, we had been active members of the Mount Vernon Place Methodist Church in Baltimore, Maryland after our marriage there in 1956. All five of our children were baptized in the church over the years. We firmly believe that the family that prays together stays together.

Mount Vernon Place Methodist Church

The church is the second oldest Methodist church in the United States. It sits on the northeast corner of Mount Vernon Place, where the nation's first monument to honor George Washington stands.

Figure 24. Our wedding at Mount Vernon Place Methodist Church, Baltimore, Maryland

Figure 25 Mount Vernon Place Methodist Church. The chancel.

This historic place is just two blocks east of Maryland General Hospital, an affiliated hospital. The proximity made the church quite convenient and ideally situated for me to attend even when I did not yet own a car. I could easily walk to Mount Vernon Place from the doctors' quarters in the hospital. Then after we were married and living in our own apartment, we commuted every Sunday regardless of where we lived. Parking was never a problem because of the church's downtown location.

In 1957, when I was in the third year of my four-year surgical residency training program at the Maryland General Hospital in Baltimore Maryland, we had prayed to surrender our lives to Jesus because of my passionate desire to serve God as a missionary. I was looking ahead to how and where I would use my skills after I qualified as a General Surgeon over the next few years.

The revelation came to us as we were taking part in a missions study program on the lives of John and Charles Wesley. In particular, I was impressed with the story of John Wesley, who spent so much time on horseback preaching and evangelizing, yet found his spiritual life an enormous struggle, especially in terms of his salvation and the problem of sin. The story of his "heartwarming" experience at Aldersgate Church coupled with his knowledge of the Moravians' peace and joy during their stormy crossing of the Atlantic, allowed him to know that his salvation was by faith and not by works. When we were made aware of John Wesley's struggle and his "heartwarming" experience, it gave us an inner joy so remarkable that we too felt the "peace that passes all understanding."

Our prayer of dedication to our Lord Jesus in 1957 led us to make our application to the Mission Board. Our first attempt was not successful because the Board as a rule does not send missionaries on a mission to their place of birth.

We continued with our lives as before, but prayed that one day our hopes of serving the Lord in a mission field would come true.

God works in mysterious ways and in the end a new door was opened. In 1959, I was given the opportunity to assume the position as the Acting Senior Surgeon of the Alice Ho Miu Ling Nethersole Hospital in Hong Kong. But that's another story ... so let me go back to relate why we came to Macau in 1994.

XXIX

God Has a Plan for You

To man belong the plans of the heart,
But from the Lord comes the reply of the tongue.

All a man's ways seem innocent to him,
But motives are weighed by the Lord.

Commit to the Lord whatever you do,
And your plans will succeed.

In his heart a man plans his course,
But the Lord determines his steps.

Proverbs 16 1-3; 9. NIV[51]

We've all heard stories or have known of someone, personally or otherwise, who claim that they had planned everything that happened to them in their entire lives and that everything happened just the way they planned it. I once read about a man who said that when he was a child he knew exactly what he wanted to be when he grew up and boasted that he would make his first million dollars by age 25, that he would amass enough to retire by age 45, and that everything turned out the way he had planned.

I would always get a kick out of my congregation at Sha Lei Tau Baptist Church during my last ten years in Macau every time I brought up the subject of God's plans for His faithful. I would invariably begin by relating

---

51   *The NIV Study Bible.* Zondervan, Grand Rapids, MI, USA. 1985

that I had planned my life very early and meticulously, and that when I was a boy of eight, studying in La Salle College, that I had planned that one day I would be standing in front of them at this pulpit preaching to them.

How ridiculous and how audacious! Of course, I was only kidding.

I told you earlier that my desire to be a missionary did not turn out the way I had planned, but God had another plan for me which ultimately turned out to be better by far. When I completed my training, in Maryland, we returned to Hong Kong and took up the position offered me at the Nethersole Hospital which is part of the London Missionary Society's mission. I was the Senior Surgeon at the hospital over two different periods — the first two years were between 1959 and 1962 and the second time was between 1964 and 1968. I had returned to the United States in the interim to qualify as a Board certified surgeon of the American Board of Surgery. At the same time I also passed the Maryland State Board examination, which qualified me to practice in Maryland. I practiced in Baltimore for two years before returning to Nethersole Hospital.

It may sound prejudiced but I did consider that in the 1950s the level of medical knowledge and training was superior in the North American medical schools and hospitals.

It was especially true in the residency training programs initiated by Dr. William S. Halstead of the Johns Hopkins Medical School, which became the universal system adopted in the United States and Canada. The reason for the advantage was because the North American continent had not been devastated by World War II. That was not the case in the rest of the world.

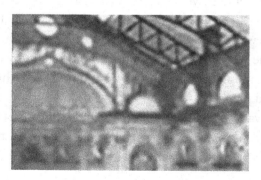

Figure 26. HKU Main Building with roof ransacked

Figure 27. HKU Main Building

As you can see from these pictures of the main building of the University of Hong Kong, the roof had been ransacked for fuel. We had to bring our own folding chairs to attend our lectures because the flooring of the Science Building had been pilfered for the same purpose.

The training I had in the United States was not purely theoretical to help a candidate to pass the examinations but was very substantially practical as well. Trainees did not automatically advance through the residency system; they were eliminated if they did not meet the standards. Furthermore, it was imperative that surgical trainees advanced to Chief Resident and held the position successfully for a year in order to complete and meet the requirements to sit for the Board examination.

I did feel encouraged and empowered when I was chosen over two other residents to assume the position of Chief Resident from 1957 to 1958. I finished my surgical residency and went on to do a residency in pathology for a year and a half before going on to Hong Kong.

You must understand that when I was going through medical school in the 1940s, Hong Kong was just recovering from 3 years and 8 months of deprivation from the war. Our teaching hospital, Queen Mary Hospital, was built in 1937. Because the hostilities started in 1941 and didn't end until 1945, equipment and supplies were far from adequate or up-to-date. Even a simple thing like a blood transfusion in 1952 was so primitive as to border on the realm of Ripley's Believe It or Not.

Would you believe that the tubing of the infusion set was made of rubber and had to be sterilized by boiling them in a sterilizer and reused? Imagine the difference then as I began my training in the United States, where we used disposable IV sets and needles!

Another advantage I experienced was being close to a world-renowned medical center like the Johns Hopkins Medical School and Hospitals and being able to learn of new advances as they happened. I remember the day in 1957 when I was operating on a healthy young man in his twenties repairing his hernia. Suddenly the anesthesiologist informed me that he could feel no pulse on the patient. In those days when a cardiac arrest occurred, the surgeon had to immediately perform a thoracotomy — that is to open the chest cavity — and massage the heart. The young man was successfully resuscitated and had no residual damage other than an extra incision in his chest.

I was pleased to learn later that Dr. Jude, a surgical resident at Hopkins, working with an engineer, Mr. Kouwenhouen successfully resuscitated patients in cardiac arrest by using external chest compression and assisted respiration or mouth-to-mouth respiration. [52] The most recent development in CPR is that the first responder should quickly perform thirty to forty rapid chest compressions to start the heart pumping and not too much about the respiration. Once the heart beats the breathing will come.

I returned to Nethersole Hospital in 1964. It did not surprise me that, because of medical politics, professional jealousies and economic competition, and despite my being a Board-certified surgeon and a Fellow of the American College of Surgeons, I was not considered a

[52]   *Wikipedia.* However, it was not until the middle of the 20th century that the wider medical community started to recognize and promote artificial respiration combined with chest compressions as a key part of resuscitation following cardiac arrest. The combination was first seen in a 1962 training video called "The Pulse of Life" created by James Jude, Guy Knickerbocker and Peter Safar. Jude and Knickerbocker, along with William Kouwenhouen had recently discovered the method of external chest compressions, whereas Safar had worked with James Elam to prove the effectiveness of artificial respiration. It was at Johns Hopkins University where the technique of **CPR** was originally developed. The first effort at testing the technique was performed on a dog. Soon afterwards, the technique was used to save the life of a child. [7] Their combined findings were presented at annual Maryland Medical Society meeting on September 16, 1960 in Ocean City, and gained rapid and widespread acceptance over the following decade, helped by the video and speaking tour they undertook. Peter Safar wrote the book *ABC of resuscitation* in 1957. In the U.S., it was first promoted as a technique for the public to learn in the 1970s.

Consultant specialist. This was because I was not a Fellow of a Royal College of Surgeons.

Therefore, I departed for Glasgow in January 1966. After being there for three weeks, I took and passed the Primary Fellowship. After that was done, I moved to London to prepare for the Final Fellowship examination in May. While in London, I got to know two doctors, one from Sydney, Dr. Victor Chang, and the other from Hong Kong, Dr. Leong Che Hung. Like me, they were candidates for the Fellowship.

Dr. Victor Chang later went to the Mayo Clinic before returning to Sydney and subsequently became a famous cardiac surgeon in Sydney.

It was an honor to entertain him when he came to Hong Kong for a visit; however, it was with great sorrow that we were later to learn of his demise at the hands of an assassin in Sydney.

Figure 28. Dr. Victor Chang at the right side of the picture
Dr. Leong Che Hung the other doctor became so well known
in Hong Kong that it would be redundant for me to attempt to
enumerate his honors. He is known in every street and every alley
and everyone in Hong Kong has heard of his name, or as the well
known phrase in Chinese says, "Gaai ji hohng mahn" 街知巷聞.

Figure 29. Dr. Leong Che Hung at left of picture

It may interest you to know that the most memorable and enjoyable memories I had of Victor and Che Hung were the times we took to have dinner together at Lee Ho Fook[53] 利口福 in Soho.

---

[53] I was told by my son that this restaurant is famous because of the song *Werewolves of London* by Warren Zevon:
I saw a werewolf with a Chinese menu in his hand
walkin through the streets of Soho in the rain.
He was lookin for the place called Lee Ho Fooks, gonna get a big dish of beef chow mein.

Chorus:
Aaahoo, werewolves of London
Aaahoo(2x)

Ya hear him howlin around your kitchen door, ya better not let him in.
Little old lady got mutilated late last night, werewolves of London again.
Chorus 2x

He's the hairy, hairy gent, who ran amok in Kent.
Lately he's been overheard in Mayfair.
You better stay away from him. He'll rip your lungs out Jim.
Huh, I'd like to meet his tailor.
Chorus 2x

Well, I saw Lon Chaney walkin with the queen, doing the werewolves of London.
I saw Lon Chaney Jr. walkin with the queen, doin the werewolves of London
I saw a werewolf drinkin a pina colada at Trader Vic's
And his hair was perfect.
ahhhooooo, werewolves of London
Draw blood

XXX

HIGHER DEGREES

In May of 1966, I passed the Fellowship in Edinburgh. While I was in London I got to know a Senior Registrar at St. George's Hospital who was from South Africa. He had already been a Fellow of the Royal College for a number of years, but he told me that he lacked one more degree before he could be a Consultant Surgeon and was hoping that he could go to the United States to get it.

I asked him,

"What degree are you talking about?" He answered,

"The BTA."

"What is that?" I was eager to know. He had a solemn look in his face as he said emphatically,

"Been To America."

I hope you see the irony of this whole game of one-upmanship. Obviously there was jealousy on both sides. But, as far as I was concerned, it was a great relief to me, once the ordeal was all over. I had obtained all the necessary qualifications on both sides of the Atlantic.

And that includes Hong Kong!

It was time to buckle down and fulfill my long-sought-after opportunity to be the full-fledged Chief Surgeon in a Christian/ missionary hospital. Dare I say that everything was working out the way I planned?

I must admit that there were many moments when I thought I had arrived and who could blame me for feeling smug at times? However, through it all, I can't help but feel that God had a lot to do with it. God has a plan for each of us if only we would seek to follow it. This reminds me of the ditty: Man proposes; but God disposes.

Lo and behold, just when everything seemed to fall into place—things began to unravel.

The year 1966 was a year that saw the world turning topsy-turvy, and before I could settle down to enjoy the fruits of my labor, riots in the streets were taking place all over the world. I had returned to Hong Kong in June and begun in earnest to assume my duties in my newly won position. Three of our older children were enjoying schooling at the Glenealy School while the youngest then was home and being spoiled by our domestic help. I was thoroughly enjoying my work and teaching the nursing students at the nursing school.

Life couldn't have treated us any better: We were very thankful and mindful of God's grace.

We worshipped at the English Methodist Church and made many friends there. We even have a picture of Stephen our son playing a part in the dedication of the new building at the church.

**Figure 30. Stephen laying a foundation stone at
English Methodist Church, Wanchai**

On December the 3rd Betty took our oldest daughter, Kay, and our son, Stephen, to Macau with my brother and sister-in-law. I stayed home with the two younger girls because I had to be on call. Betty told me later that when they got off the slow ferry at the pier, they couldn't get a taxi. A taxi driver at the pier told them that people were being killed in the city. They had to turn back at the ferry terminal and come back to Hong Kong because of the riots and the curfew that had been imposed.

The day became known as the "one, two, three" incident (3rd of December...12-3) and everyone in Macau remembers it as the day when Portuguese troops from Africa were forced to fire on the rioters, killing a number of them.

By 1967, there were riots in Hong Kong as well, but the most offensive aspect was that there were quite a number of bombs and booby traps that were laid indiscriminately all over the streets of Hong Kong. The demonstrators would display banners proclaiming "Down with Imperialism" and "Down with the American Imperialists."

The usual anti-British and anti-American slogans were painted on walls everywhere. Many innocent people were killed or maimed, but most tragically, dozens of the bomb disposal personnel of the Hong Kong Police and British military units lost their lives in the line of duty trying to defuse the devices. The situation was deteriorating by the day and after much prayer and agony, and for the sake of my family and the coming birth of our youngest daughter in October of that year, I thought it best to bring the family back to the United States.

I must have described the following incident which I encountered one afternoon perhaps in April or May. Our oldest daughter, Kay, was at the Rediffusion studios to perform in a program with her school. At the appointed time, I went down to Wanchai to pick her up.

As I walked near the studio, I was about to step up to the pavement when I saw in front of me a parked car and underneath the back of the car there was a gallon sized tin can with the lid on. I couldn't be sure whether there was a note attached to it but since "discretion is the better part of valor," I decided against getting any closer to investigate.

I was close to being terrified, but fortunately for us, it was not a bomb. We now know that this was part of their tactic — to plant many fake bombs to confuse and wear out the authorities.

Give me law-abiding citizens anytime … please.

Our youngest daughter, Yvette was born on October 17, 1967, and according to my wife, her birth was hastened and heralded by a loud bang from a bomb outside Nethersole Hospital. It was sometime during that year that I answered an advertisement in the Christian Medical Journal where a Christian surgeon was looking for a partner who was interested in sharing medical missions. As it turned out the surgeon wrote to say that he planned to visit Hong Kong, which he did. We agreed that we would try working together for a year and see how things developed.

Figure 31. How tranquil and blissful. Enjoying a meal
In May of 1968 we took our five children to Jefferson City, Missouri.

Figure 32. "Refugees" arriving in San Francisco May 1968

XXXI

God's Laws Endure—
Man's Laws Amendable

"Keep My decrees and laws,

for the man who obeys them will live by them.

I am the LORD"

Lev. 18:5.NIV[54]

Worship is honoring God. We honor the Lord by praising Him. But we also honor the Lord by keeping His decrees and laws, and choosing to live holy lives.[55]

While God's Laws are immutable, at times they change slowly and unnoticeably, but change they do. I can vouch for this personally, because man's laws have affected me at least twice quite significantly not because I had intentionally violated any law, but I had my livelihood substantially affected nonetheless.

One day in 1959, when we were living in Baltimore, I received a letter from the Federal Bureau of Investigation Field Office notifying me to appear before the officer on a certain date and time.

I arrived promptly at the appointed time and was ushered into a room with a desk and two chairs facing each other. An agent came in and introduced himself.

---

54   *The NIV Study Bible.* Zondervan. Grand Rapids, MI. USA. 1985
55   Larry Richards, *The 365 Day Devotional Commentary*, Includes Index. (Wheaton, Ill.: Victor Books, 1990), 82.

He said with a solemn face,

"I am agent so and so. Do you want to talk to me?"

Wondering to myself at the strange request but knowing what the correct answer should be, I very promptly blurted out,

"Yes, of course!" After all, I had nothing to hide and nothing to be afraid of because I had not done anything wrong.

He said that the records showed that I was employed at the Bethlehem Steel Company's Sparrow Point Plant hospital as an assistant plant physician, and at the same time I was also employed at the Medical Examiner's Office at the City Morgue as an assistant to the medical examiner and forensic pathologist.

"You were officially given a visa to work as a resident at Women's Hospital. "Is that correct?" he asked me, as he lifted his head and looked at me with a serious look on his face. I replied,

"Yes." The Agent then said that his records showed that I entered the United States as an Exchange Visitor in 1953, and my status had not changed. That meant I could be only a resident in pathology at the Women's Hospital and could work nowhere else. Then he posed the most telling question, almost with a stoic expression. He softly said,

"Would you be willing to give up the other two jobs?" Do you have any doubts as to what my answer was at that particular moment? With a very emphatic tone of voice, but with an almost suppliant and gentle voice, I replied,

"Of course I will."

Upon hearing my reply, he slowly closed his file and left the room. I heaved a sigh of relief, but all at once, there was a sense of panic in my heart. I had to give up two jobs paying $1,000.00 each. For a resident doctor in a hospital, the stipend during the fifties was $200.00 a month, with an allowance of $50.00 for being married. I was trying to raise enough to get to Hong Kong!

XXXII

GOD WILL TAKE CARE OF YOU

But godliness with contentment is great gain.
For we brought nothing into the world,
and we can take nothing out of it.
But if we have food and clothing, we will be content with that.

People who want to get rich fall into temptation
And a trap and into many foolish and harmful desires that
plunge men into ruin and destruction.
For the love of money is a root of all kinds of evil.
Some people, eager for money, have wandered from the faith
and pierced themselves with many griefs.

1 Timothy 6:6-10. NIV[56]

I was in a slight dilemma, the proverbial situation of being between a rock and a hard place – you may hate the cliché but it fit. I could have applied to get my status changed to become a permanent resident, obtaining the so-called Green Card and applying to become a naturalized citizen of the United States. The solitary conundrum at that time was that the law was clear that someone who became a naturalized citizen would lose his citizenship if he returned to his country of birth and resided there beyond three years continuously.

If I were to become naturalized, I could run the risk of losing my citizenship by working at Nethersole Hospital in Hong Kong since I would not be able to enter the United States every year to register with

---

[56]   *The NIV Study Bible.* Zondervan. Grand Rapids, MI. USA. 1985.

the Immigration Service. I therefore took the only honorable and "legal" way out for me and did not apply to become a "Green Card" holder because people in that category were required to report every year in the United States to keep their status current. Imagine my chagrin when one day, after having been back in Hong Kong for some time, I read in the newspaper about a change in United States immigration law. A German woman, a naturalized US citizen, had had her citizenship revoked for staying in her home country, Germany, for more than three years. She sued the Immigration and Naturalization Service and won her citizenship back and the law was changed.

I bring up this story to shed light on what took place after we arrived in Missouri in the 1968. I must have related this episode elsewhere in the book but I'll do it again. Missouri was among a number of states in the United States that still had a law that stipulated that to qualify for a license to practice medicine in the state, physicians had to be citizens of the United States. When we came to Jefferson City, I had a sense of déjà vu, recalling what had happened to me in Baltimore in 1958.

More troubling and irritating in this instance, however, was that I was already licensed to practice in Maryland — besides being a Board certified surgeon and specialist. My hands were tied, and I was forced to take work as a physician and surgeon in the hospital at the Missouri State Penitentiary.

Should I say that I was held "captive" as a law-abiding person among a jailhouse full of law-breakers, every one of whom claimed they were innocent or were scapegoats being punished for the wrong crime?

Meanwhile, my wife became active with the Women's Auxiliary of the Cole County Medical Association and the Missouri State Medical Association. Coincidentally, Mr. John Danforth was entering the political arena and running for attorney general of Missouri. The Auxiliary was assisting with his campaign. His slogan then was "I dare you." Betty got to know him and sent him a clipping from the newspaper of his campaign with his slogan and asked if he would "dare" do something to amend the law that limited the issuance of medical licenses to citizens only. She pointed out that there were countless numbers of resident alien physicians in Missouri caught in limbo because of this law. At the same time, other physicians in Jefferson City who knew about my situation also approached Mr. John Danforth to reverse the law. To his credit, Mr. Danforth took action and the law was changed.

The day the law was changed I went down to the Board of Healing Arts in Jefferson City, filled out my application, paid $10.00, and came away with my medical license. The previous day, I had been an unlicensed doctor and the next moment after paying the fee, I became a licensed physician and a qualified specialist in surgery.

Oh, the vagaries of the laws of human!

Could this be the root cause of why human beings often play fast and loose with the Law of God? Would this then be the reason why they spend immeasurable time and effort to also look for loopholes to circumvent the law? The talk of the town was that within days, over a hundred physicians if not more, applied for licensure throughout Missouri — so many that the Board ran out of application forms.

Much to my chagrin, my surgical partnership did not prove to meet the goal we had hoped for. I went through a period of soul-searching and even counseled with Monsignor Kaiser of the Roman Catholic Diocese in Jefferson City, on the ethical aspects of dissolving our partnership and, attorney, Mr. Robert Hawkins with respect to the legality of such a move. Since our agreement of partnership did not have any proviso that I could not practice in the same town should it break up, the main issue was whether I had enough support from the local physicians for referrals and such. Therefore, after conferring with a number of friendly physicians with whom we had become acquainted and having obtained their verbal assurance and vote of confidence, I decided to establish my private practice in Jefferson City.

XXXIII

You're A Doctor?—You Must Be Rich!

When you have eaten and are satisfied,
praise the LORD, your God
for the good land he has given you.
Be careful that you do not forget the LORD, your God,
failing to observe his commands, his laws
and his decrees that I am giving you this day.
Otherwise, when you eat and are satisfied,
when you build fine houses and settle down,
and when your herds and flocks grow large
and your silver and gold increase and all you have is multiplied,
then your heart will become proud
and you will forget the LORD, your God,
Deuteronomy 8:10-14. NIV[57]

Jesus answered, "It is written:
'Man does not live on bread alone,
but on every word that comes from the mouth of God.'"
Matthew 4:4. NIV[58]

I remember very vividly one morning in 1964 or 1965 the conversation I had with my mother in their little cottage in Shek-O Beach. I had returned to work at the Nethersole not too long before.

---

[57]   *The NIV Study Bible.* Zondervan. Grand Rapids, MI. USA. 1985
[58]   Ibid.

She wondered why I didn't start my own practice rather than work in a missionary hospital. She said to me,

"Look at your classmates! They're all in private practice and they all have a big house and nice cars...and of course, lots of money!" I answered her as gently as possible, making sure I wouldn't hurt her feelings nor disappoint her secret longing that I would become a "famous rich doctor." I said,

"It was never my ambition to be subservient to filthy lucre, in other words, becoming a millionaire was never a goal for me. I just want to be able to help people."

I related to her how one day I was urged by the Spirit of God to heed the warning sign that was given to me, which upon reminiscing, convinced me that it was a turning point in my life. The event happened one morning in surgery during the first year of my residency. On that particular morning, I was scrubbed in as a second assistant and one of my duties was to cut the sutures after the knots were tied. As I was doing that the attending surgeon turned to me and asked if I was nervous. I said, "No," but asked why he asked that question. To which he replied that my hand was shaking when I was cutting the suture. That was a wake-up call that caused me to seriously think about my future.

I did not realize I had a problem with my addiction to drinking. I did drink a lot during my days at the university but usually when I was at a party. I don't recall drinking on an ordinary day.

As I gave it more thought things changed when I came to Akron, Ohio.

Up until I arrived in Akron I had not known what a Dry State was but I soon learned. Dry States control the sale and consumption of liquor and spirits — you can only purchase them at what are known as package stores — which are specially licensed to sell alcoholic beverages. They would put your purchase inside a brown paper sack and hence the package store. Besides this, restaurants and eating establishments were not licensed to sell beer or liquor by the drink — which then led to the establishment of dinner clubs — considered private clubs with permits to sell liquor by the drink when you have a meal there. I soon became card holding members of four such dinner clubs. By the time I was about to leave Akron for Baltimore it was not unusual that I would have as many as four cocktails before the meal and sometimes would have after dinner drinks before heading back to the doctors' quarters. At other times I and two other drinking buddy doctors would purchase dozens of bottles of beer and drink them all before the TV before slumping down in bed when all was consumed.

That fateful morning in Maryland General Hospital after the attending Surgeon asked if I was nervous and when I said I was not nervous, he reminded me that my hands were very shaky when I cut that suture.

I started thinking and put two and two together. I had been drinking the night before, had very little sleep…could I be suffering from the DT's? It was time for me to make an evaluation of what I was to do with my life!

I reminded myself that I was just at the beginning of my preparation for my future role as a surgeon. If I had any intention of becoming a successful surgeon I needed to make a smart choice. This is especially true if my burden was to help the people who are less fortunate than the average. I had to stop drinking. As a Christian, I felt the urging of the Holy Spirit and I determined there and then that I should quit. And quit I did — and I had not touched a drop from that day on.

XXXIV

Surgical Specialists Inc.

Trust in the LORD with all your heart
and lean not on your own understanding;
In all your ways acknowledge him,
and he will make your paths straight.
Do not be wise in your own eye;
fear the LORD and shun evil.
This will bring health to your body
and nourishment to your bones.
Honor the LORD with your wealth,
with the first fruits of all your crops;
then your barns will be filled to overflowing,
and your vats will brim over with new wine.

Proverbs 3:5-10 NIV[59]

I commenced my surgical practice on January 3, 1972 at 915 Leslie
Boulevard in Jefferson City, Missouri.

Starting a private practice is like a venture into the unknown. My
previous practice in Baltimore was different in that I was employed in an
established Industrial Medical Center similar to a group practice which
was quite well established. In a solo practice the surgeon has to meet a
number of obligations in order to have a modicum of success.

The first obligation is to God. I am a born-again Christian and
firmly believe that Jesus is God's Son, the Incarnate Savior, who was

---

[59]   *The NIV Study Bible.* Zondervan. Grand Rapids, MI. USA. 1985

born of the Virgin Mary and lived among us. He obediently went to the Cross to die for all sinners and those who repent of their sins and acknowledge Jesus as their personal Savior will have eternal live. For this reason, I value my relationship to Jesus and I strive to read the Bible every morning and pray for guidance each morning before I start my daily work.

The second is to my integrity. I endeavor to keep a keen mind and a healthy body. I try to ensure that I continue to educate myself and keep abreast of new developments in the field of medicine and surgery. This leads to my third obligation.

The third obligation is to my patients. It is imperative that I do no harm and remain cognizant of the fact that some cures may be worse than the disease and not be blinded by the lure of my greed for financial gain at the expense of the patient's well-being.

The fourth obligation is to the patient's family. The family is obviously concerned intimately with the patient because they care for the patient's welfare and would suffer if something untoward happens to the patient. They need to be informed of the progress and prognosis of the condition of the patient.

The fifth obligation is to the referring doctor if that is the case. Most of my referring doctors are family physicians and they have a very close relationship with their patients. It is imperative that the referring doctor be the first one to know of the outcome of the surgery!

God was good to me. I had no anxiety with respect to how I would fare in practice. On the contrary, I sensed God's love and care every day.

Surely I am with you always. (Matthew 28:20)

Never look ahead to the changes and challenges of this life in fear. Instead, as they arise look at them with the full assurance that God, whose you are, will deliver you out of them. Hasn't He kept you safe up to now? ...

Do not look ahead to what *may* happen tomorrow. The same everlasting Father who cares for you today will take care of you tomorrow and every day.... Be at peace, then, and set aside all anxious thoughts and worries. *Francis de Sales.*

The Lord is my shepherd. Psalm 23:1

Not *was*, not *may be*, not *will be.* "The Lord is my shepherd." He is on Sunday, on Monday, and through every day of the week. He is in January, in December, and every month of the year. He is when I'm at home and in China. He is during peace or war, and in times of abundance or poverty. *J. Hudson Taylor.* [60]

Medical practice has changed considerably since the government instituted Medicare and Medicaid in 1966. Besides these federal programs there are quite a number of insurance programs for organizations and individuals to subscribe to. Unfortunately there are a sizable number of people who are still uninsured. At the same time, perhaps related to the multiplication of insurance coverage, medical malpractice suits began to see an exponential rise.

It, therefore, became a necessary evil for physicians to be protected from heavy financial losses which resulted from lawsuits, some of which often filed without any merit. What this has done is to increase the malpractice insurance premiums which forced physicians to increase their fees and, as an added precaution, more tests and sometimes unnecessary ancillary procedures in hopes of preventing being sued. Personally, I feel this has the effect of destroying the traditionally important friendly patient-physician relationship. On the contrary, it has led to some very unpleasant adversarial situations, such as finding yourself face-to-face with your patient in the law courts. Gone are the days when a family doctor would sit with the family by the bedside of a morbidly ill person, deep in prayer for the Almighty to place a healing a hand and heal!

As an aside, I had to incorporate my practice so that it would place my practice under a limited liability and protect me from going

---

[60] L.B. Cowman, *Streams in the desert, an updated edition in today's language.* Ed. James Reiman. Zondervan. Grand Rapids, MI. USA. 1992. p.66.

bankrupt should a law suit against me be successful. At the start of my practice in 1972 the insurance premium was US$5,000.00 per annum. After 18 years, the year before I retired, the premium had catapulted to US$25,000.00 for my partner and me.

During the 18 years, I had four suits filed against me, three of which were without merit and were withdrawn by the plaintiffs before they went to trial. The fourth case went to trial but after both sides presented their briefs, the Judge very quickly declared that the plaintiff never proved his/her case. The suit was quashed.

Were I to discount the malpractice suits against me, the 18 years of practice in Jefferson City, could be considered very productive years. First and foremost, we were blessed with a happy and close family life coupled with all of us being actively involved with our church. In spite of the fact that I was on-call 24/7, I thank God that I was still able to sing in the chancel choir every Sunday with very few absences.

Looking back, we made many friends and Betty was active in the Auxiliary and in 1982 she started the Alpha & Omega Christian Bookstore. It was well received and the bookstore was a beacon of light and was a benefit to many not just in Jefferson City but many surrounding towns.

She was able to witness to many people in all walks of life and many were blessed by the Gospel and became born again Christians. To God be the glory!

Our children all graduated from the public schools and all five of them desired to pursue their higher education out of town and some out of state. We thank God that all went beyond their college education and completed graduate training and obtained higher degrees. We praise God for their successes. They are all married and some have grandchildren which makes the old man very happy.

An amusing episode happened one day when after the four older kids, except the youngest daughter who was in dental school, were all through with their education. We were all at home and I mentioned to them that one of the things I desired most to own ever since my youth was a Bentley. They all replied,

"Why didn't you get one?" I replied,

"Actually, I already have five!"

In 1988, I felt compelled to evaluate my situation and to see whether it was time to make some alterations to my work and my life. I was 60 years old. Though my faculties and extremities were sound, I couldn't help but remember what I noticed quite starkly back in 1958.

When I was going through my residency, one fact stood out prominently and that was some of the attending surgeons were quite advanced in years. A number of them had unsteady hands and I've personally seen some of them stopping off at the bar across the street from the hospital to get a drink to "calm" their nerves before coming to do the surgery. In fact, we were reminded quite early on to be alert when assisting them to "take over" early to avoid mistakes and mishaps. I had vowed then that I would not continue to perform operations but retire before I reached that state.

I realized that my children were pretty much independent and would not need my financial support quite as much as before they started their careers and their own married lives. I consulted with my wife and intimated that I would like to retire early and find some volunteer or missionary work.

I decided that I would cease my surgical practice on June 30th, 1990.

It was a good feeling to know that my "retirement" from surgery was not forced or foisted on me. I ceased my practice of my own free will and I was not indebted to anything or anyone. I received the usual going away citations and accolades from St. Mary's Hospital and Memorial Hospital. Many doctors and nurses and hospital personnel all wished me well. But to top it all it was quite heartening to have so many of my patients express their regrets to not have me care for them anymore.

But, perhaps, the best compliment paid me was when I received a plaque from Bev Cearlock, my secretary. She came under my employ right after she graduated from Secretarial school in St. Louis and mine was the first job she had. She stayed with me all these eighteen years and we had a near-perfect employer-employee relationship. (I'm going on the understanding there is nothing 100% perfect in this world). But, as my accountant, Jim Weber said to me one day, "you are very fortunate to have such an honest and loyal employee in Bev. She will turn the office upside down to find it, if she should find she was a penny short at the end of a day." I shall miss her.

To me, that was just one more indication that God had His hand on me all along. I need to remember to be obedient to Him and stay in His Will and all will be well.

Figure 34. Bev's farewell plaque

The inscription is as follows:

> #1 BOSS FOR ME
> Dr. Siu has always been #1 boss for me.
> Eighteen years I've worked for him &
> Eighteen years I've been blessed with his
> Kindness, Generosity, Thoughtfulness &
> Concern.
> Never will there be another #1 Boss for me.
>
> I LOVE YOU!
> *BEV*

XXXV

THE GREAT COMMISSION

Then Jesus came to them and said,
"All authority in heaven and on earth has been given to me.
Therefore go and make disciples of all nations,
Baptizing them
In the name of the Father and of the Son and of the Holy Spirit,
and teaching them to obey everything I have commanded you.
And surely I am with you always
To the very end of the age."
Matthew 28:18-20. NIV.[61]

On November 9, 1990, a Saturday, a fine shiny warm day, Betty and I took time to play a round of golf. We were feeling fine. (Around the time I was planning on quitting my practice, I had a complete health check-up with my good friend and personal physician, Dr. Robert Bregant. Thank God everything was AOK.) We thought we would walk and pull our own carts.

We really enjoyed the day and eventually reached the fairway to the ninth hole and we pitched our golf balls onto the ninth green. Betty had a good shot and was on the green; however, my ball went into a depression on the right side of the green. We arrived at the green and Betty went on and putted her ball into the cup.

When I got to my ball, I began to feel a sickening feeling in my stomach. I felt a little dizzy. I went on my hands and knees to see if the feeling would go away. I stayed down for a while and as Betty picked her

---

61   *The NIV Study bible.* Zondervan. Grand Rapids, MI. USA. 1985.

ball up she turned in my direction but could not see me because I was down on my knees in the depression. She called, "Kenneth! Kenneth!"

She came over and found me still on my hands and knees and asked, "What's the matter?" She said later that I looked ashen and I was sweating on my forehead, which she said was something she seldom saw me exhibit even under very hot weather. She helped me stand up and she got a golf cart and took us back to the club house. I thought I was hungry and asked for some crackers but that didn't help.

Betty decided then that I needed to be checked in the hospital. She had the club manager call an ambulance while she got busy and called cardiologist Dr. Jeff Sanders, Memorial Hospital emergency room and all our children. When the ambulance crew arrived, I was feeling better and reluctant to be bothered with going to the hospital. However, Betty was determined that I needed to be checked and was about to drive me to the hospital herself if the ambulance would not.

Understandably, ambulance personnel would not be able to take anyone to the hospital should the patient refuse to be taken. Finally after an EKG was taken I was assured that something was amiss and so off to the Memorial Hospital we went.

Dr. Jeff Sanders was there at the emergency room when we arrived. I was given medication and taken to the OR for an angiogram. It showed that I had a saddle embolus straddling the branches of the Anterior Descending Coronary artery. Jeff showed me that it would not be feasible to do a balloon angioplasty because of the danger of causing the clot to break off and block the other branch of the artery. He, therefore, arranged for my transfer to University of Missouri Medical Center the next day and scheduled with Dr. Jack Curtis, the cardiac surgeon to do a by-pass surgery for me Monday morning at 7.30 a.m. I was admitted to the Intensive Care Unit and given anticoagulants and waiting to be transferred by helicopter the next day. I still can't get over the fact that I had no premonition that I would have a heart attack. I've never had any chest pain or chest discomfort and at this point even after the angiogram I still did not have any pain or discomfort.

Sunday, November 11th, I was wheeled onto the helicopter and met the nurse. She showed me a newly-designed "barf" bag that would not spill no matter how rough the flight. I was impressed but did not know what to expect. But the moment we got aloft, quite uncontrollably, I made use of the bag that I held in my hand very promptly. I didn't have too much time to marvel at the ingenious invention when within another five or ten minutes, I had to use it again. Incidentally, since that fateful Sunday, I have an aversion to flying in a helicopter. (Years later, when we were having our class reunion in New Zealand, at Mount Cook, when everyone took the helicopter ride to get on the glazier, I had to decline the opportunity.)

The Surgeon on the Receiving End

On November 12, 1990, I had my four vessel CABG (Coronary Artery Bypass Graft) done.

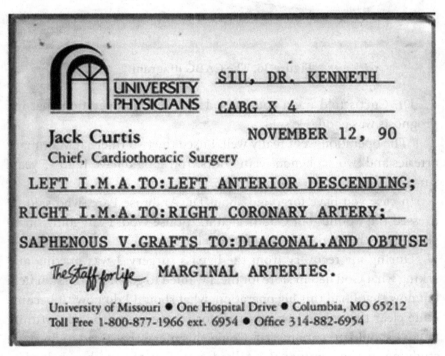

Figure 35. My CABG card

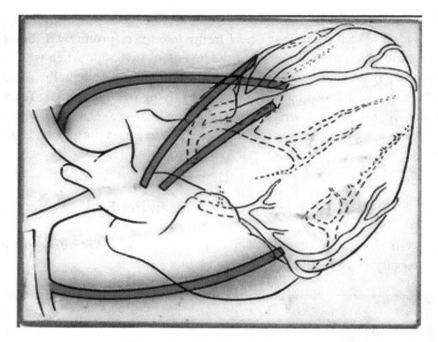

Figure 36. The CABG diagram

Dr. Curtis told me a couple of days after the operation that my prognosis was good. He said,

"The operation went really well. I used the two Internal Mammary arteries and two Saphenous vein grafts. You should have 12 to 15 years survival."

In case you have forgotten about Dr. Ambrose Pare, who said, "I dressed the wound, but God healed it." Praise God, I am going on 19 years since the by-pass surgery!!! Hallelujah!!

During my recovery from the bypass surgery, I was praying and asking what God had in store for me. I wanted to go on the mission field but now that I had this big operation, what should I do now? It became quite clear that while I was waiting for recovery and the opportunity to go, I should prepare myself. Could this mean that I had to do some studying at the seminary? I talked to a few of my church leaders from First Baptist Church in Jefferson City, Missouri and Dr. Hulitt Gloer, Professor of New Testament at Midwestern Baptist Theological Seminary, Kansas City, Missouri who was at the time Interim Pastor at First Baptist Church. We had transferred our membership to First Baptist in 1986. They all encouraged me to enroll at the seminary then apply to be a missionary with the Foreign Mission Board of the Southern Baptist Convention.

I enrolled at Midwestern in 1991 and graduated in 1994. I was licensed to preach then ordained a pastor in 1992 and was associate Pastor at Oakwood Baptist Church in Lee's Summit, Missouri from 1992 -1994.

XXXVI

Macau Baptist Mission

But you will receive power
when the Holy Spirit
comes on you;
and you will be my witnesses
in Jerusalem,
and in all Judea and Samaria,
and to the ends of the earth.

Acts 1:8. NIV[62]

In 1994 I was accepted as a volunteer missionary to Macau with the International Service Corp of the Foreign Mission Board, Southern Baptist Convention.

We arrived in Macau on August 10th, 1994 and resided at the Macau Baptist Mission on 12, Calcada do Monte, Macau. I was the Medical Ministries Administrator for the Hope Medical Clinic and after two years of sound economical principles and financial accountability, we were able finally to turn the clinic's financial condition in the black. I was asked to serve an extra two years, which was unprecedented. Once again I must admit that it was God's hand that made everything possible.

The situation of medical practice in Macau is quite foreign to me but since I was not there to practice medicine, I am in no position to comment too much on it. One thing that I found out was when the clinic doctor wanted to do more in the care of patients with tuberculosis; I

---

[62]   *The NIV Study Bible.* Zondervan. Grand Rapids, MI. USA. 1985.

found out that the government opined that they were in a better position to care for these patients.

Macau has two hospitals and when we first arrived in 1994, the scuttlebutt among the local population was that they were not too much in favor of them. The vernacular was that one hospital would "rob" you of your money and the other would be harmful to your health. Over the years, the situation had improved quite noticeably with both hospitals being upgraded with new facilities and better medical staff, many of the physicians having been recruited from Shanghai medical schools. However, one noticeable deficiency was that the hospitals did not have enough openings for the local Macau medical graduates from Jinan University in Guangzhou to obtain their training before their licensure.

Figure 37. Kiangwu Hospital and bust of Dr. Sun Yat Sen

Figure 38. Kiangwu Hospital New Wing

Figure 39. Government Hospital

Figure 40. Government Hospital

Recently, Hope Medical Clinic had started teaching and training a number of these graduates so that they would go on and qualify in the examination to obtain their licenses. Dr. Morgan deserves much credit for his efforts to make this training program a success. God had been doing great things in the clinic and has continued to do so.

During the four years with the Mission, one of the most pleasant ministries that came my way was the opportunity to help pastoring the English-speaking congregation at the Ye Long Hau Baptist Church. Dr. Osborn was in charge of the ministry when we arrived in Macau. I praise God that I have been able to participate in the ministry. Eventually by 1996, I was invited by the deacons at the Sha Lei Tau Baptist Church, one of the four Chinese-speaking churches started by the mission over the last ninety-some years, to assist them with their preaching ministry. They had two other pastors taking turns shouldering their preaching and I was happy to be able to help once a month. One particularly happy coincidence was that one of the pastors, Pastor To, who encouraged me to help later told me that he was a classmate of my brother at Kwong Wah Primary in Kowloon. I was also very familiar with his father in Hong Kong during WWII. What a blessing!

Who would have thought that what started out as a stop-gap situation in 1996 would in 1998 turn into a ten-year contract to head this church? At the time, Pastor To had passed away, and the other pastor, Pastor Lau, had left for the States. The church turned to me with their contract offer, just when my term with the Mission ended that July. Who says that God does not have a plan?

XXXVII

Sha Lei Tau Baptist Church

Preach the Word;
be prepared in season and out of season;
correct, rebuke and encourage –
with great patience and careful instruction.

2 Timothy 4:2. NIV.[63]

In August 1998, my service as a missionary with the Macau Baptist Mission came to an end. Sha Lei Tau Baptist Church just signed a contract with me to serve as their pastor for ten years. I told the deacons that in another month I would be seventy years old. I told them I would be happy and honored to sign the contract but I could not give them a guarantee that I would fulfill it.

The years from 1998 -2008 proved to be the most memorable years of my life, not the least of which was that it was also the most rewarding to my soul. How blessed it is to look back over these past ten years and be able to thank God for playing a part in helping well over a hundred persons to gain their eternal life, and when the end of the world comes, not to have to burn and suffer in Hell where the fire is never quenched!

---

[63] *The NIV Study Bible.* Zondervan. Grand rapids, MI. USA. 1985.

Figure 41. After receiving D. Min. degree at Gordon-Conwell Theological Seminary, Boston. 2005

Figure 42. Some of the youth at the last sermon June 30, 2008

Figure 43. Goodbye. Ms Deng, oldest (93 yrs) member

Here endeth the most memorable years of my life. We left Macau in July of 2008 after fulfilling my 10 years contract with Sha Lei Tau Baptist Church and arrived in Mountain View, Missouri where we bought a three bedroom house for our "retirement years." It is in the Ozarks mountain area and the town has less than 2500 people. Imagine moving from the world's densest populated area that is Macau to an area where the deer population may be higher than humans. You will understand what I mean when I say it is a quiet and sleepy town. Everyone knows who you are and on the whole everyone is very congenial. It wasn't easy, but once you get used to the quiet and hard to detect hustle and bustle of city life, it has its intrinsic charm. In full faith that my retirement was to be the last chapter of my life, I wrote the following Postlude to give the book a beginning, middle and end. However, while I am willing to spend my retirement serving God quietly, I am always ready and willing to answer, "Here I am, Lord!" whenever I hear God's call, "Go!"

XXXVIII

Postlude

No one knows about that day
or hour
not even the angels in heaven,
nor the Son,
but only the father.

Matthew 24:36. NIV.[64]

His master replied, 'Well done,
Good and faithful servant!
You have been faithful with a few things;
I will put you in charge of many things.
Come and share your master's happiness!'

Matthew 25:21. NIV.[65]

I am sure some of you, my classmates of half a century ago, remember when we were celebrating our fiftieth class reunion, having dinner at the Country Club in Singapore, when I had the opportunity to say a few words to you. I reminded you that you all knew what kind of a wretch I was when we were in medical school. I told you that through God's amazing grace I was saved and that you could, too, before it was too late. I heard one of you make a quip that you did not want to go yet because it was too soon and you were not in a hurry. However, let me remind you once more, "Be ready!"

---

[64] *The NIV Study Bible.* Zondervan. Grand Rapids, MI. USA. 1985.
[65] Ibid.

Figure 44. 50th reunion dinner. Hong Kong

Figure 45. 50th reunion dinner, Singapore

In case you are still hesitating and want to balk at the walk, let me tell you how simple it is to learn to talk the talk and walk the walk:

The Apostle Peter said, *"Salvation is found in no one else, there is no other name under heaven given to men by which we must be saved."*

(Acts 4:12)[66] Peter is, of course talking about Jesus. You just need to acknowledge that you are a sinner and repent of your sins, then claim Jesus to be your Savior; as Paul said, *"That if you confess with your mouth, "Jesus is Lord," and believe in your heart that God raised him from the dead, you will be saved. For it is with your heart that you believe and are justified, and it is with our mouth that you confess and are saved."* (Roman 10:9-10)[67]

No, this is not the end of the story. God has been good to me. He did call and I did go! He has given me yet another eventful year which I'll recount in the next chapter.

[66]   *The NIV Study Bible.* .Zondervan. Grand Rapids, MI. USA. 1985.
[67]   Ibid.

XXXIX

Sha Lei Tau Revisited

Sometime in 2010, I was making an evaluation of my life. I heard from various sources that quite a number of Christians were not attending the worship services at Sha Lei Tau Baptist Church and these included both the Chinese and the Filipino members. The church had not been able to find a pastor and was not likely to find one any time soon. In Howell County where we are living now there may be five or six churches that are not able to find a pastor. In the past two years I've had the honor of being supply pastor to five churches and besides, First Baptist Church in Mountain View can always use my help as a Sunday School Teacher. This year was a surprise too in that I had enough students to require two classes in the Fall semester. Finally, God was gracious and allowed the Lost Camp Baptist Church to call me as their Interim Pastor from October through December 2010. However, the most important outcome of my evaluation and prayers was that I was able to work it out with Sha Lei Tau Baptist Church to let me come to Macau and serve as their Pastor for a year in 2011. I also assured Larry Price the Director at the Southwest Baptist University Mountain View Campus that I was prepared to return and resume teaching for the Spring semester in 2012 if and when he can enroll enough students to form a class.

Signs and wonders happen when we respond to God's call and are willing to be in mission and ministry for His Kingdom. When we talked about coming back to Macau one of the concerns was obtaining of a visa and a work permit. When the church applied for permit the thought was that it might take at least six months, but as it turned out it took but two months. It turned out that the person responsible for issuing the permits came across my application and recognized who I was. He, Wallace, had married Heidi, who was a classmate and roommate of Levina Change Lam, who is a member of Sha Lei Tau, and I had baptized Levina's husband, Wilson years ago. Furthermore, when we got to Macau and were about to go to the Immigration Department to get our permit to stay, Ms. Tam, our Deacon and School Principal found out that the officer-in-charge was a student of hers at Sha Lei Tau School. We were treated like VIPs and got our permit to stay with the greatest of ease in our fifteen years of past experiences. It is important to have friends in high places.

Gradually, the friendly faces came back as the weeks went by and the empty seats were being filled up. We like to say that numbers don't really mean anything but for a rough measurement it was gratifying to see that while in the first couple of months we were back, we had roughly around twenty people worshiping on Sunday and Praise the Lord that lately we could count as many as forty enthusiastic souls singing their hearts out and giving God the Glory due Him.

Our experiences returning to Macau are recounted in my newsletters to the First Baptist Church in Mountain View in Missouri.

On January 20, 2011 at 11.11 a.m., I wrote:

Betty and Kenneth Siu send their warmest greetings from Macau, in the Name of the Lord!!!

It was exactly two weeks ago that we arrived safely at Macau International Airport after a thirty-odd-hour flight from St. Louis Missouri with stopovers at San Francisco and Taipei. We thank God that we were able to sleep during the twelve-hour flight across the Pacific Ocean, which helped tremendously in our getting over our jet-lag.

The weather in Macau was COLD and WINDY when we stepped out of the airport. Fortunately it was sunny, which made a difference. We were met by a small and smiling contingent from Sha Lei Tau Baptist Church, made up of Mr. Hoi, Ms Tam, Ms Ip, Tony Fong and Yvonne Wong. Somehow, before we landed, I had a premonition that when we got into the Arrival Area, we would also be "surprised "by my sister Patsy and her husband Jeffrey and, sure enough, there they were, emerging from behind the other greeters to surprise us. That was a lovely gesture on their part and we really appreciated their thoughtfulness. They even treated us to a lovely lunch at the China Hotel across the street from the airport.

Tony brought us to our apartment in his car and Mr Hoi came with our luggage in a taxi. The Church had rented a nice apartment in a new building which is just behind the church. It has three bedrooms and all the rooms have a great view of the river and the part of Zhuhai in China just to the west and north of this northwestern part of Macau. However, one drawback is that when the north wind blows, it comes right through the plate glass picture windows in every room. Brrr! It's cold. The temperature was a high of 7 degrees Celsius. We noticed right away that we did not have any heat, heaters or warm quilts and blankets. So, off to the department store we went. For the next 4 or 5 days, we plied the stores and streets and gathered all the heaters, blankets, sweaters et al that we could get our hands on...and bundled up!!! We have finally struck equilibrium and with gratitude to God, the ambient temperature has turned warmer a tad and so life is a lot more tolerable. The building is quite new and is a pleasant place to live in.

Betty did have to get pots and pans, knives and forks, spoons and bowls, chopsticks and cleavers, plus all the condiments, spices, sugar, salt, pepper and drinking water to go with the groceries, staples and fruits so we can have our three square meals.

As of this moment we are waiting for someone to come and fix the dryer but everything else is sort of shipshape and in reasonably working order. We are thankful we can have hot water for our showers and the toilets are not backing up like the time it happened to us in Mountain View. We even have a McDonald's nearby and the ice cream cones are just as good as the ones anywhere in the world.

On the 9th of January, which was the first Sunday after we got back in Macau, we were eager and happy to be able to be at Sha Lei Tau Baptist Church and be able to preach to the congregation. Praise the Lord that 54 souls did turn up in contrast to the twenty or so faithful individuals who have kept the church going these past two and half years while we were gone. I talked about making our New Year's Resolutions, using Micah as the Scripture.

Tuesday evening, Ruth, Sylvia and Jennifer came for Bible study. We started on the Book of Luke. We will meet every Tuesday evening and hope to see many of our friends join us.

Thursday evening, the young people of Paul's Fellowship will meet in our apartment and we hope to actively help in bringing as many new friends as we can into the Fellowhip and be involved with helping the church to grow. Thank God that our young people have this burden for the lost souls of those around us and are willing to get into the thick of things.

Please be in prayer for:

1. Our Revival Meeting this coming Sunday.
2. Our Tuesday Bible Study.
3. Our Thursday Paul's Fellowship.
4. Our members who have not yet returned.
5. Our hope and prayer that God will help us bring more people to our Church.
6. A committed Pastor who would be willing to come and serve at Sha Lei Tau Baptist Church.
7. Our vision for a new location for Sha Lei Tau Baptist Church.

Thank you for your prayers.
May God bless you.
Kenneth

The following is another newsletter I wrote home from Macau in March 2011.

It was a bright, sunny and slightly warm day. It was Wednesday, March 16, 2011. I had known about the monthly luncheons at the Club Lusitano, in Hong Kong, organized by Irene Osmond Ruiz, for our classmates of the Class of 1952, of the University of Hong Kong Medical Faculty for the last four or five years. This time, it was Dr. Lam Sim Fook who wrote me earlier that he wanted me to go through a draft copy of my manuscript that I wrote as part of his soon-to-be published Anthology of our classmates of the Class of 1952. We were quite eager to meet with my old friends, some I have not seen in a decade or more. We had a smooth ride from Macau to Hong Kong, though we soon found out that there was quite a dense fog over the Pearl River estuary. The surprising thing that Betty noticed when we were approaching Hong Kong Harbor was that she could see airplanes on the land to the south of our Jetfoil. She kept asking where we were. I said I couldn't help her because of my poor vision and I could not see what she was talking about. However, I surmised that if her observations were correct, then it could only mean one thing. For some unknown reason the Captain had to change course and travel north of Lantau Island, which meant that we had to go by Chek Lap Kok and the Hong Kong Airport. It wasn't long before we were able to see that we went under Tsing-I Bridge and were heading south toward the Hong Kong Macau Ferry Pier. It was but minutes before we docked and disembarked. The crowd was not big. We followed the line for those aged over 65 and were soon out of the Immigration control and were warmly greeted by two smiling faces—Patsy and Jeffrey.

We got into their van and "June" the chauffeur drove us to Club Lusitano, while they took our bags to their flat in Conduit Road. That is service with a capital "S". We really couldn't ask for more.

At the Club we met Irene and Ramon, Yeung Ming Hon and Barbara. It had been at least three or four years since I had last seen them and strangely, I felt they had aged appreciably. Yeung used to allow me to ride on his motorcycle's pinion seat in medical school between the Main Building, Queen Mary Hospital and the Sai Ying Pun Outpatient clinics. It was a great help to me to be in the same grouping with him and it saved me a lot of bus fare not to speak of the wear and tear of running after the buses. We were soon joined by Poon Kwong Chiu and his wife, then Haroon Abdullah and his wife. I looked much younger than all of them but their unanimous opinion was that I looked twice as fat as I ought to be and they all said that they would not recognize me if they were to meet me on the street. The last people that came were Dorcas Hu, Mrs. Liu Chi Ming and Lam Sim Fook and Nina. Sim Fook wanted us to approve the draft copy of our contributions to his manuscripts and gave each of us a copy for keeps. He was hoping that the publication would come on the market the following April and we would be given copies to give away. Dorcas also gave me a copy of the book "Layered Beauty" which was recently released by the Chinese University of Hong Kong, when they had an exhibition of some private collections of Chinese Lacquer Ware, including the donated collection of Hu Shih Chang. I tried to limit my intake of the luncheon since I became quite self-conscious over the remarks about my girth and corpulence. I do want my friends to recognize me when they see me. We bid our adieu and were reminded that the next luncheon would be on April 13, 2011.

Patsy came and picked us up and took us to her home. We sat around and gossiped. Actually, I did go through some of the recent X-rays taken of the impacted fracture of the head of her right humerus, when she had a fall a few weeks ago. The fracture was already filled in with callus and all she needed to do now was to exercise the shoulder and not get a frozen shoulder, in spite of the pain. We had dinner at the Hong Kong Jockey Club where Patrick joined us. We had a very enjoyable day and got to bed at a reasonable time.

We returned home on the five o'clock ferry and relaxed, while getting prepared for my cousins, Dolly Ngan Lee, her husband James, Wendy Ngan and two mystery visitors, who would be coming for lunch on Saturday.

They arrived in the late morning and it was a real pleasant surprise to see them after decades of not seeing each other. One of the mystery visitors was Vivian Ngan Lee, who was visiting from New Jersey, while the other visitor was Thomas a friend of Wendy's. We had a lot of getting acquainted and renewal to do but it was fun talking about the old days and finding out about the new things that had happened since we last saw each other. Betty was the perfect host and lunch was on the table right when everyone was feeling famished. The Lasagna and the garlic bread won rave reviews, but the piece-de-resistance was the dessert. Betty made molten chocolate cup cakes topped with cream and strawberries. They were scrumptious. We had a very pleasant midday reunion, catching up on old times and licking up tidbits of new information. It was, to say the least, altogether a very pleasant and enjoyable three or four hours. We have Wendy to thank for getting in touch with me and making this possible. We bid them farewell and rested a while from the excitement of the past few days! We thank God for making life so full of joy to those who love Him.

Later in the afternoon, Betty suggested we go out for a walk. We took a rather long walk all the way to Ching Chau 青洲 Green Island and on the way back Betty suggested we stop for some noodles at one of the coffee shops nearby. As we started to work our way home, I was suddenly seized with a very severe and sharp pain on the right side of my abdomen, so much so that I almost couldn't walk. It was a struggle when we finally made it home. Trying to figure out what went wrong, I realized that in the accumulated excitement over the last few days, my aged alimentary tract had not kept pace with all my GI, physical and emotional activities, which had completely upset my physiological equilibrium. I realized that I had not had a bowel movement since Wednesday morning when we left for Hong Kong. It was getting late Saturday and the only thing we had were some glycerin suppositories. The pain was not letting up and it was difficult trying to fall asleep. Betty suggested calling someone to help get us to the hospital but all I could think of was that we had a busy Sunday planned; we were to baptize Mrs. Lee Ga Wai 李嘉慧 at 10.30 a.m., attend worship service at 11.00 a.m. and possibly the Lord's Supper. In my prayer, I pleaded with God that He would allow me to remain well enough till after the worship service on Sunday.

I had a short period of sleep before getting up around 7.00 a.m. feeling, perhaps, slightly better. Mind you, during all this time, I did not have any nausea or vomiting. I had no fever. There was tenderness and rebound in my right side of the abdomen but there was no rigidity and the pain was nothing that I couldn't withstand. I had some cheerios and tea for breakfast after my morning ablutions, and was dressed and ready for the baptism and the sermon. I asked Mr. Hoi to purchase a couple of vials of Fleets enema and after everything was accomplished in church, we went home. We tried out the enemas and succeeded in getting rid of some gas but failed to evacuate any fecal material. I had a fitful rest the rest of the day and night but in the end, I asked Betty to call Mr. Hoi to help get me to the hospital. Sonia called the ambulance then came with Song Song to the house and we all went to the Kiangwu Hospital around 1.00 a.m., Monday, 3/21/11.

The ER doctor, checked me, and ordered a bunch of tests including blood work, EKG, chest and abdominal films, a Fleet enema, and an ultrasound of the abdomen. Naturally, I couldn't get away without the ubiquitous IV drip. By 4.00 a.m., after paying a required deposit, especially for the fact that I am only in Macau on an Alien Laborer's permit, I was admitted to the surgical floor to await further evaluation and disposition. I tried to rest as much as I could, then by late morning, the doctors finally came and evaluated my situation, whereupon, between noon and one o'clock, one of the attending doctors informed me that they would soon take me down for a computerized scan of the abdomen; the surgeon on call would evaluate it and if necessary surgery would be performed. Eventually, the surgeon came and told me that my problem was most likely acute appendicitis. He explained that he would try to use the minimally invasive technique but with the proviso that he might be compelled to remove the appendix through an abdominal incision. Of course, by this time Betty was well aware of the situation since a payment had to be made for the scan and the surgery…and so all was in readiness for surgery at 4.00 p.m. and my recovery would be in the ICU because of my age and medical history of a coronary by-pass surgery and a pacemaker.

When I woke up from the operation, it was already after 9.00 a.m. Tuesday morning in the ICU. I had a slight burning pain in the incision but I had no nausea or vomiting and by 10.00 a.m. I was able to flatulate two or three times, which is a very good sign. At eleven o'clock in the morning, they transferred me back to my room in the surgical floor. The doctors were very cautious and conservative in their management and I was not given clear liquids until late Wednesday. I was on intravenous antibiotics even though I never kicked up a fever and the drainage was sero-sanguinous in nature and within normal expectations. By late Wednesday, I was up and out of bed as much as I could in spite of the intravenous drip and the Foley catheter drainage. By Thursday, my bowels had moved and I had soft food and all the tubes in and out of my systems were removed. I was ready to be discharged! God had answered our prayers!

All told, I had about thirty visitors from the church plus friends in the Macau Baptist Mission, Dr. Stanley Wong and his wife Yolanda but last and not least our good friends John and Susanna Hyrons. I bring this up to highlight one outstanding trait that we often do not emphasize enough and that is, when Christians have an occasion to congregate to exhibit a Christian virtue, that of visiting and comforting the sick, their exemplary behavior often arouses an aura of awe among those non-believers who chance to walk by on the scene. Let me come to the point. It did not take the medical and nursing staff long before they found out that I am the Pastor of the Sha Lei Tau Baptist Church and that in the past I had an active surgical practice in Hong Kong and United States for forty years before retiring to go into the ministry twenty years ago. The point I was trying to make was that two days before I was to be discharged from the hospital, one of the nursing students asked me what being a pastor meant. She had no idea what a Christian is. She was curious and impressed with the young people who came to visit me. She wanted to know what they do in church and what it means to be in a fellowship. I explained as clearly as I could and told her that she was welcome to come and see. She noticed my business card on my bedside table and asked if she could have it. I gladly handed it to her and now all we need to do is to find a way to get connected and see if we could convince her to come and see for herself who Jesus is!

On Wednesday, they transferred a seven-month old baby girl to the bed next to mine in the semi-private room. She had dislocated her forearm. The next day, they took her to the operating room to reduce the dislocation. I was resting in bed, but as the mother took the baby to go out of the room, the mother saw me and matter-of-factly asked me to pray for her daughter. That was a sweet moment! I can only say that God moves in mysterious ways, His wonders to perform! All we are left to say is Hallelujah! Praise the Lord!

While I was in the hospital, the deacons were discussing whom they should ask to preach on Sunday the 27th and I said that God willing, I would! I appreciated very much that Steve Baker was ready and willing to fill in the pulpit should I fail to make it but I felt strongly that I would be out of the hospital and felt obliged to seize the moment to preach a meaningful sermon. I convinced the doctors that the drain and catheter could be removed on Wednesday and even the intravenous drip could be discontinued. I was thankful that all these came true on Wednesday.

Finally on Thursday, I was really improving remarkably well though I had difficulty coughing up the inspissated mucous phlegm from my lungs. They finally ordered some inhalant medication to assist my cough and I felt much relieved after that. My bowels also resumed their activities and I was assured of my recovery. It was obvious that all our prayers from around the world praying that God would heal me were answered. On Friday morning, the doctor gave the order that I was to be discharged. Betty and Ms. Tam quickly put everything in fast motion and I was dressed and soon out of the hospital on the way home. We stopped at Yue Wing Kee for a quick lunch and arrived home before two o'clock in the afternoon. Home Sweet Home!

Recovery at home was quite uneventful and sleeping in your own bed is infinitely better than at the hospital. Everything else was also easier to do and I had little to no pain at all of any sort. Eating at home is much better than the hospital fare anytime. Food in the hospital was colorless, lacking in aroma, formless like an amorphous lump and insipid when you put it in the mouth. I should not belabor the point too much. Anyway, my recovery was quite spectacular and soon it was Sunday. I had arranged to go see Dr. Matt Humphries at ten o'clock in the morning just to be sure I did not have an infection. He met us at the Hope Medical Clinic, gave a quick thorough check and gave me a five days' supply of an oral antibiotic and we were on our way to Sha Lei Tau Baptist Church. I was very happy to see forty people in the worship service including Mrs. Lee whom I baptized the last week. I began the sermon by thanking God for making it possible for me to be there that morning to preach to them. I stressed to them that the reason I could stand there was because God is Good and He answers the prayers of those who are pious and fervent in their prayers, which is well illustrated by the following quotation:

"Solomon gave orders to build a temple for the Name of the LORD"
(2 Chron. 2:1).
The temple Solomon built was not large, but in quality and workmanship it was the best he could create. We

need not do great things for God. But whatever we offer
Him should represent the best that we can do.[68]

I went on to say that I was humbled by the fact that there were so
many of our Christian friends and relatives the world over that were
praying for me, including our little two-year-old angel Constance Lam
林康晴, that I cannot see how God could hesitate to get me well in a
hurry. I suggested to them my formula for answered prayer:

God's Faithfulness + Our Trust and Obedience.

I stressed to them how important it is for Christians to remember
not to just know how to Talk the Talk, and not to just Walk the Talk but
to always remember to Walk the Walk. As I said earlier on that, perhaps
when they came to visit me at the hospital, their behavior, demeanor and
their speech must have allowed others to see Jesus in them. The nursing
staff appreciated the difference in how Christians behaved under trying
circumstances. We ought always to be on our best behavior daily in our
routine and working environments. I concluded the sermon by finishing
up on the last part of the Sermon on the Mount in Matthew Chapter 7:1-
29, and emphasizing to them to always "Live and Act in harmony with
God" and be alert to their motives when praying and offering to God.

We had a very fitting ending to our worship service when we
concluded it with commemorating the Lord's Supper especially with
our newest member in the congregation!

Please continue to pray for us as well as the Christians in Sha Lei
Tau Baptist Church.

This is another newsletter I sent on October 17, 2011.

God has been good to us at the Sha Lei Tau Baptist Church lately and
our attendance at our worship services has remained steady around 40,
which sad to say is above average for the close to 50 churches in Macau.

We were blessed to be able to baptize one lady on the 2nd of October

---

[68] Richards, L. (1990). *The 365 day devotional commentary.* Includes index. (257).
Wheaton, Ill.: Victor Books.

and a couple (a young man and his future wife) on the 9th, a week later. I will officiate at their wedding November 6th in the afternoon.

The church has elected an elderly man of around 60 and a lady about the same age plus two young men around 30 to be their deacons. They have just undergone four sessions of instructions and will be queried next Sunday afternoon then ordained November 27th in the afternoon, provided they pass the test.

All these wonderful things have quieted the concerns I had in my heart somewhat and I will feel more at ease about leaving the church and Macau at this juncture, in December. I will miss my friends here and the church and Macau...just as I have missed you all and Mountain View this past year. But now I look forward to renewing our friendship and fellowship...in 50 days.

Let me end this story about me with this quote from Matthew 24: 4-14:

4. And Jesus answered and said to them, "[69a]See to it that no one misleads you.
5. "For [70a]many will come in My name, saying, 'I am the [71]Christ,' and will mislead many.
6. "You will be hearing of [72a]wars and rumors of wars. See that you are not frightened, for *those things* must take place, but *that* is not yet the end.
7. For [73a]nation will rise against nation, and kingdom against kingdom, and in various places there will be [74b]famines and earthquakes.
8. "[75a]But all these things are *merely* the beginning of birth pangs.
9. "[76a]Then they will deliver you to tribulation, and will kill you, and [77b]you will be hated by all nations because of My name.

---

[69] a Jer 29:8
[70] a Matt 24:11, 24; Acts 5:36f; 1 John 2:18; 4:3
[71] 1 I.e. the Messiah
[72] a Rev 6:4
[73] a 2 Chr 15:6; Is 19:2; Rev 6:8, 12
[74] b Acts 11:28; Rev 6:5, 6
[75] a Matt 24:8–20; Luke 21:12–24
[76] a Matt 10:17; John 16:2
[77] b Matt 10:22; John 15:18ff

10. "At that time many will [781a]fall away and will [792]betray one another and hate one another.

11. "Many [80a]false prophets will arise and will mislead many.

12. "Because lawlessness is increased, [811]most people's love will grow cold.

13. "[82a]But the one who endures to the end, he will be saved.

14. "This [83a]gospel of the kingdom [84b]shall be preached in the whole [851c86]world as a testimony to all the nations, and then the end will come.[87]

As I conclude my testimony, I leave you with my blessing:

May the love of our Lord Jesus,
The Grace of our Heavenly Father,
And the Fellowship of the Holy Spirit
Be with us now and forever.
Amen.

11-11-11
The eleventh day of the eleventh month
of the two thousand and eleventh year of our Lord.
Sha Lei Tau Baptist Church
169S Rua da Ribeira do Patane
Macau

---

[78] [1] Lit *be caused to stumble*
[79] [a] Matt 11:6
[80] [2] Or *hand over*
[81] [a] Matt 7:15; 24:24
[82] [1] Lit *the love of many*
[83] [a] Matt 10:22
[84] [b] Rom 10:18; Col 1:6, 23
[85] [1] Lit *inhabited earth*
[86] [c] Luke 2:1; 4:5; Acts 11:28; 17:6, 31; 19:27; Rom 10:18; Heb 1:6; 2:5; Rev 3:10; 16:14
[87] *New American Standard Bible: 1995 update.* 1995 (Mt 24:4–14). LaHabra, CA: The Lockman Foundation.

.

Printed in the United States
By Bookmasters